Got Change?

Jon-Pat Myers

Published by Burning Books, 2021.

While every precaution has been taken in the preparation of this book, the publisher assumes no responsibility for errors or omissions, or for damages resulting from the use of the information contained herein.

GOT CHANGE?

First edition. April 12, 2021.

Copyright © 2021 Jon-Pat Myers.

ISBN: 979-8201701987

Written by Jon-Pat Myers.

Hello

I have attempted to write a synopsis but have failed each time so I have included the opening note of my manuscript which I feel covers what I would like to say.

The book is 11 chapters long and deals with issues such as my feelings of alienation, juvenile confusion, attempted double suicide, brushes with the law, drug addiction, establishing South Africa's premier Punk band of the day and eventual exit from South Africa.

The format is basically the story itself, interspersed with anecdotes.

Thank you for taking a chance and reading this book.

Jon-Pat Myers

Note

It's the 10th of February 2008 and I'm sitting in my little room at kibbutz Ginosar on the shore of the sea of Galilee in Israel. I started this project some time ago but somehow the first few chapters got deleted from my computer and so I am once again going to attempt to write it all down.

I'm no writer as you will soon discover and am hopeless at typing on this antiquated laptop but I'm going to give it a shot anyhow.

I have spent long hours in confused contemplation as to why I'm doing this at all since it seems such a self-indulgent thing to do and I have yet to come up with a reasonable excuse. My first thought of course is ...THE CASH! But it's a total illusion to think that I may sell enough copies to cover costs, never mind make enough to buy that elusive island in the tropics, but then...who knows?

I tried initially to write down my story but it was impossible so I took a Dictaphone and simply told the story as I remember it without embellishing the truth in any way whatsoever. It turned out to take a few days of wandering through the forest in a semi daze as I recounted the events that made up my life and subsequently scared the shit out of me as I realized what a total asshole I was to have been so ignorant and cocky all at once.

The whole thing turned out to be quite a cathartic event and served excellently as the precursor to my current mid-life crisis. As I am 44 in April, I guess that means that in theory I will make it to 88!!

We will have to see.

Other people have led far more successful or wilder lives than mine and probably are more deserving than I to be writing about past events but by and large no one to my knowledge has. To South Africans, the things I will recount may seem mundane or in some cases far-fetched and may wonder as I do why I am bothering to do this. Fact is that each time I share an anecdote or recount an experience to people that I am in contact with that are unfamiliar with South Africa except for the obvious news headlines and the general misconceptions such as lions roaming the streets and the place being in the "jungles" much like darkest Africa was depicted in the 40's, they are across the board shocked and confused and without exception urge me to put it down in print and tell a story that is as unusual to them as it is real to me. I don't see it as being too remarkable but that's perhaps due to the fact that it has been my day-to-day reality and hasn't really needed to be analyzed or justified.

This is simply my story, and although I have omitted certain things for personal reasons and have refrained as much as possible from taking a particular stance in hindsight or foresight, all of it is true and I leave it to the reader to formulate their own opinions.

Genesis

I was born in South Africa in April of 1964. It was two years after the arrest of Nelson Mandela, a fact that I would remain completely ignorant of until the age of between 15 or 16, I'm not quite sure. I was born in Johannesburg which in April is pretty cold and it happened to be one of two winters that I experienced where snow fell. I was the second of three children in a pretty ordinary family and would say that by South African standards middle class. My father's family were originally from Ireland that had spent two generations in India working for the British crown and so he was born up in the Himalayas. He had a very interesting personal history, experiencing life in the mountains and serving in Burma during the 2nd world war as a young man. He immigrated to South Africa, I think, in 1947 with 11 pounds in his pocket, a ticket to Pretoria and a promise of a job working as a motor mechanic. He carried all of his personal belongings in a small suitcase with him on the boat.

My Dad was a great designer. He would take the attitude that instead of spending money on a toy, he would make it. He did too. My first toy of this kind was when he took the motorbike apart and built a frame for it that was supported by four wheels and so would help me balance as I learnt to operate the controls. At age four and a half!!

I rode "the Tractor" everywhere he went on weekends and it attracted much interest from like-minded individuals. Later on I graduated to the bike proper and although I couldn't touch the ground with my feet, I was able to ride and then come alongside as my dad would take hold of the bike and I could hop off.

We used to ride pretty much anywhere we could without the Police coming to chase us away and usually it meant that we were on mine property. In those days the surrounding "Hills" of JHB were made from a bright yellow sand and it was here that many a Saturday afternoon or Sunday would be spent with my sister and I taking turns on the bike and trying gamely to keep up with Dad who knew the places usually like the back of his hand.

There were other toys too, like a Go cart that he designed and built in the garage and that was peddle operated. It went like a bomb and I remember spray painting it in my first of many "custom" jobs that was to haunt me for many years later as it was a habit not easily broken and much less perfected.

My mother's side were a few generations down the line South Africans and if I'm not mistaken they were a combination of Dutch and German stock. Both my grandfather and mother having been born on South African soil.

My mother was a 7th child in a commonly large family and the youngest. She met my father in the 1950's. It was a rather unusual meeting in that my dad didn't speak and still doesn't speak a word of Afrikaans and my mother's family had been active in the Boer wars which must have made the situation quite an interesting one. Although the country had been independent since 1949 feelings of patriotism were strong and the antagonism toward the British was an attitude held by many, irrespective of political orientation.

South Africa with its colorful history of occupation,

conquest, pioneers, sanctions, sport, wildlife, beer, braaifleis and bakkies, formed the backdrop to an eventful and richly variant childhood.

My very first memories are of lying in my cot at the age of about 18 months and seeing our lady servant leaning over me to attend to something. I was unable to walk, definitely before but my very earliest memories were of Aya tending to my needs. I was very fortunate in that we had just moved into a rather big house in the eastern suburb of Kensington, situated on a small hillock or as is known in SA Speak as a "koppie" A little head-koppie. The property was 2.5 acres of pretty much solid rock, bush and trees. I loved that house at 36 Hawthorn street. It was my own personal castle that I would single handedly defend against all kinds of would-be attackers that emerged from the expanses of my young and fertile imagination. All in all it was an amazing place in which to explore and grow.

From what I'm told, my first languages were a mixture between English, Afrikaans and Zulu. I used to be carried around by Aya, wrapped in a blanket and tied to her back in what was known as "pepa" while she continued to deal with the many facets of household maintenance.

Aya was a lady who had been with our family for many years and was responsible for having raised not only my sisters and myself, but quite a number of my cousins as well. Aya eventually settled with us and lived in a small room on the property with separate toilet and no bathroom or hot water as a sort of proxy family member until her death when I must have been 15 years old. She used to get up every morning, winter or summer at 5 am and begin the day's work in the kitchen making breakfasts of porridge, bacon and eggs, toast, tea and so on. In winter her first task was to stoke up the little coal stove and then do all of her many chores that enabled the whole show to run smoothly.

Ours was a house that never knew cornflakes or the like. My folks were far too sensible for that and so we would fortify ourselves with endless cups of tea and porridge made from...uh...corn! and sometimes a chocolate brown version known as Maltabella. Yum!

Some of my earliest memories are of being next to the track. Usually on clubhouse corner.

The heat, the noise, the cheering of the crowds and the smell of hot dogs that were tastier than anywhere else in the world. Ice cream, tonnes of ice cream.

My dad used to race a killer little Renault Dauphine and then a Gordini and apparently he was a pretty reckless driver and much respected for being tenacious to say the least.

Racing was my dad's "thing" he could spend hours and hours trying to figure out how to make the damn thing go faster and then go out and test his theories in person. He was a great driver though and I had a few occasions to see what he was made of and what a car was able to do in the right hands.

He had, along with some friends, built a very beautiful racing special called "the Protea" and it is still a highly successful car today in the various classic car races that it performs in. He built about 14 in all and eventually had to pack it in as the South African government taxed it all to hell as they considered the fact that as it used a Triumph motor it could be considered an "import" and so killed any chances I may have had of being a Millionaires son!

Bastards!

I started kindergarten at Belgravia recreation centre where my mother worked and it wasn't long before I was moved to another as it was thought that it wasn't the greatest idea for me to be at a place where basically my mother was the boss and called all the shots. Which she did. In fact she probably was only one of the senior members of staff but would have called the shots anyhow. I was then sent off to a wonderful little place down in Bez valley called Fairyland which to my knowledge is still there and functioning today. My experiences at Fairyland were amazing. I still recall quite vividly the scent of gravy, thickly poured on steaming rice at lunchtime. Being forced to have a nap after lunch which I was always unable to do. I'm not a very good sleeper, never was and doubt if I ever will be. I remember the lady in charge. A stormy German lady by the name of Miss Ducker or perhaps Mrs. Our only argument ever was when I corrected her Afrikaans when she taught us numbers and pronounced "four" in the German way. I remember feeling hurt and confused as I was only trying to help her fix her mistake and was treated to the "smart Alec" speech that I was to hear so many more times throughout my school career. There were also the two ladies in the kitchen who I seem to recall much better than any of Miss/Mrs Duckers many temporary assistants. They were simply known as Lizzy and Betty and it took at least 6 months full time study to learn to correctly distinguish between the two roly polies that were constantly filled with mirth and sound advice for growing little boys. We used to call them collectively Lizbet and that seemed to work. I absolutely loved them and would drop by for many years afterward to see them whenever I was in the vicinity. I made my first real friend at the crèche although we would never meet outside of school.

My folks used to refer to it as "The Bughouse!" It was our local cinema and just a short walk from home. We had two to choose from really as there was another in the opposite direction and originally it was called "The Regal" but was later taken over by the Kinekor chain of movie houses. It was then re-named "Fairway" The Gem was definitely the one on the lower end of the economic scale and it was our weekly treat to go to the Saturday afternoon matinee show for the princely sum of 10cents a ticket and a few cents in the care of my older sister for sweets.

The place was a madhouse of activity. The show would start and couldn't be heard over the noise and it was after much shouting and cat calling that the audience would settle down more or less to watch the age old shorts and wonderful footage from some archive long forgotten, showing the wonderful exploits of a guy who was possibly called "Rocket Man" and who would don a bullet like silver helmet and then take a few steps before a hop skip and jump which would automatically start his rocket back pack and off he would zoom to save the day. I remember wondering how it was that he never fried his butt! There were other movies that would run and re run. I saw "The sons of thunder" about 16 times and loved each show.

The thing was that this was the only place to get acquainted with the other sex and although I was far too young for all that, it was plainly understood that the back seats were for the older kids. The woman who owned the place would "Patrol" the aisles, armed with a huge wooden ruler and flashlight and get in between when things got too "kissey!"

Later on the movie house on the other end became more popular with the advent of what was called "The Kinekor kiddies club" This was much the same and included things like talent competitions and the like.

My folks were great movie goers and our family outings to the drive ins in and around the JHB area were a highlight of growing up. We would all pack into the station wagon and along with a huge supply of food that would have been prepared during the afternoon we would stuff ourselves with coffee from the thermos and watch westerns mostly as they were my folks' favourites.

At the close of the kindergarten day which was approximately 1 pm my mother would come and pick me up and we would go home to have a lunch of cold meats and salad or pilchards on toast. All washed down with litres of tea before I was dumped into the back of the Dauphine along with my older sister and make our way to the recreation centre where my mother worked.

My mother was a social worker in the employ of the JHB city council, parks and recreation department. She ruffled a few feathers at a stage as she had no objection to working with Winnie Mandela and was outspoken enough to say so at a general meeting and became instantly famous. My mother was relatively to her time and background an extremely open minded individual. She attended school at Afrikaanse Meisies Hoerskool In Pretoria and was brought up in an orthodox God-fearing Afrikaans home. The fact that she was able to be as open minded as she was is nothing short of a miracle in itself coupled with the fact that she had gone and married an

Englishman must have been pretty outrageous. To put it mildly. She worked in the social services dept at the recreation center and she started off by offering assistance to entire families that were living "on the outers" I remember once waiting in the car while she went to talk to a man who had his whole family of snotty nosed barefoot kids and wife living in an old abandoned Chevy just out in the veld.

These were the poor whites that the then Dept of health and welfare would try to assist. Slowly she rose through the ranks and ended up working at Patterson Park Recreation centre, a part of the newly established Parks and Recreation dept. Patterson park or "the centre" as we knew it was quite a way from home and to get to it we had to drive daily through Bez Valley which was a rough and economically challenged area to say the least and then through Cyrildene which was an old suburb populated by well to do, predominantly Jewish people with their own synagogue and houses/ mansions that were sometimes double or even triple storey affairs. We would then go down Sylvia's Pass to basically the Orange grove Norwood boundary that was populated by predominantly English-speaking people with a fair assortment of Portuguese and Italian kids and adults that would attend the various activities at the centre. It was only much later when the Norwood Police station built two enormous blocks of flats adjacent to the centre that we actually associated with kids with an Afrikaans orientation. Even then there was a distinct separation between English and Afrikaans.

My Grandfather was a good man. I respected him a lot. He worked in the bank and used to drive a grey Opel if I remember rightly. It was strange, we would go and visit the family each weekend and pig out on too many different kinds of food to mention. Each aunt and niece had their special thing and it was all a big competition to see who could out do the other. I was usually pretty quiet and would keep to myself in the beginning and then slowly get involved with the other kids of around my age. There was this gooey ritual of having to kiss everyone hello and goodbye, including the men.

My grandfather would sometimes pull me aside and secretly slip a 20cent piece in my fist and always comment on my instant smile.

"Ja! A true Scotsman!" he would say....

I went to an English kindergarten or crèche, call it what you will and somehow before I went to primary school I went to the kinder at the centre due to the cost or convenience or perhaps a combination of the two. This created many problems since once again I was the "Boss's son" and everyone thought I got preferential treatment which, truth be told, was quite often the opposite as my mother wanted to make it clear that I was just the same as everyone else and would punish me accordingly as an example on many occasions. Also true is the fact that as the kid of one of the staff, many doors were open to me after hours that were not open to the average member of the centre.

At the age of 5 I was shipped off to the Afrikaans school in Bez Valley where my sister had been attending after starting off in an English school. The reason for this escapes me. I think that my mother felt that since we were in any case bilingual and our home language was English, Afrikaans schooling would be a good way to create a balance that would be beneficial in a country such as South Africa.

I hated every moment of that school and could write a book about it but I'll try to skip over as much as I can and just give the basic picture. This was an institution run by God and policed by God fearing "opregte mense" who were living somewhere in the pioneering past in a world of bitterness and delusion. It was an enclave of right-wing politics and strict measures, cut off from the rest of the world. A lot of the kids that attended were from poor families that had the myriad of social problems that are associated with alcoholism and unemployment. Violence for these kids was simply a part of life and for the most part they were a rough and tough bunch. My overriding memories of this place are fear and violence from the students and from the teachers. The women were as bad as the men. If I hadn't just received a hiding I was about to get one or being threatened with one. The men used to cane us on the behind for infractions such as speaking, incorrect school uniform, long hair (hair touching ears or collar was deemed unclean and evidence of bad character) Practically any excuse was acceptable as the premise of "spare the rod and spoil the child" was the creed to be followed. The women would hit us on our hands with a large wooden or plastic ruler and often hard enough to shatter the implement. Girls were always punished on the hands and never on the backside as it was indecent? I guess... Anyhow we were in a constant state of fear and trepidation. I went to this school and was introduced to all the "wonders" of our "great" forefathers who resisted the British during the wars and killed the "kaffirs" wholesale with Gods full and hearty approval. The word "kaffir" was used as standard practice at school by teachers and students alike and only a few of us would say "swarte" which means "black person" Some of the more cultured teachers would use the term "Bantu"

I'm in primary school and school is over and I step into the car. My mother says "what's the matter?" So not being able to bottle it up any longer I relent and confess the there are some boys at school bullying me. Nobody ever stands up for me and I am just tired of it all. She responds " I never want to hear that you have been fighting except if someone calls you a "moffie" then you have my permission to give them a smack, OK?' If you fight I will give you 20c for a blood nose and 50c for a blue eye.

I was conflicted as to how fighting would be taboo except in certain circumstances.

Some weeks later I am pushed in the line and slapped over the back of the head. I react by telling the boy to piss of which is exactly what he wants. An excuse to fight and challenges me. I tell him fighting is dumb and I'm not interested. He calls me a "Moffie." I punch him square on the jaw and he flies off the corridor, over a flower bed and lands on the lawn which is out of bounds. He picks himself up and runs as fast as he can to return to his place in the line before a teacher spots him and tans his hide. Tears in his eyes. No more problems from that boy.

I feel like shit.

I was active in the seasonal sports as all the students were expected to do some sport. Expected meaning that it wasn't legal to make it compulsory but God help you if you don't. Sport was a BIG thing and Rugby was by far and away the main religion. I played rugby from the first grade but only in organized teams from around the third. It was very rough and we played barefoot on the unforgiving red earthed fields of the Transvaal highlands. Those Afrikaaners were as tough as nails and it is no surprise to me that South Africa is usually on the forefront of the sport internationally. I eventually soldiered forth and due to fair coordination and grit, I made the "A" team and played in the Lock position which as far as I can gather was my punishment for a previous life as a torturer during the inquisition. I used to go home with the tops of my ears slightly torn and the underside of my toes bleeding from the dry and cutting grass that we used to play on. It was absolute hell to get into the bath at night. It was better playing a match against an opposing school than have an active practice with the older boys as the dirty play was more or less accepted and seen by the masters as a mechanism to make you tougher and keep you in line at the same time. We played most of the other Afrikaans schools in and around Johannesburg and did well enough to make it to the district finals. The only thing I excelled at at this time was swimming. I was the second fastest swimmer at school which was quite a big deal and it earned me as much respect as derision from the older boys.

I'm at school. I am perhaps 10 years old and one of the boys challenges me to a fight which means that if you back down you will be called a chicken. So. I accept.

A chicken seemed to be a fowl thing...

One of the other boys is elected referee and my conditions for the fight is that it will be just us three at the venue. After school we meet at the appointed place and the referee marks out the boundary of our makeshift ring.

At the signal of the ref, we square off against one another.

I try for a peaceful settlement and attempt to talk my way out of it and the offer of a truce is rejected and so off we go. He is too chicken to punch me and I am chickener than him and so we circle each other wearily until the ref loses patience and eggs us on, desperately trying to draw us out of our protective shells...

He is one of the toughest boys in the school and he is squawking to both of us "donner hom" " is jy bang Ingilsman?' I don't want to be thought of as a dumb cluck so eventually I choose a spot on the boy's cheek take a deep breath, pluck up my courage and lay one on him whereupon his mouth explodes in a spray of blood and I am declared the winner instantaneously. The winner of the fight is usually decided as the first one to draw blood or the other guy submits or starts crying.

I move one step up the pecking order and its not long before I am once again challenged. This time by one of the boys roosting above me, eager to maintain his perch.

A referee is elected. A location chosen.

I feel cooped up as usual but my feathers are unruffled as I know there's no use in brooding...

My memories of the place are just dark and dismal and I feel better when not remembering it so I'm going to skip it and move forward.

Whilst at this school I had somehow paired up with a guy by the name of David Steinbach. He claimed to be Jewish although he went to a Christian church when he wasn't off trying to catch the ever-elusive fish in the local pond and spoke both English and Afrikaans at home. He was a total outsider and me, due to the fact that I was called amongst other things "Rooinek" which means redneck, an insulting term for an English person derived from the fact that the English were fair skinned and would always be terribly sunburnt on their necks and not connected to the American 'Redneck' The irony is that the Afrikaaners that I knew were more like American Rednecks than American Rednecks were themselves!! I was also called "Joodtjie" which roughly translated means – Jew! This was due to my surname which in the Afrikaans pronunciation resembles the Jewish Meyer. Anyway...we ended up having to sit next to each other and struck up a friendship. We would practice Judo together during breaks and attended the same Judo club and would speak in English all the time. This resulted in a semi seclusion from the others but also a more secure platform from which to resist the taunts and insults that were common and quite often encouraged by one of the more rancid masters. We weren't complete outsiders as this may suggest just a little different from the rest and thus a natural target due to our association with the archetypal "enemy"

I'm in primary school and all the boys have begun to make GANGS!

Once again 10 or perhaps 11 years old.

I refuse to join any gang since I'm not prepared to butter anyone up to become a gang member and nobody wants me in their gang anyway. I go off behind the school to the rose garden and say a prayer in which I inform God that I want to be in HIS gang. "Tell me what to do!" and so, I wait. And I wait. And I wait and wait some more.

Some weeks later a new boy arrives at the school. His name is David Steinberg and in some weird and wonderful way he claims to be Jewish. An Afrikaans speaking Jew no less... It turns out that he is a student of Judo and has a wonderful voice and is not in the least bit shy to blast out at the top of his voice in front of the entire class at the slightest provocation. We become friends.

Every break we go off alone and practice Judo on our knees. It is the only permissible way to do it as standing would be considered fighting and was deemed to be too dangerous. David is one of the best young Judokas in JHB and we develop a close friendship. I would accompany him on weekends where we would stand all day in the pouring rain and try in vain to catch fish. Weekend after weekend.

David slowly becomes more and more connected to the more brash boys in the class and I become more distant. Eventually through the pressure and coercion of the other boys he challenges me to a fight. Knowing that I'm the weaker one I'm naturally reluctant but arrive at the appointed time. It's really a hard moment for me as he is really my only friend and I don't want to fight him and I know that he is only doing it to gain acceptance from the others. So we fight and I throw no punches or kicks and eventually he gets me in a strangulation grip and I'm forced to submit. I'm angry, sad and humiliated all at the same time. The boys of course turn me into a laughing stock and David is naturally the hero.

I go back to the rose garden and cry in private wondering what exactly it is that God is trying to teach me.

This was my main friend at school and at the Dojo but for the most part I still spent my afternoons under the watchful eye of my mother at the centre. I became good friends with the son of the regional supervisor and we both shared a similar situation as kids of members of staff. They lived in Craighall park on the other side of town and I would often sleep over and enjoy fantastic weekends of relative freedom and mischief together with other kids who could hardly speak a word of Afrikaans and for sure had no Afrikaans friends and would have been hostile to me had they known that I attended an Afrikaans school. It was a strange set up and one that caused me to question why I indeed had to attend such a school at all since all of my friends were English speaking anyway. I was amazed by the openness and easy communication between these kids and their parents as they were far more liberal and Democratic than anything I had been exposed to. Not that they didn't suffer corporal punishment or anything like that, it was just that according to their accounts they were at least allowed to contest the caning and in some cases the parents would intervene with the school authorities on their children's behalf. I found this hard to believe and in my case unimaginable that my folks would intercede in any school matter.

I eventually took it upon myself to approach the district school inspector on his regular visit to the school and managed somehow to secure a private moment with him and explained my predicament to him. He was most understanding and tested my bilingualism thoroughly with the verdict that I had his approval and word that he would keep the subject of our discussion private as he understood the implications of the staff and students hearing about my desire to go to an English school. I told my parents and based on a discussion that they had with the inspector I was finally allowed to go to the very school that my sister had started off at and it was just a short walk up the main road. I had become a student at one of the oldest educational institutions in SA. A group of schools originally founded by sir Julius Jeppe comprising an elementary school or preparatory school affectionately known as "The Prep", a girls and a boys high school all situated on individual properties with spacious grounds and well-equipped facilities.

I would like to say that I entered a new world but it was more like a totally new parallel universe that had been existing for all this time just a kilometer or so from my front door. The funny thing was that due to attending the school and being able to walk there, I finally met the kids who lived in my street and the next one down that I had for years simply just driven past. The experience was overwhelming. I could grow my hair over my ears. There was a lot more tolerance. You could have something to say for yourself before you got punished. The punishment itself was meted out in less rabid fashion than before and paled next to the kind of abuse that by now I was well used to. It was more like a consequence of failure to respond to other measures such as writing lines or detention and not simply a kind of knee jerk reaction to any and every minor infraction of an absolute law.

Somehow, based on what exactly I don't know, I was made house captain which of course did wonders for my popularity with the kids that had been vying for the position since the first grade and it immediately set the tone for the year to come. It was short lived however as soon things settled down and I ended up having the most fantastic year of my school life. I would say that it was possibly the most influential formative year of my life in mainly positive ways and played a major role in creating the person that I am today. I worked hard that year. I got good grades and unsurprisingly won the academic prize for the year for Afrikaans. I started playing cricket with a real ball and pads! Not the usual tennis ball affair that I was used to. I was embarrassed the first time I went up to bat as I had never before seen a "box' and for the life of me couldn't figure out what the hell it was used for. When I was asked by my captain " aren't you wearing a box?" I replied "Naah! I don't need one!" I immediately scored points for being hard core. I also went out first ball... I loved cricket.

I was completely hopeless to begin with and worked extra hard to improve and made the first team at no 11 due to the fact that I would catch anything and had a good arm. Cricket made me some new friends and established me as "one of the boys" and fairly well up the pecking order.

I arrive at Jeppe prep. A new boy. We go to class. Everything is strange and familiar. Boys with long hair and speaking Portuguese, hardly able to use English effectively. No longer does Rugby take prime position. It has been relegated to the sidelines by Football. Soccer is the in thing. These scruffy foreigners are good at it. REALLY good. So Soccer is what we play and I go into Goal as it's what I know and it proves to be the best position as the games are always "Porras v English" and the thrash us 20 to 30 goals to nil in the average break. As keeper I'm the most active English player.

My maths teacher was a beautiful lady called Miss Markus and she had the best classes. We could have discussions about practically anything as long as there was reasonable order and the work got done. My English teacher was a total dragon lady called miss Steenkamp. I thought it ironic that I would have an English teacher with an Afrikaans surname and such a name at that! She was an amazing teacher though and I loved her class since it was most difficult and due to the fact that each Friday's lesson was given over to reading a comprehensive booklist of classic literature. You could read any book you chose but had to complete the list by the end of the year. It was hell for the other students but absolute bliss for me and awakened a love of books and reading that continues. We would read Dickens and Shakespeare in simplified forms and were expected to write reports which I found a real challenge.

I did quite well academically and managed to achieve a high enough grade to be accepted to the higher-grade course of study in my first year of high school. For me the choice of schools was simple. Jeppe! Not only did I now feel a loyalty, but more importantly the school was situated right at the bottom of my street.

It turned out to be a year of total rebellion that I'll cover next chapter.

I would just like to close this chapter by going over some of the more prominent aspects that come to mind regarding this stage of my life.

Growing up at 36 Hawthorn street was a unique experience since basically we lived in a country house situated in the suburbs and close to the center of the city. The connection between us and our neighbors was virtually nonexistent in terms of socializing as they never had children in my age group and there simply wasn't a need to communicate except for the occasions when I would get caught stealing peaches or plums from the fruit trees in their gardens.

It's pretty late one night. I don't remember my age exactly but it's about 10 or 11. We hear screams from outside. The dogs aren't barking and its really strange. We hear the terrible screams and they are getting louder as whoever it is, is approaching the house and we realize that they're coming from Nozizwe. Aya's grandchild. Aya has a leather belt in her hand and she's beating the young 15year old like I have never before seen anyone being beaten. We don't know why she was receiving a beating. To this day no one knows. We knew better than asking and interfering in the " black business"

My dad stopped the violence as it was his house and told them to take it elsewhere. Aya as always being respectful, desisted and went outside and stopped the beating.

The following morning Nozizwe was gone. She had been sent back to wherever she had come from

The people in my "circle" were situated in other parts of the city and we would only meet in preordained circumstances and for clearly defined time periods. Never at home. I was kind of an outsider from the very outset and as a young boy it used to bother me quite a bit that "I don't have any friends!" but it turned out to be a sort of blessing in disguise since it forced me to learn how to occupy myself and above all to utilize my imagination by creating games and making tools in the huge workshop and so on. It was a time that I became connected with nature as the house was surrounded by huge Eucalyptus trees which attracted many different birds including at one stage a couple of Eagle owls. The night sky was more visible due to the absence of street lighting and the view of the valley quite spectacular, especially on Guy Fawkes when the place would erupt in an explosion of color and sound. There was a variety of fauna and fauna that you wouldn't find 200m from where we lived and that the average kid would never see as the "Koppies" were pretty much out of bounds for most children. The koppies were in many ways quite dangerous as you could suffer a fall and no help would be forthcoming due to the area being fairly remote. The other major reason given for staying off the koppie was the fact that it was used by black people as a shortcut through to the valley and for hoboes to idle away their time drinking alcohol or quite frequently, methylated spirits. Not to mention snakes and scorpions. I had first-hand experience a number of times attesting to the dangerous nature of the place. One time in particular I remember awaking to the sound of screaming coming from the bottom of the property and sternly told by my dad to close the door and for all to stay indoors while he went to investigate, "rollie" in hand and a determined look on his face that I was unaccustomed to seeing. It turned out that some poor young black woman had been raped and beaten and left at the base of our "Christmass" tree. My parents called the ambulance and Aya went down to give her some sugar water to help with "Shock" while they waited for the "Black" ambulance to arrive from the Hillbrow hospital. On another occasion there was "Black on Black" violence that spilled over into our property and then over the fence into our neighbors and was dispersed with a few shots from his shotgun and rather explicit language that I had not thought possible to issue forth out of the mouth of a devout Christian and officer in the Salvation army.

It's really late one night and I'm down on the main road with my skateboard alone taking advantage of the lack of traffic. I'm disturbed by the sound of screaming and cursing and as it turns out, one of the boys that works at the boarding house in our street is beating a woman. She's walking away from him as he is hitting her repeatedly over the head with a fist sized rock. I go closer and am about to intervene and one of the boys that knows me sees this and orders me sternly not to get involved as it is between them. He doesn't interfere and neither do any other passersby as this woman is walking, screaming and the guy is battering her with the rock. Her head is a mass of mangled hair and blood as she stands waiting while the guy tears a fair-sized branch from one of the trees and proceeds to beat her with the broken hoof shaped end, not the leafy part. He beats and beats and she doesn't run. Just continues to walk. Leonard, the man that knows me explains that this man got into a taxi to find his girlfriend there with the driver who opens up the conversation by boasting about the great time they just had together unaware of the fact that they are involved with each other. They both get out at the traffic lights and this is where the beating starts.

Leonard explains that if one had to get involved in this type of situation that both parties are liable to turn on you and it is not a good idea to intervene.

A very similar situation occurred a few weeks later not very far from this incident where two black men were fighting over a woman and a white guy stopped his car to try to prevent them stabbing each other and they both turned and stabbed him. The man's wife gets out of the car and tries her best to stop them from killing her husband and somehow manages to get him into the back of the car and races off to the private clinic just a few meters from the place. They drive past me with the back window smeared in blood and handprints as the man struggles with his injuries. I follow them down the drive, curious as ever and see the woman standing in the lobby of the clinic as the man is rushed to intensive care. She is shaking and hysterical, with a clump of hair and scalp in her hand that she is unable to release.

I walk outside and sit in the garden that I know so well and am reminded of Leonard's advice.

My memories of "home" are special and they always seem to include in one way or another the cherished memory of Aya. Her real name was Lina but we called her Aya or Gog. My memories of the centre include "the Boys" Such a completely degrading term since a 9-year-old referring to a group of grown men as the boys is ludicrous yet somehow didn't seem so at the time. Anyhow, the "Boss Boy" or rather the accepted leader of the group was a man called Andries who I absolutely adored. He was tall and athletic. He had played as a semi pro footballer in his day and took it as his responsibility to act as my guardian angel and was exactly that. There was more than one occasion that he saved me from a scrape or two and would always reprimand me afterward in private. His nickname for me was either "Misterrr" or "Hey Useless" depending on his mood. I had utmost respect for him and due to his enthusiasm for football he groomed me into a fairly decent goalkeeper in our late afternoon kick abouts when he was off duty and I was waiting for my mom to finish work and we could go home.

It's a regular weekday afternoon. I'm at the centre and at this time usually when the shadows begin to lengthen, Andries would be finishing up and then come down and we would kick the ball to each other or dribble or more often, I would be in goal and he would send scorchers through for me to try and save. Sometimes the other boys would join and they would play amongst themselves while I kept goal as best I could. So I would either be planted up against the side of the old hall's wall and have shots taken at me or alternatively have to try and not be outfoxed by the marvelous skills of the guys wearing heavy boots without being in the slightest way hindered by their bulk.

This was the way they would love to relax.

I once asked Andries why the black people so loved football and not Rugby and his reply was that in football you use your whole body like dancing. In rugby you have to rely on your physical power whereas in football you have to develop skill and rhythm.

This particular day the rest of the boys don't arrive and Andries and I and as usual very little is said between us except for the occasional taunt " Ha!...lucky!" "hmm. Good save Useless!" "You're too old Mafuta" and so on. My shoes serve as the goalposts and we could be at Wembley for all the seriousness of applying ourselves to the task.

All of a sudden the afternoon stillness is shattered by spine chilling repeated screams coming from the back cells of the police station. The distinct sound of some poor person being viciously beaten. A man is screaming and screaming and screaming and it chills me to the bone. I want to scream too.

Andries looks at the police station and says something under his breath. I ask, "What's happening? A fight?" and he says "no, it's the police" ..."let's play somewhere else."

So we take the ball and move to another spot where we can continue our game in peace.

I discover when I'm older that this is a common practice at the station. Beatings are frequent and brutal.

It is one of the locations at which corporal punishment is administered. The offender, burglar, car thief, minor, whatever, would be strapped face down to a bench, stripped naked to expose the buttocks and a prescribed amount of "cuts" would be administered with a cane that may have been dipped in vinegar and that would open the skin. I found out from some of the delinquent white youths that had been punished there for offences such as motorcycle or car radio theft that they would receive anywhere between 1 and 4 or maximum 6 cuts administered for repeat offenders. What I learnt from the black men was that they would simply get the shit beaten out of them.

Both Aya and Andries have my eternal gratitude for instilling in me a sense of pride and honor that carries me through difficult times and helps me to maintain a sense of perspective in a crazy world. If I had to choose the people who influenced me in my most formative years in would be without any doubt Aya and Andries that would top the list.

Both have sadly moved on but I think about them regularly in my day to day activities and am grateful time and time again for the gifts that I inherited from them. When I think about Andries I immediately hear his laugh. His whole body would shake and he would manage a smile no matter how dismal the situation. He never ever spoke about politics and there never seemed to be a gap between us. Not like most black and white people. I remember going to see him many years after I had left school and had traveled and so on and he was in his tiny room busy praying. I waited outside for him to finish and he walked up to me and took my hand and just stood there with his smile and with tears in his eyes for some time before he said " so?" and I told him that I had just dropped by to say thank you. We never exchanged another word and it was the last time I ever saw him.

Looking back at it today I see it in a very different way of course but back then it just hadn't dawned on me yet that there was such a big difference between us.

I wake up just after sunrise one morning to hear the dogs barking at the garden gate which meant that something or someone was trespassing on our property that wasn't fenced off or patrolled by the dogs. My dad grabs his gun and a flashlight as its still quite dark.

Attaches a lead to the largest dog, Freddie a vicious mix between Boxer and Ridgeback and goes to investigate. He discovers a woman at the base of our Xmass tree who has been raped and badly beaten. She's lying semi-conscious, and half naked. I'm told to stay put as are my mother and sisters and Aya goes down to try to help the woman and perhaps find out what happened. More screams as the Maids from the surrounding properties move forward to observe the scene. My dad takes some heavily sugared water to Aya so that she can give it to the woman to apparently prevent shock and discreetly retreats while my mother calls for an ambulance and notifies the police.

There's not really much more we can do and so get dressed and ready to go to school.

I think I was fortunate or perhaps unfortunate in that I had the privilege to travel a lot even at a young age. My parents both liked traveling and the whole family would go caravanning at any opportunity. Instead of going to Durban as most people would do, we would go all the way to Mozambique which was more exotic in a sense and exposed me to a very different way of life that I would not have known existed beyond our borders. When I was 9 years old my dad took my older sister and I on a touring trip of the UK in which we had to keep a diary of all the very well organized itinerary that my dad had set up consisting of museums and castles and museums and racecourses and museums and historical sights and you name it that we saw over the period of a month traveling in a camper van that could do about 50km per hour flat out on a hill with a tailwind. It was the most amazing trip of my life. I think, looking back that it was possibly the main contributing factor to my daring decision to corner the school inspector and change schools.

The world I lived in was in many ways magical and scary at the same time. I was fortunate in that I spent time with my father riding motorbikes from a ridiculously young age and having traveled and so on exposed me to a world that was a little different from the on that my so called peers were living in and so I guess it could be said that "I wasn't quite one of the boys"

Thank God.

High School (rebel without a clue)

I was a year younger than average high school starting age. I don't know why. It didn't deter me in any way though and I at least had some people I knew from the Prep so I wasn't completely alone on the first day. The schooling at Jeppe Boys was much more free in many respects than primary school in that you were expected to be more responsible and were treated in a semi adult way. Due to the fact that at the Afrikaans school we had been so strictly drilled in handwriting skills and wrote in a type of script that was uniform, tedious and constricting, I hadn't developed a "print" style of my own and thus my initial attempts were slow and at best partially legible to the trained eye. It was pure murder for me to try and keep up, especially with dictation of which there was plenty. The natural result was that I soon fell behind in my notes and even soonerer afterward stopped taking notes completely and used to sketch as a disguise so that the teachers would think I was writing. It was at this time that I became fanatical about skateboarding and it was of course far more interesting to pursue my goal of becoming a pro in the afternoons than to actually do ridiculous stuff like homework or perhaps even catching up with my notes. I was friendly with a Mormon guy by the name of Keith Dell and together we would skate all the hills in the area and arrive home in the evenings with the most horrendous scrapes, cuts and bruises. I used to spend of much of my time in my dad's huge garage/workshop making my own boards and in a way it was an education in itself. We were dedicated and absolutely loved to skate. Keith stopped soon after puberty but I continue to skate quite actively to this day and still love it although I'm considered by most of the youngsters to be an old fart and by their parents as a kind of Peter principled anomaly. Nobody knew much about skateboarding in those days and there were not really any boards for sale yet, but for me it was my lifeblood and the result was that I got pretty good at it and spent most of my first year at high school traveling around and doing demonstrations and skating when I should really have been at school learning the intricacies of algebra and how to multiply apples with pears and calculate the resulting fruit salad which made and still makes minimal sense to me. The friends I made at high school were all about two years older than me and I didn't really associate with the boys in my class and of my own age. So in effect I didn't have a so called peer group and the boys I fraternized with were the naughty boys who used to sneak out the back at breaks to have a smoke and although I never smoked and they never pressured me to, I was quite welcome to hang with them and act as a sentinel to warn of approaching prefects or wandering masters. I think since I used to cut school a lot I was accepted into the group.

Two of the guys in this group were very good skateboarders and well connected with the slowly emerging skateboarding scene that was about to boom in mid-77. At the end of the year one of the boys Peter Clark broke and set a new world speed record of 100km per hour plus which was no mean feat on the equipment available in those days. I remember that the official speed was about 112kph. Peter, Raymond Hoey and I tended to go around together as we were from the same part of town and we would do demonstrations around the country and get paid for doing them. They were a lot better than me but I could hold my own and had no real interest in attending school as I thought that a career as a skateboarder was much more appealing.

It was the first few days before the official opening of the "Rand Easter Show" at the Wits University grounds. Raymond and Peter were part of a skate team called Solo Sport and it was the top team of the day. A sports chain had been convinced by the skate teams' manager to include the first real Skate ramp to be constructed in SA in their exhibition hall. It was a huge affair and as I was friendly with the team,

I would go with for the first few days and watch the rehearsals for the demonstrations and also to help work on the ramp itself which was a horrible job. I had to crawl into these tiny little spaces under the ramp and stick pink insulation fiberglass to the bottom of the construction to try and reduce the noise. I was in agony for the entire week.

I wasn't good enough to make the team though and one evening after working all day I walked past an exhibit where the guy had decided to include skateboards into his lineup of pool cleaning things to capitalize on the growing fad. What caught my attention was the small ramp that he had constructed outside his stall. I immediately went up to him and asked him if he had anyone who could ride the ramp and upon realizing there wasn't anyone besides his son, I grabbed the opportunity to try and get a job for the show. I soon got my friend Keith along to join me and so we would demo every half-hour or so and get paid to do it.

I guess it was my first "real" job!

The result was that by the middle of the year I didn't have any notebooks to speak of. It came as quite a surprise to my parents as my mom went through my bag one day to discover that my books were filled with sketches and many subjects were crammed into one notebook as the teacher would sometimes check what we were doing and I would cram it all onto a clean page and got away with this for months. The result of this was that I was forced to go to the vice heads office and copy my backdated notes in each subject while that particular class was in progress. It was the stupidest solution I could have imagined as no boy would borrow me his book to copy while he was actually supposed to be in that class. So I used to sit there while he snuck shots from his halfjack of brandy and await the inevitable beating that would ensue on average once a week when he was in the mood to torment me more than the usual string of abuse and reminders of what a miserable waste of creation I was. His name was Mr. Thomas and he was a bastard. He took pleasure in tormenting me, asshole.

The headmasters name was Mr. Hofmeyer and he was a spineless fool. What all of this amounted to was that my father threatened me with boarding school if I didn't pass my first year. Which of course I didn't. I managed a 13% aggregate for the first preliminary examinations which absolutely shocked the school authorities and so they had me do IQ tests and psychometric and aptitude tests. I was called out of class one day on the intercom which by then had become routine and I was sent to the library and sat with all the nondescripts of the school. Boys that had gained notoriety for having stabbed someone or punched a teacher or simply being so stupid that they couldn't write their own names, etc. So here I was in this class with kids with glasses five inches thick and prospective serial killers and we were expected to complete a battery of tests in a given time. I didn't think too much of it at the time but applied myself as I wasn't sure whether failure may mean a lunatic asylum or a lobotomy or both. It wasn't long after that I was summoned to the heads office and all hell had broken loose due to the fact that I had scored abnormally high marks. I was apparently one of two people in the JHB area that had managed to achieve such a result, but who knows? That could just have been more bullshit to keep me in line. It's also the point at which all my real troubles began.

The first time I left home was actually officially the second. The first time I didn't get much further than sitting at the bottom of the garden with a suitcase packed full of tinned food waiting for the sun to go down when my Mom came out and tried to talk me into forgetting the idea. Her approach was always "you want leave home!? Please do! I'll pack your bags" It was a kind of reverse psychology she thought was really nifty and sure to work. The second time was in the evening and I was about 12 at the time. I grabbed my skateboard and out the door, down the widow making Roberts Avenue and off to the park at the entrance to JHB before not knowing what to do exactly. I spent the night in the flower bed freezing my buns off and the next morning walked slowly back in the direction of home. I hadn't had supper the night before and was starving.

Eventually I went to our corner fish and chips shop and got a packet of chips from "The Beaver" as we used to call him. He took one look at me and said "Go home!"

Now that I was officially a smart alec the pressure to excel was applied in ever increasing daily doses. I was expected to catch up and move ahead super quick with no excuses and they took the attitude that my lack of achievement was due to lack of suitable stimulation resulting in boredom and not so much due to being a misfit.

Some time later during the Xmass holidays, I was at the Cresta centre skateboard park enjoying the final day of the break when much to my surprise my dad arrived carrying what looked like a box of pizza. Needless to say, I was quite puzzled as it was totally out of the ordinary. The package contained a school uniform for Athlone boys high which was a rough school down in Bez valley that had a rotten reputation. To put it bluntly I was scared shitless of the place and used to give it a wide berth on my various skate safaris around the area. To think that I was actually supposed to attend was beyond my comprehension. One hour later there I was with two beefy matriculant boys carrying my suitcase into an old manor house that had been converted into a "hostel" for the boarding school boys and was one of many in the area that was used as such. The rooms had been converted and contained double bunks and lockers. I walked up the stairs and they let me in and were very friendly and put down the case, closed the door and punched me full on in the stomach. I was doubled over and more in shock than anything as I had never been hit that hard by anyone ever and fought the impulse to retch all over their shiny black shoes. I was flabbergasted and from that moment onward my living hell never ceased. First there was initiation by the older boys which amongst other things comprised being struck on the chest with the bristle side of a toothbrush that would create a matrix pattern of small blood droplets that were not to be touched and had to coagulate to produce a "mark" that you had received initiation. There were 101 things that were expected of you as a boarder that was not required by the "day boys" and they had to be learnt double quick. The boarding school was a tough place to be. The "inmates" as I liked to call them had come from broken homes and some had been "boarders" since the first grade and knew the score in much the same way that an experienced prisoner would be familiar with prison life and so were automatically placed higher up on the pecking order. These kids had practically never known "home life" as many of us new boarders had and they were comfortable and adept at the ins and outs of boarding school life.

I'm in high school. The tennis club and my friend's house is just down the road that goes past the girls school. This for me is a regular and traumatic experience. It seems to be the same for the girls too. We are separated and repressed and are clueless as to how we should relate to each other. My biggest fear at this time was boarding a bus filled with ...schoolgirls!! A bunch of them together would terrorize the lunkiest muscle bound hulk with ease and a measure of perverse glee. They as a group could instill the fear of God into the meanest of the boys, more so than any teacher wielding a cane could.

Having come from the rival school across the hill I was most unpopular from the start and I arrived at a time when the headmaster of the school was serving his fifth year as head which meant that he had seen the matriculant boys from their first year through to their final one. His name was Buddy Heard and he was the most charismatic person I have ever met. He ruled the school with an iron fist that clutched a cane and meted out cuts to anyone and everyone at the drop of a hat and would have caned the masters too if he could have. He had seven children of which the first one was adopted and the rest simply flowed afterward. He treated them more severely than the other pupils in many cases in much the same way that I was treated on occasion at the centre. The word *severe* here deserves its italics. Within the first week he knew every new boy's name and at least a little about them. Their mothers name, previous school, distinctions or more frequently lack of distinction and so forth. He would interrupt the school's proceedings at any time and for any reason at a whim. He would grill teachers in front of the students or in public the same as he would any student irrespective of status or background. Nobody was above his wrath, no favorites, no excuses, no compromises, just the perennial "reign of terror" as he would announce when he deemed that things were getting out of hand. I was in awe of the man and petrified at the same time.

I was quick to adapt and suffered much less than boys who were having their first boarding school experience. I think that it was because I was used to the group mentality that I would come in contact with at the centre and at youth camps which were in a way a form of boarding in themselves.

Sport was compulsory and of course the shortest route to any kind of success. The head of the boarding school shocked me on one of the first few days of school by idling up beside me with his ever present cigarette and stating quite matter of factly. " Hmm, Myers...are you playing wing this year or fullback?' Without hesitation I announced " fullback sir!" resisting the urge to snap to attention, click my heels and scream SIEG HEIL!! He just sneered and said " Hmm, we will see" and drifted off in a cloud of choking smoke. This was the first day or two of the term and Rugby season was months away yet which serves to illustrate the fanaticism of these people and in particular this master who was to be our main coach for the next few years. I of course had little choice but to play rugby and never made the A team as hoped since the guys were basically much better and far tougher than me. Also, they had played together the previous year as a team and I arrived as an outsider and presented little opposition to the already established positions. I made the B team and played my guts out the whole season in the wing position. Somehow the coach thought I was fast enough but I truly wasn't and spent most practices and matches running my ass off just trying to keep up and rarely if ever saw the ball for more than a split second before I was summarily bulldozed by a pack of rabid animals out for blood. Repeatedly. I of course shrugged it off as I was a member of the elite and was in the continual pursuit of excellence that would enable me to have a successful school career and go on to become a rocket scientist and part time brain surgeon without batting an eyelid.

It's another late evening and we are surprised to hear a knock on the kitchen door. It's basically impossible as no one could come within 25m of the front gate without disturbing our large and vicious watchdog. "Miesies! Miesies!" We hear Aya's voice calling. Confusion gives way to panic as I rush to the door as I know there has to be something seriously wrong for her to disturb us at this hour. I open the door and there she is standing with a wad of bloodied toilet paper over her nose. My immediate thought is that she's been mugged but it turns out that her nose had started bleeding on its own for no reason some hours age and she is unable to stem the constant flow. She was losing blood at an alarming rate and was weakening rapidly and so without further ado my dad and I get her into the car and off we go to the Kensington clinic only half a km or so from our house. We are told that she cannot be seen and has to go to the black hospital. The closest black hospital is in Hillbrow so that's where we go. True to form she is told to take a seat and wait her turn. Its 10 pm and there's a line of people right out the front door and into the parking lot. Many had been there for most of the day to be treated. We were the only white people there excluding a few doctors. Mainly Indian doctors.

A hemorrhage in her nasal passage.

In some ways I was more afraid of the boys than the masters. The senior boys in particular as they would deal out physical punishments with impunity and it was run of the mill for me to have to bend down and receive a caning with a cricket bat or hockey stick from one of the seniors for any minor breach of the rules , laws or whims that frequently took the boys in question. I once carried the scars on my butt for weeks of a "caning" with an athletic running spike for basically challenging an older rather brutal hostel prefect. Cricket practice proved to be painful as the coach would reward a dropped catch with a whack of the bat and it would go on for ages. It was horrendously painful and I remember seeing one particularly outspoken but badly coordinated boys grey/yellow/purple backside in the shower after a catch practice. To me it was unbelievable but it was simply a fact of hostel life to be beaten each day starting at around 7am when we had to stand inspection and the housemaster would deal out cuts for clothing being badly folded or a bed being sloppily made and this would continue at morning assembly and throughout the school day for the day boys and into the evening for the boarders.

I was the captain of the u/15 A cricket team It was my job to look after the kitbag and as is my nature I was a little negligent and everyone would help themselves to whatever they needed whenever. One fine day I was called into the "Boss's" offices and Mr. Heard calmly and matter of factly told me while not even looking up from his stamp collection." Myers, it has come to my attention that the under 15 A kit has many items missing. You have until tomorrow 7 am to replace everything. I don't care how. It's your problem. If anything is missing from the original inventory you will be held accountable. Do we understand each other?" I duly replied "Yes Sir!" and got out of there as quick as greased lightning. I never even went back to class.

Straight to the hostel and into the 2nd teams kit. "Two bats and a pair of pads." Then off to the staffroom..."Sir I have been asked to fetch *the 1st team kit!" "Ok Myers! Make sure you don't bowl those stupid inswingers on Saturday." "Yes Sir!" And so it went. Eventually I had accumulated enough equipment to start my own Cricket Ranch and hefted it onto my shoulders and took it home! Straight into the garage and swiftly to work with the sander to remove any tell-tale signs such as permanent marker or brand names. I sanded the most expensive Cricket bats clean! It would have given a heart attack to the purist!*

Scoot back to make supper and roll call and hide the goods till morning.

The next morning at 7 am I was standing outside the office and Mr Heard arrived." Is It all there Myers?" He asked/accused/commanded.

"Oh YES! Sir!"

He proceeded to idly rummage through the huge bag of sweetly scented Willow and commented " Very unusual brand names these, aren't they Mr. Myers?'

"Brand new, top of the range Sir!" I said with absolute confidence!

I remember one incident in particular when the headmaster gave me an impromptu caning. It was one second after the bell had rung and I bounced a golf ball on the corridor floor and placed it back in my pocket. The head was standing on the next floor up and grabbed me by the hair and stuffed my head into a recess for a fire hose so that I couldn't "ride" the cut by bucking at the moment of impact and proceeded to give me about four cuts, screaming and ranting all the while. He had no qualms and immediately grabbed a few tardy onlookers and dished out the same to them before sauntering off down the corridor in search of more victims. He had on occasion walked into a group of rowdy boys with cane swinging and beat the crap out of the lot of them. That was our headmaster! It sounds very cruel and base but it has to be seen in perspective. When Mr Heard took over at Athlone boys there were boys that didn't even sleep at home. They would carry a plastic bottle of thinners or benzene in their inside blazer pockets and be high as a kite all day long. I knew of boys who would mug people at night to get money for food or just to play pinball at the arcade. It was a shock to me. A completely different world, unknown to me and one which I had watched from my house on the hill only two km's away for most of my life. That was a sore point actually. I was in the hostel and prohibited from going home except on Sundays and I could see my folks' bedroom window from my bed. Many of the kids were products of semi mixed marriages and were racially in what was known as "grey" areas. They were obviously of mixed blood but according to the law, possessed enough "white" blood to be legible to attend a white school such as Athlone. Some things about school life at Athlone were much the same as they had been at Jeppe. The dress code was strict and punishment was swift for those who over stepped the mark. No hands in pockets, hair two fingers above the collar and not to touch the top of the ear, black socks and trousers with upturned seam to be of the length that touches the top of the shoes, blah, blah, blah. The only real difference was that at Jeppe detention was a more common punishment for such offences whereas at Athlone it was corporal punishment all the way. Hair inspection was a constant and as a result of one particular incident I earned my first nickname which was a good thing as it was an identifying point that for the most part was positive even if the name was derogatory.

I was a male model!

Not the square kind that had square faces and lots of square abs and that would walk up and down the square.

I was the cheap kind. It was my mom's idea originally. She had heard about people doing adverts and getting paid for it and so she signed my younger sister, me and herself up. It meant going to a lot of auditions which were a real ordeal for me. You would sit in a queue with all the other hopefuls who were mostly asinine thespian self-obsessed types with huge egos and vacant headspace. I hated it.

When I was about 10 years old I went to an audition for a movie called "eLollipop" and it ended up that I got to the final selection and lost out to a guy called Norman Knox who got the main "white boy" part. The young black guy I never got to see and the same goes for the movie which was quite a success from what I could gather. I was dead shy and possibly this is what swung the decision in the other guys favor.

I would go to all these interviews and it was great as I would be allowed time off from school to do so. I landed a few jobs which were for the most part still shots and we would marvel at seeing our pictures in magazines and so on.

My most famous job though was for Coca Cola. I was 14 at the time and it was a job that most of the aspirants aspired to as to them they were destined for stardom and it was good for their so called "careers"

I got the job and went to the shoot and was told that the photographer was some really hot, hot shot. I was nervous as hell and sat and watched while this photographer's assistant ran around like a fly on dung and did EVERYTHING! He set up the set and the tripod and focus and the whole thing while the "hot shot" stood around being "muy importanto" and did diddley squat. I tried to act as cool as possible due to the fact that I was sitting next to a very pretty young lady and was trying to hide the fact that I was scared shitless! Not of the shoot. Of her! Girls drove me nuts and I had no idea how to behave.

Eventually the "light was right" and so the Hot shot walks up and looks through the camera and says something to his assistant who adjusts something and then proceeds to say stuff to us like..."smile!" "that's right" "uh...you! tilt your head back more" and so on. I cover up my embarrassment by whispering things straight, fixed, smiling faced at the lady and get her to giggle and the shoot goes swimmingly. Eventually the hot shots finger must have gotten tired as he declares "it's a wrap!" and we go home.

It's some weeks later when I'm in the car with my mom and with my head in a book as usual. She stops at a traffic light and says to me "hey! Look at this" I ignore her as we are not really speaking and she's insistent. Eventually I relent and jerk up my head "WHAT!" and find myself staring at the back of a Coca Cola delivery truck that has my grinning mug splashed all over the back. It's HUUUGE! I don't know what to say and my first thought is "Oooh boy! What are the guys at school going to say about this!"

When I get back to school I get dubbed "Coca Cola boy" amongst other things. The kicker is that almost to a man, I am chastised for having worn a KES rugby jersey!! Even the masters take up the chant. I don't know what to say. I try to explain that red is the color of the company and its not up to me what costume I will wear. They play it all down and accuse me for not being loyal enough and insisting on wearing the Athlone colors! I just shook my head.

I continued to do this kind of work for years and would get a small percentage of the cash only. My mom would take most of it and say that I would get the rest as needed or some such crap. I never saw it mostly. The Coke jobs money I did get though, and it was used to buy my first cassette tape Walkman which I used continually. I didn't have enough for the machine and was about 10 rand short which my mom put in with the clear understanding that it was my birthday present!

I later used this experience to be more confident at other auditions and worked in the movies a lot as an extra as well as doing ads for film and television. I got to meet some of the local and international stars and it supported me at a time I would have starved otherwise. I liked the movies and could happily work on set again. I wasn't much of an actor though. In real life I have pulled off some incredible parts and mostly off the cuff, but to do a scene over and over with all kinds of people watching is really hard. I have great respect for the good actors. They work hard. The downside is that I can hardly get caught up in a movie as I'm always aware of the technical things that go unnoticed by most people. It's rare that I'm emotionally involved in the film.

A funny twist to the story is that years later I did a Pepsi ad and was (I'm told) one of the main characters. I never got to see the ad as it appeared in cinema theatres and I could never afford to go and see a movie. A few weeks after doing the Pepsi shoot, I was accepted to do a shoot with the band Mango Groove If I remember correctly and it was for Coca Cola. The people who were doing the shoot were also many of the crew that had done the Pepsi one and so I was told " sorry! You can't be used! You have to go!" I thought "Bugger this" and went to the director and told him that I had come all the way from JHB to Pretoria to be told "Sorry!" it was uncool. I should be compensated! And I was!!

I got paid not to be in a Coca Cola advert!

70 rand!!

One evening I arrived back at the hostel and realized that Monday was a whole school hair inspection and these were usually carried out by the head and the vice and usually were more severe than usual. I had no one to cut my hair and it was borderline but not short enough to escape unscathed so I took it upon myself to cut my own hair.

The resultant creation was an unusually avant-garde rendition of contemporary British punk rock style. That my wonderful locks had all these aesthetically pleasing attributes was unbeknown to me as I had no idea of punk rock at that time and neither did anyone else for that matter. Needless to say, the next morning I was tossed out of school and sent to the barber to repair the damage which he was unable to do with any success and I returned to school and was promptly referred to as "spikes" or "spiky"

I was a straight C student for the most part and really only paid any attention to art which I loved. We were forced to sit down every evening for "prep" which was a two-hour homework session in which I basically sketched under the pretense that it was art and copied my homework religiously from one of the more duty-bound and shall we say "malleable" students. We were allowed to read when homework had supposedly been completed and this is how I occupied most of my time.

The single contributing factor to me becoming more aware of the kind the kind of shadow life that was being lived right under my nose was when I first started smoking dope.

If you wanted to get some you knew that a black person would know where to get it. It wasn't so easy. You had to get it from the right person as whiteys were generally not to be trusted. So through word of mouth and introduction you would meet the right guy. Quite often the person you least suspected. A woman who tended to geriatrics, or a simple house maid who you may have known for years may be knocking out matchboxes of ganja every night from her rooms window at the bottom of your very own garden. It was weird.

Quite often I would go into the compounds where no white people besides policemen might ever have been. An entirely independent world from the one you may have been familiar with. There the tables were turned. You were the outsider and your laws no longer applied.

I was very much into music and I suppose you could say it was my major interest at this time. Having had a sister who was older and had introduced me to what was then termed "underground" music I was quite knowledgeable and familiar with a genre that was shared by boys a little older than I was and so I struck up acquaintances with some of the more marginal characters at school. These guys were not only familiar with the music but also with some of the associated peripheral activities such as drug use and so on. Many admitted openly that they smoked dope and would boast about getting drunk at parties on the weekends that of course I was unable to attend due to being involved with sports and having to stay in the hostel. My mother had effectively scared the daylights out of me by telling me what a one way ticket drugs were since she was a victim of all the propaganda and had worked with kids and adults who had abused drugs but had no real first-hand experience of her own and so carried over her fear of the unknown to me with interest. I had an almost inbred fear and since I never smoked cigarettes there was no natural intermediary step for me to take on the way to experimenting with grass which was the most commonly used substance at the time.

I was atypical hostel boy with my straw basher askew on my head and attending all school functions across the scope of activities and leading the rest of the school in the war cry at sports events. The whole atmosphere of the school, just like that of Jeppe and a few others was molded on the English model and followed similar endeavors such as a debating society and a chess club, all reminiscent of the Goodbye Mr. Chips kind of environment. It was all very much in the shadow of the British ideal environment for boys education. The school tie and all that shit.

It was years later when looking for my first apartment that I had the good fortune to experience the "School tie" thing. I was sitting in a line at the estate agents and was wearing my rugby jersey. I was well at the back of the line and when the door opened I was immediately waved through the door. I pointed out that I wasn't next but it was ignored and the estate agent said" Yes! What can I do for you?" I proceeded to explain that I was looking for a flat and had found one after searching for months and was desperate. He asked me" Job?" " Uhh not yet!" How much money do you have in the bank then?' " Uhh... 35 cents!" He looked up at me sharply and got straight on the phone. "Pease bring me Mr. Myers' bank statement" It arrived from downstairs and he looked at it and then at me. "How do you expect me to trust a man who doesn't know his own bank account?' He asked... "I ...Uh?" " You have 39 cents not 35!" "Ahhh! Interest! Of course!" I replied with an apologetic air. He was pretty matter of fact about it to me. " If you were a KES boy I would have no problem with you but you're from Jeppe. I'm not in the habit of supporting our rivals but as you have been pathetically honest with me,

I will have to make a concession. Get your father to sign and the place is yours. Late with rent and you're out! Next!"

Sport took up practically all of my so called spare time and I developed into a pretty fair cricketer, consistently in the A team of my age group and then being on the reserve list for the first team along with two others that showed promise early on and eventually team captain, opening bowler and batsman. To add to this I also played for the old boys team on Sundays which meant that I played cricket 7 days a week throughout the season. Having been considered by others to be someone with talent was a view that I never shared. I suffered from extremely low self-esteem and probably it was the reason that I would work so hard to make the grade. I never involved myself in physical fights and so was thought of as being a wuss which was an open invitation to the cowardly boys from higher forms that would bully the younger ones to compensate for their obvious inadequacy with their peers. Fact was that although I refused to fight, I could take a knock on the rugby field and often give better than what I got so I was in a shady area for the ones that would be inclined to pick on the weakest and by and large they left me alone. My noninvolvement in fisticuffs was probably due to the fact that it was a severely punishable offence and due to my exposure to the various institutions in the past was more afraid of that than the jeers and insults of the boys that I knew I could easily get the better of physically. The other major contributing factor to my so called pacifism was the fact that I had practiced Judo and achieved a respectable rank and non-aggression was bred into us by the instructors and main teacher, so I never really felt a need to have to prove myself and knew that I was adhering to the martial code of only using your art when all other avenues had been exhausted and only if your life was in danger. I know how it sounds but I really took that stuff to heart and followed the precepts of our school to the letter. I still practice the Chinese arts and take it even more seriously today than I did then.

I was in love. I was in love for a long time too.

It was my habit to go over to my girlfriend's house at night. Late, late at night. I would climb out of my window and then go straight over the wall onto the koppie and walk swiftly through the near pitch black to the border with Bez Valley. I would then walk straight across and then make my way through the huge park on the other side, keeping a keen eye out for anyone and avoiding them like the plague. It could be police or civilians. Either wasn't welcome. It was too late. I would then make the last leg of the 7km walk and sneak down the drive of my girlfriends next door neighbor, taking special care not to alert the dogs or be heard by her Father as I passed dangerously close to his window. I would then throw small bits of gravel against her window and when she woke, would go to the back door and unlock it. I had to then sneak back down the drive and into her driveway and round to the back door and as quietly as possible open the door without having the dog go berserk, and then lock it again so it wouldn't arouse suspicion if discovered. Then, with my heart beating like a conga I would hold my breath and walk the scariest walk of my life in complete darkness down the passage, past the open door of her father's room and into her room next door. Close the door quietly and then a few more steps before diving under the covers and becoming re acquainted with the necessary activity known as breathing.

The rest of the night would be dedicated to a slightly different but just as necessary activity until exhaustion would set in and a short , fitful hour or so sleep before hearing her father awake and then ducking under the covers as it was his habit to take a peek into the room and then make his way to have his mornings bath. I would listen to the water running and the rustle of newspapers and the snap of the first beer of the day that he liked to drink whilst reading the paper in the steaming bath. This was my moment and it was a critical one. I had to sneak past him while the door was open and he only a few feet away from me. Then out the door that had been unlocked for me and run like hell all the way home to sneak back through my window before my folks would wake up.

I would go through this routine for YEARS! Not once being caught but on many occasions getting so close I wouldn't believe it possible to have gotten away.

I got caught by my folks but never by her father. He showed me the shotgun that he said he would shoot me with when he saw that we were in fact serious and having a long-term relationship. The bloody gun would be right next his bed.

The closest shave I had was one day when he arrived unexpectedly and I had no choice but to dive under the bed. He spoke to my girlfriend for a while and it was getting later and later and eventually she had to leave for school, leaving me in the house with him. It had happened once or twice before and it was just a question of waiting in out on the other side of the huge house, but as fate would have it. This time would be different. After she left he came into the room and flopped over onto the bed! He was lying a mattress thickness away from my sweating and hardly breathing body! He stayed there for the whole morning! I nearly died. He was snoring and farting and I was praying my stomach wouldn't growl or something to alert him. Eventually he got up and went to the kitchen and I somehow ducked past him when he went to the balcony. I was locked in due to the burglar proofing and had to use the door. I hopped the back fence and ran like blazes through the next property, praying that the dogs would be too startled to give case and that the owner wouldn't see this skinny teenager running like a bolt of lightning through the vegetable patch.

My troubles were not over as I had not been to school and my folks were more than curious to know where I was at breakfast time but as fate works in both directions sometimes, they believed me when I told them I had left for a pre-school tennis practice with my doubles partner as the club championships were coming up.

I couldn't believe it and when I next saw my girlfriend we just looked at each other and shook our heads, not sure if laughing was the right way to go. It's not something we could very well share with our friends.

As in most schools countrywide we had two mornings per week where we had to do what was called cadets. This meant dressing up in a military uniform and marching around like morons to the screaming and shouting of higher ranked boys and masters who tried to re live their failed military lives vicariously for two hours each time. The whole point of the exercise was to prepare for the El Alamein parade that was held once a year and in which boys who didn't wiggle their toes effectively would pass out in the heat and fall unceremoniously flat on their faces and lie there till they were placed on a stretcher and carried off to be revived by being placed under a running tap on the side of the parade ground. I did this the first year and wondered how the hell these boys got to be stretcher bearers. That was a cool job. You sit in the shade of the trees and run out sporadically to fetch the fallen and cart them back to be resurrected and ready for next year's parade. It got even better when I realized that they were all members of the musketry squad. Now I loved to shoot, in fact it was one of my major pastimes when I was a kid roaming the koppies with my air gun and was a pretty crack shot. Problem was that it was practically impossible to join the squad. In order to join you had to be able to shoot and in order to prove that you could you had to get a chance to do so and there was no trial or notification whatsoever. It was a closed club of super elite boys who basically got in through word of mouth and status, so it was comprised of the first team rugby captain and the athletic victor lad aurum and so on. I stood no chance. None. That's exactly why I decided to simply report to the shooting range the very next time we had cadets. The teacher was my other rugby coach and threatened to cane me on principle but I insisted that I was a good shot and made a deal that if I wasn't up to par that he could dismiss me with a thoroughly good caning and there would be no further argument. It was agreed and while he warmed up to tan my hide I stuck 5 rounds straight through the bull! I was in. No more marching for me and to top it all I managed to become the best junior shottist that year and later the best senior. Not to mention the added bonus of being included with the best of the best.

Cadets was officially referred to as 'Youth Preparedness?"

There was stiff competition between the masters to acquire the best sportsmen for their teams and in my case this was quite comical. My cricket master knew I could swim and due to the fact that the headmaster was fanatical about swimming he ordered a swimming trial in which every new boy had to participate. If they were half good they were sentenced to be swimmers which meant pre-school 100 lengths each morning regardless of the temperature and irrespective of whether the boy actually made a team or not. My cricket master who was also my hostel master knew that if the head saw me swim he would take me and my cricket career would effectively be over before it started and there was precious little the cricket master could do about it. I was pulled aside before the trial and ordered to "fake it" and was shadowed step by step under the pretense of encouragement but actually having to listen to his admonitions..."not so fast Myers...not so smooth...do you want to swim at 7am or play cricket?" and so on. I was passed over for the team and all went well until the school gala. This was a serious affair as all house events were to be and the division was always day boys vs. boarders. I was on the team of course with the school's best in the relay and not only did we win both the crawl and medley but set up a school record that stands to this day in both events. The head understood immediately what had transpired and true to form never mentioned it except for a straight-faced compliment to me for my miraculous improvement in such a short time. I thanked him with an equally straight face and added that I was quite surprised myself at the transformation. He was like that. He could beat the crap out of you at a moment's notice for no real reason and then inquire as to the health of your ailing grandma in the same breath. All with absolute sincerity.

I had some terrible teachers and some great ones. One that comes to mind was my English teacher Mr. Connor who was a total bastard and never paused for a moment in making my life hell. He would punish me by making me write out Mark Anthony's speech ten times as often as he could and ridicule me as a standard procedure. I think he hated me out of respect and I respected him out of unadulterated hatred. It was a compatible arrangement. I went back to that school years later and approached him and asked if he remembered me and his response was "Unfortunately yes!" and I said thank you to him for teaching me many things that I only realized afterward. He smiled and said something to the effect that the penny is predictably slow to drop and dismissed me with a smile. No questions about my current life or occupation or what you would expect. He was completely disinterested. He was a dedicated teacher though and I respected him. Funny thing is though I only remember the first two lines of the speech and couldn't continue if my life depended on it! Go figure...

I had finally managed with great difficulty to convince my parents that I would be much more successful as a day boy than as a boarder and continued to attend Athlone much to the disgust of my masters who wouldn't even speak to me and the boys who called me things like 'Traitor" and 'Sell out" I thought it was all a little childish and had made up my mind to try my best to return to Jeppe. I still had friends there and it seemed to be a far more civilized place to be.

The master that had encouraged me to fail the swimming trial had recently moved to Jeppe as a teacher and I met with him and discussed the possibility of him putting a good word for me with the new headmaster. He agreed to help as long as I agreed to be on his high jump team and represent the school in athletics. I was at this stage very serious about Tennis and he understood that I wanted to come back to Jeppe as they had an unusually strong first team and I wanted to be on it and so didn't mind that I was uninterested in cricket or rugby. Tennis was the only activity that my father had said I was *good* at. Whenever I had achieved something extraordinary the best praise I could hope for would be "Hmm you're coming along nicely" period. He was an enthusiastic player and a great badminton player and one Sunday after knocking around with him he said with great solemnity " you're a good player. You should work at it" I was speechless. I had never heard him say that to me before or since. It's just the way he is made. He was brought up to be stoic and he would praise and chastise with equal reserve.

So... I played tennis. Athlone had a pretty dismal team and I managed to make the first team as a pretty dismal player to emphasize the point and the sport itself was generally looked down upon by the school as a whole. We played all kinds of even dismaller schools which we would thrash. I had joined the local tennis club and was improving rapidly and knew that although I may not make the first team at Jeppe, at least tennis players were respected and the guys from the club would be my classmates.

It was a trend for me to focus more on the individual activities such as skateboarding, high jump and tennis as opposed to the team sports at this time. I didn't have to rely on anyone else or let people down if I was having a bad day.

Getting back to Jeppe was great for me. I was now in a class where most of the guys were my age and I was respected by the class above that were now seniors as we used to be together and things were good on the whole.

This time I got mad and left home. For more than one night. I went and got a job as an usher at the civic theater and saw Evita 51 times. I hate Evita! We were referred to as "hosts" as it was thought that it was possibly classier and actually you didn't show people to their seats you just told them where to go "Good evening! G 27? Seventh row down on your right-hand side!" I wore my dad's black suit jacket and my big black boots and my school shirt complete with bow tie! I stayed at the tennis club and slept in the bar for close on two months!!

The following 2 years were turbulent. Although I was actively playing tennis and physically very fit, the emphasis was slowly starting to focus on the more adult activities like chasing girls and going to parties. I started experimenting with drugs at this stage and fluctuated between being goal oriented in my studies and tennis and not caring at all about anything really. I had a girlfriend for the first time and was hopelessly in love which as foolish as it may sound was a deciding factor in keeping my stability both mentally and physically. My relationship with my parents was abysmal and especially the tension with my mom was getting to breaking point. It was always bad. At the age of 11 I refused to speak Afrikaans or to go on the mindless Sunday visits to see the family and it created a rift between us that never healed. Bad went to worse and worse became a new dimension of anger and abuse that I couldn't believe I was capable of and yet was actively engaging in. Our relationship had always been a tempestuous one and as the gap widened into an abyss I was shocked to realize that I truly hated her and all the hypocritical bullshit that she stood for. True to my promise I have never uttered a word of Afrikaans in her presence and only on the rarest of occasions have I seen any of my many uncles, aunts, nephews and nieces since. If one of them walked past me in the street tomorrow I would not be able to recognize them.

As I was quite open about my experimentation with drugs, it was seized upon as the root cause of all my dissention and blamed wholesale for everything that was happening to me. This frustrated me no end as I saw that the people who were supposedly trying to help me in effect didn't know shit from sugar and I lost faith entirely in the so-called establishment and their supposed omnipotence. I felt like I was surrounded by self-righteous fools and the sad fact of the matter was that I was but I must add that there were a few notable exceptions. It meant nothing to me whether I passed or failed, whether I was accepted or not. Nothing made much sense and I suffered from severe bouts of depression and sleeplessness. Of course my grades plummeted and clashes with the authorities became more and more frequent.

It was a hard year and I narrowly survived. I would steal any bottle of alcohol from my dad's liquor cabinet and hit the streets to gatecrash a party or simply wander around.

Having a capacity for booze (possibly due to my Irish heritage) I was soon bored with throwing up all over my shoes from over indulgence and it wasn't long before I made the transition to experimentation with over the counter drugs. Cough mixtures would be knocked back and then a day of disorientated wandering around. My drug of choice became Toluene which I would obtain by sniffing my mother's industrial strength leather glue and unlike others I knew that abused it by breathing or "huffing" it with a plastic bag, I would meticulously prepare the mixture and seclude myself and literally "sniff" it through my nose. I loved the smell anyway and found that my experiences were markedly different from those of my friends. I had a long and far more tempestuous affair with toluene than with anything else. My experiences with glue deserve a book of its own and I won't relate them here except to say that under the influence I experienced the full range of human emotion, both positive and negative.

The year was a disaster and culminated in a double attempted suicide which landed me in a psychiatric ward and totally re arranged the landscape of my immediate future in a way that's hard to relate or even begin to try and describe.

I had decided to "check out" consciously some time before the actual attempt. I chose the day and cut school and locked myself in the caravan at home where I would not be disturbed and proceeded to ingest a cocktail of pills that was guaranteed to take me out for the full count. My father, for some reason started feeling uncomfortable at work and for some even more mysterious reason followed his instincts and came home to investigate and upon passing the caravan he called my name. I was completely quiet and there was no way he could have known I was there and yet he took it upon himself to force the door and found me passed out on one of the bunks. He slapped me around a bit to revive me and decided that the best course of action to take would be to take me down to see the social worker at SANCA (the South African National Council for Alcoholism and drug Addiction) where I had become an outpatient on the recommendation of the schools social worker. Before leaving home I snuck into the bedroom and raided my mom's medicine chest or chemistry lab whichever you like to choose and swallowed 140+ tablets without anyone's knowledge. We went off to the clinic and I remember sitting, facing the head therapist/doctor and thinking what an asshole he was to be rabbit ting on about something totally unrelated while my life was percolating away right before his eyes. I eventually fell straight over on the chair and my dad who was present realized that something major was up and dragged me through the streets to the car without any assistance from these stupid pricks and rushed me off to the closest hospital. When I reached there I started going berserk as I was trying to prevent them from pumping my stomach and had to be restrained. I remember only snippets of the whole scene. At one stage a senior doctor came into the curtained off chamber and in an authoritive tone told me to shut up and cooperate or something equally dumb and my response to him was " If you come any closer I'll puke on you motherfucker!" he ignored my threat, advanced and I sprayed him with bright red puke. I have no idea if it was a drink I was given or what but he turned on his heel and left cursing all the while. I then remember losing coordination entirely and the buggers managed to stuff this rippled tube straight down my throat after prizing open my clenched jaw. That's it. I was in a coma for a week afterward and regained consciousness in the Johannesburg general hospital's closed psychiatric ward.

I spent about a week in this crazy place with the craziest people imaginable. People who had lost the plot completely. I was drugged to the gills and obviously unable to assimilate the experience in any way whatsoever. What I do remember was how I felt when my girlfriend arrived and realizing how much I loved her and how much I would miss her and the pain that she would have had to endure had I been successful. A comical moment was when I took her aside and whispered to her that "they" had put magnets in our feet to prevent us from running away and at the same moment I realized what I had said and the absolute ridiculousness of the statement and we both broke into gales of laughter until we had tears in our eyes.

I would have to get up each day and stay out of bed and be grilled by a particularly cruel, stupid and very gay doctor who practically demanded to know why I had attempted to kill myself with such determination and the more he would persist and threaten me with institutionalization for life as a "state presidents patient" with no hope of release, the more I would clam up and refuse to comply. He was a total asshole and I had nothing but contempt for him and all his Freudian bullshit and I told him so to his face. Often. I thought it interesting that "they" had, or were about to decide that I was incapable of taking responsibility for my own life and so "they" would ever so kindly step in and take it upon themselves to be responsible for my life for an indefinite period of time. In fact, PW Botha himself was to hold the course of my precarious little, insignificant life in his hands personally and do so at the tax payers expense!

How cool is that?! I was and still am amazed. I of course considered my attempted suicide a highly personal matter and wasn't about to spill my guts to this fool or any other. It left me in a rather sticky predicament and I had to take some kind of action and so one day I locked myself into the lecture room that had a double blackboard in it and chalk and proceeded to put down in words what I called " the Jon-Pat Manifesto!" It was basically an overview of how I saw life and what I wanted from it, complete with illustrations and I was hoping to present it to the authorities at my next grilling session. Unfortunately, halfway through my masterpiece one of the orderlies discovered the locked door and panicked as they thought I was trying a third attempt and so I had to complete my life's statement super quick while they tried to talk me out of knocking myself off, convince me to open the door and surreptitiously force the door as quietly as they could without causing me to panic! Ha! Ha! It was a pathetically ridiculous scene. I managed to stay ahead of the pace and when they eventually broke through and rugby tackled me unnecessarily and subdued my resistant free resistance with well-practiced full pretzels I shouted for the doctor to come and read for himself and then decide how insane I really was in his own time and at his leisure. Well, he did and so did many others that were invited to visit and within 24 hours I was released and went home with a collection of bags containing the tiniest little pills that were supposed to be administered by my folks and guaranteed to turn me into a happy carefree youth with an insatiable appetite for the oyster of life or something like that...

I wish I had managed to record what I had written on the board. I remember the picture that I drew of a small house on a cliff overlooking the sea. Beach buggy parked in a carport with a surfboard on the roof rack. A simple life.

I wanted to live in a world where I could fulfill my potential as a human being and not in one where I fulfilled the need of a society geared toward exploitation and service for cash. This is what I felt I was being groomed to be by the school system and the society with its group mentality that I found so hard to relate to.

As is to be expected, my recollection of these events is not very coherent but that's the way it is with my whole life. I can recall the most mundane things with absolute clarity but I'm buggered if I can tell you when it happened according to date. I can place the events chronologically pretty well mostly but I'm unable to put them clearly into the context of time. It's strange.

I would go to many "Therapy" sessions and sometimes the usual therapist would be absent and I would get a substitute. On one such occasion this rather pointy cornered young lady walked in after very recently having been unwrapped from the packaging material she had been sent in by the university and seeing me sitting staring out of the window at the street below inquired " What do you see when you look out like that?" Soft soothing tone of voice and all... I replied " Ants!" She hesitated for a while and said very ordinally. " Ants?!' I said "Yeah Lots of stupid little ants going here and going there and ending up where they started their day so they can rest and continue the same stupid activity tomorrow and the next day!" There was a pause and she said ".... I seee...Hm..."

The session went as it had come and the following meeting I was cornered by my regular therapist. "Tell me straight! Have you been abusing again or not? Did you arrive stoned for the last meeting?!" Now I NEVER went to my sessions stoned and challenged her to mention one occasion on which I had done so. "The other therapist has scheduled a urine test so you better come clean with me!" she said with annoyance. I replied that I'm ready for a test if she wants. "What's going on?" She replied with a shaking of her head. " Its written here that you have been having hallucinations and reported seeing INSECTS!" When I explained what had transpired we weren't sure whether to laugh or cry.

It was a turning point for me. The staff at school as well as the boys seemed to have a completely different attitude towards me. It was a quite shocking thing for them to realize that I had undertaken to do such a serious act with such single mindedness and for the most part I was left with much more freedom than ever before. I was told that I could return to school when I felt ready and did exactly that. I never carried a schoolbag and also never bothered to write my examinations and naturally never progressed to the next grade and had to repeat the year.

Before the end of the year I was approached by one of the masters who was head of department as well as being the headmaster of one of the boarding schools. I knew him well and he taught languages and had a reputation for being strict and quite liberal with the use of the cane. He called me to his office one day and offered me the opportunity to live as a boarder at his hostel and placed very little restriction on my movements or actions. He was a highly intelligent and compassionate man with a great deal of insight to match and I took up the challenge and started the year as a "hostel boy" only a few hundred meters from my home. The deal was simple and with only the proviso that I would inform him of my movements and complete all my homework assignments. Failure to do so would result in immediate expulsion. I was to be his own personal boarder with my own room and not connected to the rest of the place at all except for the eating of meals. It was a great set up and I immediately applied myself to improve my academic standard and participate in school activities.

He was a man true to his word and always had an open door to discuss anything and everything. He wouldn't beat around the bush and would come straight to the point and had no tolerance for fools whatsoever.

I am greatly indebted to Peter van der Wolf for the period that I spent with him. He allowed me to be me and to analyze and discover what it was that I really wanted. He would not let me off lightly for anything and re instilled the desire to be excellent at whatever it was that I chose to do and what's more, respected the choices I made whether he was in agreement or not.

To jump forward a little...I did very well while I was lodging at the hostel. I had achieved my half colors for tennis and excelled academically. More importantly I complied with Mr. van der Wolf's stipulations and the result was that I no longer abused drugs at all except for the occasional drunken party. I decided to leave school before the end of the year which not only shocked everyone but badly let down Mr. van der Wolf and it was years later on one of my many visits to him that we breached the subject. I, it was said, would have achieved my full colors for tennis and no doubt been the captain of the first team. Being a prefect at Jeppe was out of the question but whilst at Athlone it was quite sure that I would be one of the two vice head boys. I was unaware of this fact until I spoke with one of the masters years later who told me this, much to my disbelief as I would never have guessed that they thought so highly of me.

In my opinion I am definitely not cut out for that kind of a job.

The eventual reasons for me leaving school early are based on internal politics and its useless to discuss. I reached a point in my life at that stage where I felt I had to make a decision. I knew there was no going back and that my choice would affect me for the rest of my life. It was a hard thing for me to do at the tender age of 17 and it took all of my willpower and resolve to undertake, but I did. I made a choice and its one that I have suffered for many, many times throughout my life but one that I have no regrets whatsoever about.

Quite the contrary.

Besides...at school they tried to teach me what to think. Not how to think.

Veldschool

I grew up with a black person in my house. She was my proxy mom and carried, fed, changed my nappies and cared for me with as much love and attention as any mother would. She was a special woman as it was said that she was a "Sangoma" but whether that's really true I couldn't know. She definitely knew about herbs and treated people on occasion as well as acting as midwife to friends and strangers alike. She was also one of the elders in her church which was an African church whose congregation met each Sunday out in the veld and would sing and chant in the rock lined circle they had established in the earth. She was a kind of "in-betweener" in that the traditional values and beliefs of the African people at that stage were still firmly entrenched in their minds and actions yet they also incorporated a European approach to Christianity by singing hymns and prayer and so on. So they would worship in the bush in a sort of hybridized version of organized religion. I have mentioned Andries at length who taught me so many things and particularly what it really meant to be a man in the true sense of the word.

I grew up with all this and absolutely no knowledge whatsoever that Nelson Mandela existed. The first exposure I had to his name was noticing some graffiti on an underpass where there were slogans like "Power to the people" written hastily in black spray and also "free Nelson Mandela" Someone had added underneath 'With every box of Kellogg's cornflakes!" I asked about this and was told that it was the work of "the terrorrrists." Terrorism, of course was the huge blanket of fear that we were all brought up beneath. Communism was the buzzword and as I understood it "they" were infiltrating "us" at every turn and mostly attacking our subconscious minds... If we weren't extra vigilant, we would end up being nothing more than slaves to the "Blacks"

This is typical from the time that I grew up.

For me, I think, the main split happened when I decided to leave the Afrikaans school. A few experiences that I had had compacted my decision. The boy who acted as the referee to many of my fights, lived just around the corner from our house and we were quite close for a time. He was the "uber kind" and was the best academic, runner, rugby player and 2nd best swimmer in our class of course! He had convinced my mom that he would help me with my homework and so a few days each week I was allowed to skip the centre and I would go and visit Deon where, true to his word we would do homework, for 1 minute and then spend the rest of the afternoon raising hell in the neighborhood. Usually the "game" would be a test of strength or simply stupid activities to see how much punishment we could tolerate from his older brother before we lost consciousness or were decapitated or both. The thing that struck me was when we would go and have lunch at his house. He like everyone had a black domestic servant who he would call " die meit" which means "the maid" but which has a rather negative connotation much like "nigger bitch" I suppose. He was only 11 years old and he would speak to this woman with absolute contempt which shocked me as I was taught to respect my elders regardless. I was not only shocked but more confused in a way as I simply could not understand his hostility toward her and towards all the " die fokken kaffirs" But at school even the teachers would take that tone and you would hear them ranting in the staffroom at breaks how it would be a good idea to blow up the mines to take care of the lot of them and suchlike talk. Them and us. I just didn't feel so much like I was one of us so much anymore. I have never called anyone a kaffir in my life and it's a form of address that when I hear it just boils my blood. Even just relating this story my skin crawls to write it. It's such a stupid term anyway as the real meaning of the word would apply to the Christians automatically as it is an Arabic term meaning "non believer" in Allah of course. Anyway, Deon used to order her around and she would bow and scrape and then go outside and curse him in Zulu which he couldn't understand. I would though and would treat her with respect which would earn his derision and on occasion she would get fed up and tell him that he could learn some manners from me and his response was to threaten her with a beating. This from an 11-year-old. With total impunity. For Deon it was the right thing to do. He was merely behaving as he was taught. He didn't want to be seen as weak. I couldn't relate to it and it bothered me no end. It was a total contrast going to visit my English friend Grant. If he had spoken that way to his servant, he would have received a beating from his father that he would never forget. Daisy, their housemaid was more like a friend or perhaps colleague than a "Worker" She also lived outside in her own little room and so on but she was treated with a lot more respect and I would be intensely aware of the difference between Deon and Grants home.

Perhaps reading this you may be thinking how crazy it was for practically every household having a servant but growing up with it was accepted as a part of life. You grew up saying " the garden boy" I remember one day at age 23 saying "where's the boy?" realizing at the same moment...Oh my God! I'm talking about Elvis here! Wow! Is this me? The man who works with us. A man old enough to be my father and I'm calling him "the garden boy" For Chrissakes, is it that deeply ingrained in me?

It was the kind of life that we lived. We wouldn't consider things like that and yet if someone had addressed or referred to you in that fashion you would be immediately insulted. Looking back I'm amazed at the way our realities were "conditioned" There was no freedom of the press so you would never know what was actually happening and it may be happening just down the road.

The first main event that literally rocked my boat and in fact everyone's boat was in 76 on the occasion of the "Soweto riots" The day of the event, I was in my street playing cricket with one of my neighbors when we were interrupted by the boys mom who told him to get straight inside and told me to go directly home. I asked her what all the fuss was about and she said "the blacks have gone berserk! and are on their way. Go home!" I remember standing there and said " Anyone comes near me and they will get a taste of this!" waving my bat threateningly through the air while taking a good look at the bottom of the street to make sure that it actually was safe. The fact that THOUSANDS of people were dancing in unison and creating all kinds of havoc never occurred to me. I had never seen a single picture of a demonstration, riot or any such thing and there simply wasn't anything in my mind that would come close to providing me with a conscious image to relate to. Today, with the internet and cable television news it is inconceivable but in those days it was simple cold fact. The news that we did get was of "them" burning down the schools which had been built with white tax payers money and naturally just impacted the rift between the races. The standard gripe was that 'we build their schools with our hard work and this is what they do!"

I'm in my 20's. My friend Shaun and I, the two skate punks, decide we are going to go to Vereeniging, a town some 40 or so km away as there is a skateboard park there. We decide to jump the train and go in the 3rd class compartment as there is no conductor checking these carriages.

Now we hopped the train that went through Soweto due to the fact that we had never actually seen the place from the inside and were curious.

We enter the place shortly after leaving JHB station and the first impression was of row upon row upon row of small houses which were aptly named "matchboxes" I had seen such images before in paintings by the more politically orientated artists that would depict these images and I truly thought that it was exaggerated to produce a dramatic effect. I was amazed to discover that the artists never could have captured the immensity if they tried.

We enter and I expect that soon we will be out into the country and on our way. It takes <u>three hours</u> for us to get through this endless expense of "matchboxes" It's not a pleasant trip. At the stations, there are young kids who run beside the train and hop on clutching desperately and beg through the tiny open slit of a window. When they see us in "their" train they go ballistic and hurl abuse, spit and try to throw rocks through the small window. Eventually one of the many package laden ladies comes to us and suggests that we sit on the floor and in so doing will not attract so much attention and be safer. We hastily take her advice and although the trip is not as intense it is still pretty hairy as when the kids see us, they uniformly take an aggressive attitude.

I am shaken to my boots. Not by fear but by the enormity of the place. Hill after hill of these small houses. At one stage I suspect we are traveling in circles but it's not that simple. The black adults on the train are quiet and more than a little uncomfortable with us being there and more than one moves to another carriage at first opportunity. I am always amazed how some people will risk so much to help us as reprisals are swift and brutal for so called "collaborators' Taken to its extreme in the horrific images of people being "necklaced" by having a tire placed around their necks and filled with petrol and being set alight. More than one lady was friendly and helpful.

We eventually get to Vereeniging, a dismal enclave of right wing, ultra nationalist thinking and walk no more than 20m from the station before we are pulled over by the police and roughly searched and pushed around when nothing is found.

We go and skate and decide not to stay overnight as planned and hitchhike back to JHB the same day. We were both deeply moved and disturbed by the experience and the fact that we were stopped by the police so soon after our experience made me feel how very out of place we were.

It is the only time I have ever been "into" Soweto.

Consider that my house was located almost exactly 15 km from the beginning of Soweto. It was a straight drive on the freeway and one that my dad and I often did when we went to ride our motorbikes in the veld in the vicinity of the township. Soweto stands for South Western Township by the way. I had never been there. I hadn't even seen it from a distance.

My dad used to take his point 22 revolver with him "just in case" I was never sure of what. Snakes I thought. I never considered how in hell you were supposed to draw, aim and shoot a snake while you were screaming along a dirt track at a death-defying speed or for that matter, what danger a snake would pose in such a situation.

My dad, being basically an immigrant and completely immersed in his cars and bikes, took no interest in politics whatsoever and for the most part could be considered apolitical. I don't think he was legible to vote in any case. He became a South African citizen at the age of 83! And only because he thought he could wangle some pension money!

The 76 riots were a turning point for many people as regards their awareness of the unique situation that we were faced with in South Africa. For me it was undoubtedly a major event. I would return from a vacation in Mozambique and the conversation at school would be centered around the black white situation.

Although my knowledge of South African history was fairly comprehensive and I could tell you all about battles and heroes, I simply would not have been able to tell you very much at all about anything beyond the time that the Republic was established. My exposure to sculpture consisted of seeing a bass relief on the library wall of a bunch of oxen and wagons and guys with floppy hats riding horses. All from a much earlier time. There wasn't much from the 50's for example. To me the 50's were a time when roadhouses became popular and Chevy's and greasy haired guys with boxes of smokes rolled up in the sleeves of white t shirts.

In my home we practically never discussed politics. It wasn't a conscious thing, it just didn't seem relevant with all the activity in our various lives the conversation would centre around day to day events. My folks were not what I would call politically oriented like some other people's parents were. I would probably say that they could be classified as "rationalists" if there is such a thing. My dad's attitude was that black people were simply a little primitive and were so due to the fact that the British Empire was a little slow in colonizing the place. Blacks weren't bad per se, just a little ignorant and needed to be educated to catch up to the Europeans much in the same way that the British had done in India. He never felt hatred or animosity of any kind and treated everyone with dignity and respect. My mom was conservative and based her opinions more in line with those of Christian charity than of right-wing politics. My folks were quite typical and a world away from the archetypal image that has been propagated by the international press of every white person being a Nazi and every black a slave. That's basically a load of horse and I'll fight anyone who wants to argue with me about that.

Apartheid was something that I didn't even begin to understand and one of the first questions I asked Aya at the age of about 14 was, "well, you're black and I am white, what do *you* think of this Apartheid?' It needs to be stated that I didn't even know that Apartheid was a law. I didn't know it was the name for this collection of laws. I had just heard the word and knew that it referred to the separation of blacks and whites. The fact that they and we would have separate public amenities such as busses and toilets and even park benches. There was a toilet for 'Whites" and one for "Non-Whites" You would never go into the non-whites one since it always stank and didn't have seats or paper and you could get raped so it was out of bounds. Aya was reticent, to understate, and said we shouldn't really talk about it since it leads nowhere but I was persistent and eventually one day while I was helping her in the kitchen she relented and turned to me and said' If you have a cow, and it's black and white and you want the cow to be black. So you take your knife and you cut out the white pieces. What have you got?" ..."and if you have the same cow and you want it to be white and you cut out all the black pieces...What have you got? Hmm?" I thought about this and wasn't sure what to say and she turned to me and looked me straight in the eye and said ' You have a dead cow!" she turned and continued with her work laughing and shaking her head the way she would do so often. That is the only time and the only thing ever, that Aya said something pertaining to the political situation. She was a devout and God-fearing woman and considered everything below the Almighty a waste of time to sit around talking about.

My first exposure to political thought in a formal setting was when I was 15 years old. It happened at Veldschool. Literally- Field school. The very name conjures up images of bubbling streams and huntin' and fishin' straight out of National Geographic. I thought we would learn to identify edible plants and track wild beasts and identify each and every star in the southern sky...but sadly... I was mistaken.

Veldschool turned out to be nothing less than an intensive week of indoctrination and basically preparation for our soon-to-be-undertaken National Service. As I had changed schools during this period I had the dubious honor of attending Veldschool twice. Both times at the same location.

The first time I went there, there was the main master who dressed in khaki safari suit complete with hat and a leopard skin band. I swear! He would rant and rave and have us marching up and down the square and leopard crawling through the dirt and thorns at 5am. He pissed everyone off. One morning it was particularly rough and a little later in the day he was supposed to deliver a lecture. All the boys were sitting sullenly waiting for the fool and as he strutted up, one of the boys said "here comes Hitler!" He heard it and screamed" WHO SAID THAT?!! HA?!!" Nobody as much as squeaked. He said something to the effect of " somebody got something to say? HA!? Cummon speak up. NOW's the time" I thought to myself..."better get your hand up quick" and so up it shot. It was the only one... to the accompanying groan of the rest of the boys...

So I put it to him like this in a very calm and respectful way." Sir your attitude works with the Afrikaans school as that is what they understand but we are used to debate and don't respond very well to being ordered around. We are quite capable of superseding their achievements but we need to do it as a team and basically if you changed your attitude somewhat we will prove it to you. So yes, the boys think of you as a Hitler as that is the way that you present yourself to us" and I sat down. Everyone was speechless and I was ready to pee in my pants. The funny thing was that only ONE boy stood up and supported me when he asked the boys if they agreed. All the tough big mouthed bully boys were as quiet as churchmice. I'll never learn.

It was late afternoon at the camp. We were all billeted in tents and slept on metal bunks. The boys were divided into "groups" and there was stiff competition between the better ones who took the whole thing very seriously.

As is quite usual at this time of year, late afternoon thunderstorms were commonplace and brutal. One was brewing and the boys scurried around trying to retrieve as many important things they could and deposit them in the dubious security of the tent. I, being the group leader and well aware of how hopelessly outclassed my merry band of bandits were when compared with the main group of "Jocks" who beat us hands down at everything, decided to use the elements to our advantage and take this golden opportunity to strike like lightning and loosen the guy ropes on their tent!

The result was awesome! The storm blew in with stroboscopic lightning and thunder and just before the wind and hail pelted down, the gale force wind billowed out the tent like a hot air balloon and launched it clear, to eventually come to rest about 1 km away!

The physically fit "Jock" team ran physically after it and finally after much dragging and wrestling, managed to re pitch said tent after the storm had abated and completely soaked all their belongings to the bone.

They spent the rest of the week squelching round in the mud pool <u>inside</u> their tent!

It was magnificent!

A few weeks later, after I had changed schools, it was our turn to go to Veldschool and as fate would have it we went to the same one! Out of a whole country with a whole network of them we had to go there! As I got off the bus he was there like a drill sergeant and recognizing me he exclaimed " welcome back comrade" and kicked me so hard up the backside that I honestly thought he had fractured the bones in my coccyx. Bastard.

The reason he had addressed me in that way was due to a lecture that we had been given by the headmaster of the Veldschool on the previous occasion.

It was entitled. "Communism"

The headmaster was a shortish, powerfully built man who was feared by the rest of his staff. He gave a few talks and was intolerant of any kinds of "nonsense" his punishment exercises were killing and he didn't accept anything less than the parameters he had set. If you had to run around the square in 30 seconds. 31 was unacceptable and there was no quitting until the target was reached even if you were still there crawling around the following day. It had to be done. He gave a very basic overview of the communist system and when he got to the part where, as he put it " the 10th phase is when the government dissolves and the country is ruled by the people" My hand shot up and I said " wow! That sounds like a bloody good idea Sir!" He went ballistic, accompanied by the knee jerk comments from the other boys, vigorously voicing their indignation and doing the expected thing. " Ooh! Aahh!" He went on about the atrocities committed by Stalin and the lecture went way beyond the allocated time. At the end he asked me if I still thought the same and I stood up and said "Yes Sir, I do" It brought the house down.

That evening I was summoned to his quarters and was expecting to be caned but it turned out that we had the most intensely illuminating conversation ever. He informed me that what he was about to say was between us and not for the boys to hear about and proceeded to tell me about his activities as an agent in Russia and some of the crazy things he had experienced. He was way smart and better read than anyone I had ever met and at the close of the evening he confided to me that he also thought "it was a bloody good idea" But sternly reprimanded me and said that it would be far better if I didn't voice my opinion so openly. The comical end to the evening was that he said. "well everyone is expecting that I punish you so play the game OK?" he then took out a cane and proceeded to raise his voice and shout abuse and then whacked the note book on his desk loudly and shouted " NOW GET OUT OF MY SIGHT!" I wasn't sure whether to laugh or cry as, when he took out the cane I was sure he was going to tan my hide and upon seeing the show was both shocked and relieved. When I got back to the tent the boys asked what happened and I just said " I don't want to talk about it" The next morning, Hitler himself stood grinning at me with a look that said clearly "see what happens to Kaffir boeties like you HA!" I Looked away and continued "to play the game" as I had promised.

This is the first time I have ever related that story to anyone. It was an experience that was pivotal. It served to confuse me more than anything as the clear definition between the "goodies" and the "baddies" was beginning to blur and it would be years before I would realize how much of a risk the man took in confiding in me.

It was common for the naughty boys to smoke and on Veldschool it was also a common thing to see how much hell you could raise and get away with. The naughty boys in my vicinity decided that it was time to "Get High!" And so all the stories came out but no material with which to get high on. No, it was a common story that if one would be so inclined, one could smoke "Cowshit!" and be guaranteed of an amazing 'Buzz" So off we go to acquire some dryish cow manure of which there is an abundance in the area. True to form we all have a puff and settle back for the promised "Trip" and of course. Nothing!!

Except a crap taste in my mouth!!

Hitler pretty much kept his distance from me throughout the week. I refrained from provoking him which he must have thought was due to "the lesson" that I had been given by the headmaster but on the last day, as we were boarding the bus. I spotted him and walked over and told him exactly what I thought of a man who likes to kick someone from behind without provocation or warning. In fluent Afrikaans!!

He just gaped at me as I walked away.

Other "talks" we were treated to dealt with subjects such as the subliminal war being waged and enlightened us to the REAL meaning behind wearing jeans for one. Buying records by the pop group ABBA was giving funds directly to the enemy to buy arms. Jeans were a secret sign of membership in the banned communist party. The peace sign was actually a secret Satanist symbol as it depicted a cross with the horizontal pieces broken and leaning on the upright. Soweto was an anagram, for what I don't remember...and so on and so forth...

Subsequently I would be a lot more aware of what was going on around me. I would listen to political conversations by the other students and do my best to remain rational and try to understand this system that I thought qualified as one of the dumbest ideas ever conceived by a head of state.

The absolute use of force and Gestapo tactics...how long did they think it could last? It's beyond me. Still.

I know that the way I have portrayed things so far is to kind of cover the Afrikaaners with the racist blanket and cover the English with the liberal one but things are never so simple.

South Africa was not simply comprised of Blacks and Whites. It is a vast tapestry of cultures, backgrounds, religions and attitudes that cannot simply be divided in the typical pie graph, geography class manner. It comes as a shock to me that even today in a world that knows the internet and cable television that I encounter educated adults that take the view that South Africa is White and Black. I teach English online and my first question to students that give me this picture is "which blacks?' Invariably I am faced with incomprehension. People have no idea of what I am asking. My response is to give a short lecture outlining in the broadest terms the societal framework. I'm going to do that here but must insert as a disclaimer that it is very, very simplistic and based on my own subjective view and should be taken as such.

Whites come in two general flavors. English and Afrikaans. The English dudes (and dudesses) come from England! And for the most part controlled business and private sector activities. They would be liberal in terms of political orientation. Except for the ones who were not. The Afrikaans dudes and their spouses come from Holland and France and their dogs from Germany. They were, by and large right wing and lived in government houses because they were Policemen, Firemen or worked in the post office. Afrikaners played Rugby and Englishmen played also Rugby but knew how to play Football too. It was called Soccer. Both drank lots of beer.

The Jews were English and controlled all the money. They were the Doctors, Dentists, Orthodontists, Lawyers, Bankers and Rabbis. South Africa's Jewish population was large and so were their houses.

They drank both beer and wine and preferred golf and tennis. They didn't mind if other people played Rugby or Football.

Now for the Blacks...There are a lot of them and they come from South Africa but not all from the same place. I don't know all of them but the two largest groups are the Zulus, a proud and fierce warrior nation and the Xhosa who have a name that can only be pronounced by South Africans who have put in the sufficient hours of practice and don't chew gum and talk simultaneously. They are by contrast, a fierce and proud warrior nation. Both are ruled by a king...I think, but they live on opposite sides of the same river. There are a number of other nations too. Notice I don't say tribes as they are much smaller and don't make the cut. There are many tribes too but I won't get into it. Sotho's both north and south, Swazis who live in Swaziland! But travel frequently, Shangaan, Griquas, Bushmen or San people, Tswana, and a whole array of others I just don't remember at this point or have omitted due to lack of certainty of national status. The fact remains that there are a lot of them and what's interesting is that they are all distinctly distinct from one another in terms of language, mythology, tribal law, social customs and so on. Men worked in the mines and women in the houses. They all like football and drink lots of beer. They are not all friendly with each other though and some are traditionally enemies and hate each other's guts.

But love each other's women.

That would be very simple if the proverbial pie would stop there.

But what about the Coloureds? Coloureds, you ask...Well yes. During Apartheid there was the clear distinction between the rights of whites and lack of rights for blacks but what about If you were an Indian? Chinese? Malayan? Egyptian? Where did the law provide for you?

Good question!

These guys are easy deal with as they have clearly defined cultural and national identities but the "coloureds" are a different story. They are people who are the result of interbreeding between the early mariners and settlers in the country and the slaves that they either were transporting or had brought with them to do all the hard work. Many people from Malaysia who are predominantly Moslems. Indians would be lumped into this category along with all the other nationalities mentioned that were unfortunate enough to have a less than milky complexion. Here we find the merchants. Greek and Portuguese were traditionally the café owners and greengrocers. Italians the restaurateurs. Indians owned haberdasheries and curry houses. These guys preferred drinking wine and cricket was sport of choice except for the Portuguese and Italians who drank wine but loved football, didn't understand rugby and hated cricket.

The political orientation for the last two groups is not of any consequence as the majority couldn't vote anyway.

They sleep under the wide and ill-defined blanket known as. The grey areas...

So there it is, The South African socio-political structure in a nutshell.

Simple.

National Service

The word blasted through my mind like a fart at suppertime. FaaaaaaaaaaaaaaaaaaaK!

In its wake I lay peering out of the window at the dismal, cold, overcast winters day outside and knew it would be the last morning for the next 2 years that I would awake as a civilian. It was the day that I was expected to report for my National service.

The first thought that struck me was "I wonder what I need to take?" I got out of bed and dressed in jeans and my school rugby jersey and took my sisters cotton laundry bag, went to the kitchen and started piling in tinned food. Vegetable curry mainly and a tin of black boot polish. I asked my dad what he would recommend that I take and he replied with complete confidence "Nothing! They will give you everything!" Straight into the car after a quick toast and tea and off to Pretoria.

A few weeks prior to this I had left school and thought that perhaps an education would be possible through the military. It was a common ploy for young men to use and a successful one at that. It had worked for my uncle who had stayed and risen through the ranks to end up as a Kommandant in the parachute battalion and everyone was very proud of him, including me!

I had this idea but was only semi convinced that this was what I wanted to do but as I had to undertake my national service anyway since all males had to by law. I decided that I could wangle my way into the Air force by declaring that I wanted to join the permanent force and so get out of the infantry which was where I had been called up to serve. I chose the Air force for two very clear and logical reasons. Firstly, I thought that since these guys were flying about in Jets and Helicopters, they would have to at least be semi-literate and probably more civilized than the guys who would need essentially no more skill than walking or more probably running to engage the enemy in battle. The second and more important reason was of course that the Air force wore black boots and the Army brown. As a dedicated Punk Rocker I could simply not compromise my identity and so the choice was clear. Well....at least I got the black boots I so badly wanted.

The basic training was to be 14 weeks of running about at the Air force gymnasium, situated in the suburb of Valhalla on the outskirts of Pretoria. An ironic twist was that this was where my Sunday family meetings were held at my uncle's house just a block away from my bungalow. Now, a barbed wire fence separated us.

With a name like Valhalla it was clear that unseen forces were definitely at work and no doubt lurking in the wings giggling madly

So in through the gate I went as my dad turned around and headed for work. I dutifully took my place in the line that was before me and stood patiently waiting for my turn to come. For three days! Having taken the in initiative by wearing my very prestigious rugby jersey paid off when a short shit of a corporal stopped behind me and shouted in his own particular language " did jou play rokbee!!? I stood up and gave the affirmative and he shouted back " KOM WIF MEE!" And so I grabbed my washing bag with the clonking tins and followed him. He put me straight through the procedure and before I knew it I found myself kitted out with uniform and blankets and standing in a long open barracks with 21 beefy looking young men all with particularly bewildered looks on their faces. It turned out that this corporal was wandering around and grabbing as many fit, sporty looking people and shunting them into his squadron so that he would have an advantage over the others in all the physical competitive activities that had to be undertaken. His name was Barnard and he hated my guts about half as much as I hated his. I of course did not play rugby and stowed the jersey at the first opportunity. He has the dubious distinction of having left me with a scar on my shin, where he kicked me one day on the parade ground and opened up a huge gash that required stitching and left a neat little scar.

I was in Flight 1, 3 Squadron and our corporal was a psychopathic ultra-fit sadist with not a single brain cell to spare. His father was the commanding officer at the base. He was a veteran of the bush war and an advanced PTI (physical training instructor) This guy had completed a course that in all honesty could have killed him just as easily and we were all scared shitless of him. So were the other corporals, the sergeant and all the officers except his dad who I think was too but never let on. At the end of basic training I volunteered to polish his boots which were special jumper's boots and he never saw them again. I wore them all through Europe Ha! Ha!

My initial deduction that the Air force would be just plain sailing was blown right out of the water by the officer in charge of the basic training for our intake. A newly promoted Major by the name of Butler decided to set the record straight and refute the commonly held view that it was "easy" in the Air force. Thanks to him and at his own admission at our passing out parade, we lucky devils had completed the toughest basic training that the "Gym" had known in its history. His highly inept staff had had us running, jumping, rolling in the mud, swearing, sweating, puking, jumping, hanging from ropes, shooting, marching and cleaning, constantly for the 14-week duration of the sentence. We learnt such vital skills. How to comb and iron your bed for inspection. The hair on the blanket was brushed into a particular pattern and then starched into place. The corners would be literally "chewed" to get that perfect box finish. How to run 2.4 km with full kit. How to do press ups and other important exercises after having drunk a liter of water and then rolling over the earth until every man had had the opportunity to chuck his cookies. These and a wide range of other mindless things were designed to make us impervious to the attempts of the enemy to subject us to the humiliation of defeat while we were standing guard with our dogs at the various military airfields around the country.

It worked! Not one Mirage or Helicopter went missing in all the time that we were there.

Being a new recruit was an immensely refreshing experience for me. I was an observer. Not only of the others around me but also of myself. Sometimes it would feel like an out of body experience. I knew some of the other recruits from school and knew them pretty well. I would watch as the intense pressure created by the corporals and flight sergeant would erode their resolve to remain calm and rational and before very long they would be caught up in the panic of the whole thing and be trying to achieve the set goals which were impossible to reach by even the wildest stretch of the imagination. It became "each man for himself" the irony was that the whole "group mentality" ethic was being observed so we had to behave as a group and did but couldn't care less about the other guy in reality. I kept a relative equilibrium by immersing myself in my music and constantly trying to keep my head and think for myself. I was super fit due to my intensive tennis training and could take whatever the corporal would and did throw at me and still come back for more. I was used to getting up at 5 am and running the 411 steps on the koppie and then often cutting school to train at Ellis park with the pros. This infuriated the other guys who were mostly smokers and really, and I mean REALLY suffered. I would complete the run in second place behind the marathon guy and then go back to help carry the others that could never make it on their own and so we would be able to complete the given time for whatever as a group. I sucked at inspection and soon realized that there was no way in hell that it was possible to do an inspection perfectly as the whole training was geared against it. The others never seemed to cotton on and would be up all night polishing boots and all kinds of ridiculous things while I would have my bed pre made and starched and doss down on a stolen mattress that I would hide in the ceiling during day time. Getting my rest was smart as each day we would be extended well beyond our limits and I needed all the energy I could muster. The others hated this and I was often the focus of their resentment. I never gave a hoot.

I was officially the 2nd fittest guy in the squadron. The fittest dude was a Springbok Karateka and he would do one hand knuckle press ups while picking his nose or scratching his butt with ease and more than a little flair. The other very fit guy was the marathon runner. He knew how to run. I think he had studied it as one of his courses at university as he was also a Doctor of Physics! He disappeared about two weeks into basic training and the next time I saw him he was a Captain being driven around by his personal driver. On the other end of the scale was a man we dubbed Oupa which means Granpaw... He was in his 30's and had been dodging the call up for years but had been sold out by his wife and so was one of us. He was a chain smoker and there were times that I thought he was going to die right there on the spot. We also had a few older guys who had been doing time in jail and they were for the most part quiet and it was clear that they weren't to be messed with. Together we made quite an interesting if not happy little family.

The first week of training managed to transform 21 of the 22 people in my flight into certifiable Zombies. The lack of sleep and physical exertion combined was an effective means to get the individual to the point where it is simply reaction. Response is not the correct word. Tempers were frayed and although it came very close on occasion I managed to complete the course without any serious scrapes.

There was no reasoning behind anything. It was all so seemingly pointless and I had real difficulty in maintaining my sense of motivation and self-control. I kept waiting for the moment when they had finished "breaking us down" and started to " build us back up" but it never came. It was just senseless. And had to be done.

It wasn't without its moments though and I had many laughs. We had two corporals in our squadron. One was named Smith and couldn't speak a word of English! The other was Smit and didn't understand a word of Afrikaans. I had some fun with them as for each I pretended not to understand their language which would create the most comical situations and which were fully tolerated by the rest of my squad. The corporal would scream a command at me and I would remain immobile. Eventually he would inquire how to say it from one of the troops and he would crack us all up by repeating the command in a hilariously authoritive way in the other language. This would occur regularly with both and provide a welcome respite from all the military seriousness. It was all good fun until I was asked a question in one of the lectures where both of them were present. I answered and watched with glee and trepidation as the 1st corporals face clouded over and when he boomed across the hall at me, the others look of confusion. They then looked at each other, realizing that I was fully bilingual and that they had been had on, then took me outside for a punishment session I have yet to forget. It was fun while it lasted though.

Towards the end of the training we were supposed to go to the shooting range to shoot for our grading as shottists and this was something I really looked forward to. On the day though, I woke up with my jowls swollen like tennis balls and not feeling too good at all. The corporal refused me permission to report sick as he thought I was trying to get out of shooting and so I took my place as we were marched off. I suffered physically that morning more so than in all my training and caught flak from everyone as they thought I was putting it on. When it was my turn to shoot I made a clean hole out of the bulls-eye and my corporal who was a "Gold" rated shot accused me of "leaning" which was not allowed. I insisted that I had not and he made me run around some more whilst he checked my rifle. He took a few shots and then challenged me to do the same and I shot a good grouping although not as well as before. Immediately I had become a completely new person in his eyes and was now on the cusp of being tolerated. It was a miracle.

At one stage the Flight sarge sent me on a run up the embankment behind the targets. A not very safe thing to do and I struggled up. Two steps forward, three steps back till I reached the top. I was supposed to go and "greet the pole" I was totally spent and thought "bugger it! They can wait till I get my breath back" Eventually a rookie pops his sweating face over the edge and says that the Sarge and the corporals are going nuts as they are screaming for me to come down but I don't respond. I make my way back down and stagger up to the Corporal who is red in the face from all the screaming. "What's going on? Why did you take so long? Are you crazy?' I am near to passing out and I tell the corporal in all honesty " I tried to speak to the pole but it was no use! He doesn't understand!" He stares at me incredulously and screams 'WHAT!??" I explain" Corporal, he's Polish!"

Before it can get out of hand though the flight sergeant came over to see what the fuss was about and asked me what my problem was as he had seen me struggling with the physical exercises which he took as a sign that I was somehow hung over. I told him about the swelling and as he inspected me went pale and told me to get the hell away and report to the doctor. I did and it turned out that I had a severe case of mumps and ended up spending the next month under quarantine at 1 military hospital! The kicker was that the corporal, wanting to cover his butt at not allowing me to report sick, wanted to have me charged with something akin to insurrectable activities as mumps were highly contagious and I could have done it purposefully to jeopardize the whole of the basic training. It was like I had committed an act of terrorism!

Luckily nothing came of it and I spent the next month confined to my small room and day by day my level of fitness would diminish till finally I returned to base and took me place as one of the stragglers.

The highlight of my stay there was having the pleasure of watching my room/cell mates facial expression while he was subjected to a lumbar pump by one of the interns that was two years younger than Doogie Howzer and being informed that I would be next if there wasn't a rapid improvement in my condition or if the doctor felt like it.

At the end of the training we were supposedly to be sent to the dept of the Air force where we would be most productively utilized and this was supposedly decided by the batteries of "tests" we had to take. It was a farce though as the best positions went to those who were the best manipulators and it was a question of who you knew and not what you knew. At least one third of the whole intake would be shipped off to dog school regardless as that was the only thing that they could think of to do with each intake of national servicemen. It was the irony that as the Air force needed skilled labor and this skilled labor was taken from the regular soldiers, it didn't have much use for the average school leaver with no skills. The solution was to make one third dog handlers who would "guard" the bases

and a good portion of the remaining third would become gate guard or "boom pilots" as they were commonly termed.

What was left were the best educated and skilled who may become officers or pursue the work they had been doing as civilians.

I became a 'Doggie"

I went to dog training school for 5 weeks where I, along with most of the base, contracted dysentery due to drinking contaminated water and then was posted to the largest northern base in South Africa in Hoedspruit in the Northern Transvaal. It was notorious as the worst place to be sent to and for all the lucky ones that went elsewhere, the maxim of the easy Air force held true and they had a great time for the remainder of their service. For us though, the fun had just begun.

The base was surrounded by a 27 km long double razor wired electric fence. Most of the facilities were beneath ground and for the most part out of bounds at all times. We lived 15km away in the living quarters which was above ground and from the outside resembled a holiday resort complete with country club, swimming pool, tennis and squash courts and an 18 hole immaculately maintained golf course.

From the inside it resembled a concentration camp.

I arrived at the base a week late due to a convoluted and confusing series of events that I won't go into and was met at the train station by one of the troops who drove me straight to the base at 170kph while I was forced to sit in the open back of a light utility vehicle or in SA speak 'bakkie" As soon as I arrived the rest of the troops gathered around me and proceeded to shout, threaten and jostle me around for the afternoon with one or two other 'roofs" or rookies. By early evening I found myself standing stark naked in the headlamps of a troop carrier and forced to roll around in the ashes of a still smoldering fire after which we were ordered to jump into the small swimming pool but were not allowed to make the pool dirty. The other two rookies had already had a week of this kind of nonsense and stayed put while I hopped straight in as I was burning my arse off in the hot ashes. All hell broke loose and I was beaten around a bit and then had to spend the rest of the night with a teaspoon trying to clean up the pool. At about 4.30 am a troop came round with a vacuum cleaner and cleaned the pool while I was ordered to get dressed and stand next to my bed and wait for the sgt major's inspection. Of course this was the first time I had seen the bed and it served as a natural introduction, courtesy of my fellow comrades in arms. It was the beginning of a wonderful relationship with the sgt major that was to last until my last day at the place. It was the opening round in a match that would have us at each other's throats daily.

Having arrived late proved to be a kind of blessing in that I had to now run around the base 'clearing in" by myself. Clearing in meant that you had to go and get your bedding from one place and your uniform from another and tetanus shots from the Doctor and of course ...drawing a weapon. Now I had at some stage prior decided that I was to object military service for conscientious reasons and had to go through the system in order to do so. The upshot of it all was that it culminated in a meeting with the Major who inquired as to my reason for wanting to object. I told him I thought that violence was wrong, but understood and accepted that I was to do service and only wanted to do so in a capacity whereby I didn't have to carry a weapon. He then said "on what grounds?" I wasn't sure what he meant and repeated "uuh, I think it's wrong" He was curt and demanded to know whether it was religious or political. I thought for a moment and replied " personal Sir, I don't need an institution to lend credibility to my convictions" He fumed and said that I had to choose one of the two as that's all that was allowed. I wavered and then he told me that I had two choices; do your service with a gun and shut up for two years or plant cabbages with the Jehovah's Witnesses for six! Decide! I knew there would be no middle ground and as I had mastered the rudiments of arithmetic whilst still at school I made the calculation and promptly saluted, about turned and got the hell out of his range before he decided on my behalf.

So to return to the original subject...I was now in the unique position that not only was I expected to clear in on my own without supervision, I was also not yet on the roll call lists and so would not be missed at morning parades and other such unnecessary activities. So I never took a weapon and I never ever went to the shooting range and I practically never stood an officers inspection for the duration of the stay. I think it must qualify as some kind of record. I would borrow my seniors pistol for pre guard inspections and I would get my roommate to lock me inside my locker for inspections. Once a week for over 20 months! I was never caught. I was however caught at other things and paid the price with interest.

I'm in the Air Force. It's the day that I will finally leave on my 14 days annual leave. It's the highlight of a year spent in the twig light of a world stuck in the dark ages.

Before leaving the base I have to pick up my paycheck and then it's party time!

I go to the HQ building and see the endless line waiting to get paid and so I go off to the base barber and sneak in while he's out and shave off both sides of my hair to produce my fist "real" Mohican! Before it would always be to cut it as short as possible but it was never shaven clean. I reckon "to hell with it" and figure it will grow back sufficiently in my 14-day vacation from base. I go back to the HQ and with my peak cap pulled securely down as far as it will go to hide the new clean and very white skin, I walk confidently over to the table to collect my pay. I stop in mid stride and do a neat about turn as I notice the RSM enter the lobby. I bound up the stairs and go and hide in the Chaplains office hoping that I was not spotted. It isn't very long before I feel the familiar malignant presence behind me as the RSM enters quietly and sneaks up behind me. I look at the Chaplain and smile "here it comes!" kind of smile much like a smile you would crack as a passenger on the Titanic while watching the approaching iceberg.

He lifts my cap off my head and lets rip with the customary volley of insults and curses. He catches himself midway and apologizes to the Chaplain and shouts at me "Now jou made me swear in the fokken Dominees office!...Uh Jammer Kapelaan" Grabs me by my collar and hauls me down to the office. I duly stand to attention while the corporal assistant gets out the charge sheet and begins to write all the nonsense down. The RSM comes back in and screams at me Get Out! Go to the barber and fix.... THAT!" I run out and go directly and don't even blink as I go into the small office that doubles as a barber shop. I tell the barber who is a friend "shave it clean! FAST!" he does so all the while telling me that now I have really done it and so on. I rush back to the RSM's office and stand to attention. He enters and with much glee waves the charge sheet in front of my nose "HA! No 14 days for you MEYERS! I got you now! HAHA!" I ask him with usual dead pan face " Excuse me Sergeant Major. What is the charge?" He goes a beautiful shade of violet and fumes at me "DAMAGING STATES PROPERTY!" I quite calmly tell him "sorry Sergeant Major but I cannot sign that" He goes ballistic "WHAT! WHY NOT!" I turn to him and state " Where is the evidence?" I'm poised between lying

on the floor convulsing in my own urine and laughing hysterically and just simply peeing my pants where I stand.

He looks at me incredulously "But you cut your hair!" I respond "no sir I did not. The base barber did so at your order! If you want to charge anyone you have to charge him for obeying an unlawful command or yourself for issuing it. Sir!"

We stood there for a millennium before he quite calmly and quietly said "get out Meyers"

I soon discovered that the system has an amazing ability to tie itself up in red tape and I became expert at making this work in my favor. Certain heads of dept would not be on speaking terms with others and I would play them up against each other to gain the advantage. I learnt that in the SA military the 2nd in command on any base is the Chaplain. It does not matter what his personal rank may be. That means that a Lieutenant may be the 2 IC even though the 2nd highest rank below the commanding officer may be a brigadier!! Now, our Chaplain, I discovered, was an avid tennis player!! And I of course would know when his usual match with his partner would take place and so I would innocently be on the next-door court smashing serves at 200kph+ or practicing against the wall. It did not take very long before I was quizzed and sadly had to confess that I had no one of a decent standard to practice with. He, being a gent and practical thinking man, would then re assign me to a job that afforded us both the opportunity to apply ourselves to the important task of honing our skills. I would then show more interest in my spiritual life and eventually make martial clerical history by becoming the first non-Christian to become the chaplain's clerk!

And ...yes...I am sitting here with the same smug expression on my face as I had then! So there!

This did not go unnoticed by the RSM and he would then try to outmaneuver me and get me to do some crappy job by way of a direct command from the commanding officer. He was seldom successful as I had become the head of securities squash partner soon after!

It didn't stop him from succeeding to make my life hell for the most part, culminating in clandestinely ordering me to be beaten by the more mentally challenged members of the base rugby team. My head was covered by a blanket while I was sleeping and the group proceeded to beat me with the metal rods of the squeegees that we used to clean up with.

The protagonist in this affair later went on to serve 14 years in prison for armed robbery.

I had many different jobs for short periods of time. I was shunted here and there and eventually job number 14 became the chaplains dept clerk. I had worked there on and off but finally made it permanent. Whilst there I met one of the chaplain's junior officers, a man by the name of Albert van der Stock who eventually took his vows and became a Franciscan monk. I have a lot to thank him for and we kept in touch for years afterward. We shared similar political views although his were from the Christian perspective and he educated me in many of the more profound concepts underlying the Christian faith. Without him and the Chaplain I'm not sure I would have survived the ordeal.

To me, national service was one long stretched out nightmare that distorted my thinking for years to follow.

I would receive a weekend pass once a month and have four days off. 2 days to travel and 2 at home. The base was about 600 km from JHB.

My activities with Albert were both in and out of the base. As an ordained priest and officer, he had the right and responsibility to lead a congregation outside of the base and we would drive to weekly prayer meetings in the nearby towns as well as rural areas to minister and try to offer assistance to the black communities. Albert saw his calling in a very typical English liberal way and ministering to the black people was top of the list. The authorities would try to hamper his efforts at every turn. The living quarters area was much like a small village complete with hospital and a food factory that used to can food. The hospital was for the residents only and only whites. The food factory would throw away literally tons of food each week and at one stage Albert tried to get permission to distribute some of this to the surrounding communities that were desperate as there was a devastating drought in progress at the time and animal carcasses would lie in the fields and rot in the unrelenting sun. There was widespread famine and the resultant malnutrition. Permission was of course denied and no reason needed to be given. I was livid. So was he.

I was at this stage far more politically aware than most of those around me and had managed to get my hands on a few banned books which I would re-cover and read while standing guard. I remember reading the story of Stephen Biko like this and keeping the book well hidden at all times. I was always reading anyway so I didn't attract too much attention but I shudder to think what would have happened had I been caught. It is one thing to be caught as a civilian and quite another as a piece of state property. Technically that's what I was. State property. If I cut myself shaving I could have been charged for damaging state property much the same as if I had sprayed graffiti on a policeman's motorbike. I seriously doubt if anyone would ever have done such a thing but it was possible by law.

The funny end to the national service story is that technically, I'm still in the Air force!! The day that I finished it all, I had to of course "clear out" and get signatures from all over attesting to the fact that I had returned all the returnable things and so on. At the conclusion of all this the form had to be signed by various officers and last but by no means least, the RSM. When I had gone the whole ritual and secured the signatures by hook, bribe and lots of crook, I went to the RSM's office where I was made to wait for the next 3 hours while he sat inside and ignored me and I stood dutifully outside trying to wear him down. Eventually I thought "bugger it" and knocked, walked straight in and without permission told him in a calm voice that I respected him and his authority and hold no grudges regarding the past nearly two years head to head. I have all my signatures and am ready to leave. Would he please sign? His reply was "well Meyers. You don't have mine. Now fuck off!" So I did. Without my clearing out certificate or a look backward.

Six days later I had sold my car, kissed my girlfriend goodbye and gotten on a Jumbo jet with a Guitar I couldn't play, a football and collection of books. Destination: LONDON!!!

London

I arrived at Heathrow early in the morning and took a tube to Victoria. My first impression was, "Home!" I recall how strange it was to feel that since it couldn't possibly be.

I was accompanied by Grant as my folks thought that he would be older and wiser and was asked to keep a watchful eye over me. It was a disaster from the beginning as I saw my childhood hero in a completely different light and very soon realized how far apart we had developed as people and after a few short weeks went our separate ways and have never really met up again since.

I had 700 pounds to spend and started right away. I was stone drunk for two weeks straight and did what I wanted when I wanted.

London was intense. I had just come from spending more than two years in the sticks and was plunged into the noise and activity and the youth hostel was a planet in its own right where I could party down 24 hours a day as long as the cash lasted. I took anything and everything, I went to gigs and met the people I never dreamed to see and realized that they were not the rock stars at all. Just simple people with very few if any aspirations to become "mega" It was sobering even though I was totally pissed most all of my waking time. The music of course just blew me away. It was awesome. I never believed that it could be so loud. Grant had played in a multi-racial band and was pretty into the "ethnic" music scene in SA. I thought it was total crap. A bunch of well to do white suburban kids hanging out with the black musicians and mostly just as an excuse to smoke dope. There were of course the dedicated people as anywhere but the scene at large was just a bunch of hooey to me. I hated it. I was PUNK! I was proud to be punk as I understood what the hell it was all about. It was a social movement and about tearing the blinkers from your eyes and seeing the true reality. The music was energetic and powerful. The alternatives available in the 80's were pretty tame and bullshit for the most part. I think it can be said that the Reggae scene was probably the closest genre in terms of attitude at the time. Reggae of course was not mainstream and the red flag for white dudes to be involved with Ganja. Sounds contradictory but there it is. The people that understand what I'm on about don't require the explanation.

I arrive with Grant. There is a line outside the hostel right out into the street and so I drop my pack and sit looking around me at the street and the young girls in front of us in the queue.

Grant has a "friend" who is supposed to help us out with getting a room and although he has found the guy nothing seems to be happening and so I get impatient and walk ahead to see what's happening at the front of the line. Its chaos! There are people trying to book in and all kinds of languages are being spoken and its just crazy. I make the quick calculation that at this rate, even if we reach the front of the queue in five days time, we probably won't be able to get a room anyway.

I go to the toilet and haul out my dollars that I have changed for an emergency. I walk to a huge pile of sheets that are supposed to be taken to the laundry as I have seen some of the workers do and haul it onto my shoulders and start pushing and screaming my way through the throng. When I get next to the desk I put the bundle down and walk straight up to the young and very flustered looking young lady. " Scuse me! Please would you move? I haven't got all day!" and I push my way through as if I am a staff member. I get to the desk, haul out my cash and say "private room for two" and stuff the money into her hand. About 30 seconds later I have the key and go outside to where Grant is waiting and grab my bag "you coming?" I ask while dangling the key in front of my grinning face!

We drop our bags and I make straight for the pub while Grant sits around talking to his friend. I grab a beer mug and tell the barman "fill this up with Southern Comfort and cola please" and hand him a wad of cash. I walk out and explore a bit. It isn't long before I notice many people coming and going from the same door and so I do the same. I open the door to a huge room that used to be a hospital ward before the building was converted into a hostel and stand agape at the scene before me. There are two rows of double bunks with an aisle down the center and the place is a hive of activity. No one pays the slightest attention to me as I stand staring. Here there is a guy playing his guitar, there are two girls sitting with headphones on, on another bed there is a guy shouting at the people below to keep still for a second as he is rolling a humongous joint and they are having very active sex under the sheet and its shaking the bed!

Someone hands me a joint and I respond by offering a sip of my drink but just get a huge grin as the person holds up a long cool glass of lager and a thumbs up!

I think to myself" This beats the crap out of the Air Force!"

I'll breeze through the whole trip in Europe and perhaps just highlight the points that were the most influential formative experiences. I had special times In Germany and hitchhiking solo solidly for weeks visiting libraries and art galleries wherever I went and it would require a whole book just to relate it all but I'm going to put the focus on London as I spent the longest time there and had the most deeply imprinted memorable times.

I sought out all the sleaziest places. Back street pubs that would have 'Real" punk gigs with the good bands. It was heaven.

The first point for me of course was the freedom of expression. There were 'BOOKS!' not just pulp but all kinds of bookstores that stocked the most esoteric titles. I was astounded and caught myself on more than one occasion looking over my shoulder to see if I wasn't being watched and that it wasn't some kind of trap! Paranoid, I know but that's exactly what I did. I could take Kropotkin and Bakunin right off the shelf! In SA I had to fake a university student ID card and lie that I needed this or that book as part of my studies to the assistant at the JHB general library and she would then go to the "back" and fetch this book and then note my name on some kind of register! I had managed to cover quite a lot of ground in this manner before my nerve started to fail me and I called it quits. I'll bet that the SA security police are still searching for one Robert Sole. R Sole as it appeared on the card!

I remember going to Shakespeare's book shop in Paris and spending a week inside, hiding from the rain and immersing myself in anything and everything. In London I went to a college and sat in the corner in an Anarchism lecture for two or three meetings before I was quizzed by the lecturer. I must add that it was total crap. The lecturer and all his cronies were a bunch of wankers and I remember thinking that they were like casualties of such a free society. They would complain about things related to the dole and things that I would have considered privileges back home. In SA, you don't work, you don't eat. Simple. I didn't enroll, not that I could mind you as I was fast running out of cash. The music stores were out of this world too as they had all the stuff that in SA had to be specially ordered and a lot was in 2nd hand shops that were dirt cheap.

I noted too, that there would be flyers posted on tube walls and so which called for an end to "The Botha regime" and "stop apartheid, Free Mandela!" and so on. It struck a nerve. In Amsterdam I was blown away by a HUGE wall mural on a building sites containing wall. It depicted a marching group of black people, supposedly people like Mandela and Biko, etc. all who were active in the "struggle" the words were "the spear of the nation. Mkonto wesiswe" and a block long spear being held by everyone. I took a photo of it as I thought it was unbelievable I came from a place where you could get into deep doo, doo for wearing a yellow, black and green jumper and here was a wall with the letters ANC emblazoned on the wall with full acceptance from everyone. One of the things that struck me was the fact that here, in Holland, people knew more about apartheid and particularly the history and current state of the struggle than I did. I had done a little illicit reading but had never heard of the military wing of the ANC. WOW!

I was really taken with the amount of opportunities that had been created for artists to show their work. People seemed to have a sense of respect and the Mr. Average had an inbred soft spot for art as a whole. It was great. The art on the walls in Amsterdam was truly unbelievable and it is the place where I made the conscious decision to become an artist. A painter mind you. I remember the moment clearly. I was wandering aimlessly through the rain and came across a window that for some reason had a painted picture displayed in it. It wasn't a gallery. More like a radio shop or something. The picture was of a face with hands held up in front of it. Claw like and the feeling was total despair. It was excellently done and I stared at I for ages, even returning a few times later in the week to see if I would be moved in the same way. I was and marveled at the power of visual art. How a few strokes of color on a piece of masonite was able to stir me to my depths. Magik! I wanted to be part of that. I didn't want a part of the stupid politics though. I went to South Africa house where there was an ongoing demonstration against apartheid for years and was disgusted. It seemed like the whole thing was staged and the "rent a crowd" kind of misfits that were chanting and walking around with their pickets were pathetic at best. They were total assholes and I was very angry and confused. On the one hand it was fantastic that people could be there in public and protest something without fear of reprisal but on the other it was clear to me that these ignorant fools had no idea at all and looked like they simply had nothing better to do and so had embarked on a "mission" to save the underprivileged. None of them had even as much as looked at a map of the country and most of the opinions that I heard seemed to be based on the propaganda that was used to sell newspapers at that time. I don't question the validity of what they were doing. Not at all. It was an unjust system and it was right that they should be disgusted, but by the same token I feel that things have to ring true. I have to stress the things that were never covered by the mainstream press that a particularly one side view to the world at large. Why didn't they also mention the good that the "Whites" were doing? Why didn't they mention the fact that there were more black millionaires in SA during apartheid than white? Granted, if you take the vastly different numbers in population into account it's not that spectacular, but black people from all the African states north of the country would dream at night about the wonderful life they could have in SA as the conditions in Africa in general are abysmal. Famine, war, corruption, ethnic violence, disease, the list is unending. Life in Africa is harsh and difficult and comparatively to most other countries, the black South African lived a charmed life. In other countries the people could vote, or so it is believed. Could they vote without fear of reprisal? Could they drink clean water from the tap in other countries? Name one, because I want to know which one it is. The fact that SA is so absolutely wealthy all round was a blessing to all the people. The whites who controlled the cash lived like the kings they thought they were. They laid an infrastructure that was comparable with anything international and did so with the "cheap labor" that the black people provided, in record time. But the whites, although predominantly so were not the only ones to benefit from it. America at the same period was engaged in a civil war and let us remember the slavery issues that contributed to the rift. Let's stay there and compare the civil rights records of both countries or rather let's not as I'm on a roll that can be maintained for an indefinite amount of time.

Fact is that the world was never aware of the positive things and there were many. That's wrong. Period. It's life, I know and I'm being a little naive here but it's essentially wrong. From any rationally sane perspective.

So I was angry and irritated but I never caught any flack and moved freely among them as I put on my newly acquired cockney accent and no one was the wiser. My cockney sucks by the way. There were a few South Africans there for a Rugby match and were challenging the demonstrators and the ever-present police stepped in and broke it up before it started and a funny scene as they moved off. There's me, spiky hair, boots and leather jacket standing off to one side and one of the South Africans takes me for a local and asks " hey man, were do the South Africans go for a drink around here hey?" I told him in my best cockney "Earls court mate" Thinking that it was so typical. You travel 14000km to go for a pint with your buddies! Here I was avoiding the familiar things from home and here they were seeking them out. Some things never change.

Confusion, elation, euphoria, despair, hunger, hangover, exhaustion, cold. Nothing was lukewarm. It was boiling or freezing. A wonderful see saw ride from extreme to extreme. Just how I like it.

I was having the inevitable fall out with Grant. He had met a guy who he thought was "clued up" and I thought was a wanker and so, while they walked up and down the Champs Allleeesay... Ek Se!... looking for a homosexual to mug! I went looking for alternatives. I found a truck that had about 75 parking tickets stuck to it and realized it was probably not going anywhere and so tried the door which to my surprise slid open and I jumped gleefully inside away from the incessant rain. I had spent a night or two at the Metro entrances and wasn't to chuffed with the smell of urine and the hungry mosquito's so to me this was a couple of stars up in the hospitality department. The bonus was that inside I found a huge cardboard box filled with tinned food! I couldn't believe it.

I went to the job center and looked for jobs but couldn't read a word and it was useless so whilst wandering around one day I came across a tennis court and sat watching the coach give a lesson when I got the idea. "Hey! Why not try to help out here!?" I went to the coach afterward and asked him and although he was a little skeptical due to my boots and so on he said "OK meet me here on Saturday and we will see how you play" I thought "Great!" but hadn't really thought about what I was going to use to hit the ball with. SO... I went to Les Halles, to the largest sports store I could find and checked the place out. My initial idea was to ask the shop owner if he would perhaps forward me a racquet against my passport or something, after telling my sorry tale and hoped he would take pity on me. That idea lasted a full 10 seconds. I saw Grant and the other guy again and wondered aloud if it was possible to "take" a racquet from the shop. The other guy sneered at this as he was constantly trying to outdo me by doing the most outrageous and totally stupid, reckless things he could to impress Grant and myself. It had landed us in the police station twice and me, being a stupid fool myself decided to put this asshole in his place. I told him "you think I can't steal a racquet? I'll steal two!" whereupon they both laughed and continued to patronize me as was the current trend. I was really pissed off! Both at them and at me, but I knew that I could do anything I set my mind to and so went each day and continued to check it out.

First thing I did was to march in and march out with a brand-new pair of top of the range tennis shoes. The next day I marched back in and selected two racquets and got the assistant to advise me and wangled with him a bit but it was clear that I knew a bit about racquets and so told him "Ok String them up at 63 pounds with Victor Imperial and I'll collect them tomorrow. Do you take American Express? Good! OK Then!... Uhh... Au Ree Voor?? Hahaha!"

Before I left I went back and said "Hey, you work for commission yes? Well then I want to make sure that you get the sale" he was really grateful for that and so took the racquets to the stringer and as I had taken the labels off one of them, he did the same. The next day I was really nervous but decided there was no turning back. I walked in and with my slip for the racquets I approached the stringer and asked him if they were ready. He replied that they were and so I took them and "tested" the tension by whacking them against each other to listen to the sound as I am so used to doing. I perked up immediately and smiled at him "good job! Thank you uhh...Mersee Bookoo! Hahaha! By the way where are my covers?!" "Ahh sorry Monsieur... Here you are!" I took the two technological marvels and walked straight out of the door with a smile and a wave to the cashier and a nod of thanks to the salesman!

The next day I arrived ready for work!

Here I was. Down and out in London and Paris. Literally. I thought it apt that as I was sleeping in the metro and "earning" my pennies by bashing public telephones to dislodge any trapped coins and reading Mr. Orwell's book at the same time. I was a South African and as such could not draw from the welfare state in England as the Europeans were able to and I was also not about to take an illegal job and was sustaining myself by shoplifting a can of beans able shredded red cabbage once a day, not to mention chocolate, books and lots and lots of cider! I'm not proud of it but it's what I did. I had met a couple of Irish guys at the hostel when I stayed there and would bump into them from time to time. The one guy was a crack thief and could pick locks. I saw them one day and shouted across the road "top o the morning to you Paddy my boy!" in the best Irish accent I could muster. They came across almost wetting their pants and explained that NO Irish person speaks like that. I said "what? Is my accent that bad?" and they all replied " no! not at all. You sound like a bloody Dubliner" One of the shiftier guys said he wouldn't be surprised if I could con my way into a dole check with that accent. I laughed and shrugged it off but they all went kind of quiet in the typical "criminal scheming mode" and looked at me with deadpan faces. I laughed " you really think so?" "Naaah!" And so I was thoroughly drilled in the intricacies of getting a "Gyro" They had done it countless times. Getting second and third unemployment checks with false credentials and so on. I was apprehensive but exited at the same time. I never seriously thought I could or would be able to pull something like that off. But... I went to the local Woolich building society and opened and account with 1 pound that I had got from begging at the tube station. It was called "poncing" (I could never figure out why. I guess it's because you "Pounce" on your victim!!) and it's how I used to get a few pence together to go to the supermarket and buy a chocolate or something and walk out with half the shop stashed down the front of my pants. Anyway, I opened this account and made my way to the local DHHS office just before closing time rehearsing my speech and remembering the pointers I had been given and especially the danger signals that would serve as a signal to run like hell or be caught and arrested. Deportation would surely follow so I was quite nervous to say the very least. The bottom line was that everything went exactly according to plan and in the space of one hour and forty minutes I did the routine at two offices and had cashable checks in my grubby little paws to the tune of 77 pounds! I was rich!

I only tried it once.

The downside to taking lots of different chemicals to make you feel better is that they're not free!

The downer side of the deal is purchasing them from the dodgiest characters the planet has to offer. Both are forgotten as soon as the deal is struck.

At one stage I had enough cash to stay at a youth hostel and as was our habit we would nominate one or two people each day to go on the "run" As it was a dodgy business, the more upstanding travelers would leave it to ruffians like myself to do the dirty work and take the risk. I would go to a pub on the other side of town and meet the "right" guy and do the run for a small cut. The "right" guy wouldn't always be there and so a chance would have to be taken with some unknown and then it was very risky. You could get robbed or caught by an undercover policeman or worse.

One night I was there with a friend and we were forced to go with an unknown and so down to the bogs we went and hoped to make the deal. This guy and his friend were pretty rough looking and all four of us squeeze into the cubicle and out come the packages. It turns out they were "above board" and the stuff is genuine and a fair amount. At the close of the deal the rougher of the two invites us to join him "jacking up" I am totally against it and decline and without further ado he hauls out a needle from some hiding place under the bog and proceeds to go through the ritual he obviously knows so well. I, although by no means innocent, am curious to see how it is done as I have never actually seen someone do this except for the movies. He takes a teaspoon and places it with some powder in it on the top of the toilet and flushes the bog. He then takes the needle and fills it up with water taken from the bog! I do a double take as he squirts a little into the spoon and mixes it up before slurping it back up the hypodermic and sploosh, straight into his arm. "Yeah!" he says "you sure you don't want to use my works? It's cool with me mate, as long as you ain't got hepputitias or summink!"

I declined a second time

The cheques were turned to cash and the cash to liquid assets which I promptly drank and soon was in the same position as before. I spent two weeks in the freezing cold living on the streets in London. I would sleep in the greenhouse at the Chelsea gardens and sometimes on the church's lawn. I was totally drenched by the sprinklers one chilly night and so moved on. Parking lots, rolled into a carpet on a truck once and generally moping around aimlessly. I would still manage to see bands by sneaking in through the back doors or helping to carry equipment before opening time and so met a Canadian guy who was much in the same position as I was. We teamed up and as all my things had previously been stolen by a junkie (one of the Irish guys in fact) I only owned a sleeping bag and the clothes on my back.

He was "sussed" (street smart) and together we made quite the team. He was a great companion and a very smart and well-informed punk rocker. Together we managed to secure a "squat" in Elephant and Castle that had just been renovated and was in mint condition, complete with central heating and flushable toilets.

London is the most amazing city I have ever been to. I highly recommend to anyone not to go there if you are planning to be homeless during the winter. It SUX!

I know because I was, and had become fed up with it very quickly. I had met a Canadian guy on the streets a few times. Vic. He was a smart and clued up guy and much more in the know than I. He was in much the same position as I was and together we found out that it was possible to "Squat" a place. Now I had been to a few squats in my time and they were horrendous. I wasn't keen at all and it was with much persuasion that I eventually went to find out more about having a "real" squat.

The ones that I had seen were really bad. They had all the floorboards ripped up out of them as people had used it for firewood and the result was more like a cave than a flat. The soot encrusted walls were only one aspect. Usually the windows had been smashed too and a squat was yours only as long as you could protect it from other homeless people. Of which there were many. It was the time of the miners riots and things in England were on the brink of civil war in many places. I'm not exaggerating.

We went down to Elephant and Castle and went to a place called "Snow" which was an office situated inside an old Ambulance station that had been occupied by a group of activists. I knew the place quite well as I would often go there to see the most out of the way bands you can imagine.

On one occasion we went to see a band that played for a "donation" so was basically free. We went out together after being let in and "ponced" for an hour or so before the gig to try and make a donation to the band who had come from far inland to play.

The performance; Woman gets on stage and starts to play a saxophone while her friend does a kind of improvised belly dance to it. She is then joined by a guitarist and then other members come and go at their own cues. Sometimes playing together and sometimes not. In the middle of the "gig" a guy wearing a ballet tutu and goggles, snorkel and flippers gets up and starts reciting poetry. Sometimes his own and sometimes from people like William Blake. It all flows as one strung out chaotic disorder. I'm not sure what to make of it.

Anyway... This place is basically a fortress in the city. The windows are welded shut with steel plate and there is a major security door that no one will bother answering unless you have the correct name. It is amongst other things the home of "Snow," The squatters association!

We enter and as arranged meet Psychedelic Alvin! I kid you not. It's the dudes name. He reminds me of the hippy guy in "The Young ones" He has a rather interesting homemade wooly jumper and is as stable as Uranium. We get straight to the point. "Got the barrel?" "Yup" "Got the girl?" "Yup" "Pliers?" "Yup" "screwdriver?" Got any gum?" "WHAT?" "Gum asshole!" "Uhh Naah" "Go get some fucking GUM!" and stalks out into the bowels of the castle. We get the gum. We wait. He arrives and with just a look we know not to pull that one again!

"Right! Gimme some gum! Let's go!"

We move off at a jog into the freezing night and straight to the "Squat" we have found.

The place is boarded up from the outside and basically impenetrable which is the whole idea since the housing estate have renovated it and are about to have rent paying tenants move in. We only have a few hours to work with as the waiting list for such a place is usually about 6 months and places are hard to come by.

We get to the block and walk down the corridor towards the end where the boarded place is situated. Vic and I know our drill backwards and Marie our Norwegian Punkette friend and her dog are ready to play their part. We know that from the moment that door goes down we have approximately 2 minutes before either the council bully boys or the police arrive. We're hoping for the police.

Alvin takes out a bunch of keys and searches for the right one. He knows exactly which one it is and has all the master keys for the council's locks. How he knows or has them I wouldn't know.

Key goes in. The brutish outside padlock comes open and the door panel comes off. I boot the door. Bang! Alvin becomes a puff of smoke, as does the lock he has taken off the door. We enter and I am already half way through opening the lock to change the barrel inside while Vic has the "Gum" that Alvin has given him to attach a typed a4 sheet on the inside glass of the door. This is to be our "safety catch." Basically it states that we are occupying the premises as a "political act" and to try to forcibly evict us is in contravention of the law. I haul out the barrel and Vic clips the shaft of the new one to size and we re-insert it as quick as possible with the door securely shut from the inside. It's done! Vic and I retreat and take the wooden panel from the door to a place well within the flat. We sit down and wait quietly while Marie stands giggling next to the front door. It is no more than half a minute later that we hear the boots running down the hall.

A sharp knock. " Open up it's the police!" The dog goes ballistic. No response." Hello! Open up it's the police!" Marie replies " Sorry gentlemen but I'm not opening the door and you can read the note. Go away!" There is a short pause. " Look we just want to talk, won't you please open the door?"

Marie is trying her hardest to be serious and stifles a laugh before responding " If you don't go away I'm calling the police! I'm warning you!" Vic and I nearly wet ourselves but make no sound " We are the police! Are you alone? Is there someone in there with you?" Marie takes a sterner tone and tells them " You know the score, now piss off and leave me alone!" This continues for a short while but the police know there is nothing they can do. They are bound by their own law. They eventually leave.

We have won only the first round. Now it's a question of having one person occupy the flat at all times to ensure that the council bully boys don't kick the door down and pour cement down the toilet and then run away as they can't occupy the place but they can make it un livable.

We go through all the ins and outs like paying 15 pounds to ensure that the water and lights cannot be turned off and so we have a newly renovated flat to live in for the rest of the winter complete with central heating and a huge bath!

I remember lying in the steaming bath for a whole day once. My feet were cracked and bleeding and it was a few days of rest before we all went down and nicked the lights off the Southwark Housing Departments Christmass trees and had a multi colored house to live in!

It possibly saved all of our lives.

We would jump the tube and go to gigs all over London and "ponce" for beer money and eat at the traveling soup kitchen that went around the stations late at night and provided food for the homeless. We must have been the only homeless people ever to gain weight due to being destitute. Winter in London was no joke. Minus 11 at one stage and sleeping outside was less than fun. I got to know the city well. I loved and still love the place. I would walk each day. Walk and walk and walk and walk. I loved it. I realized that there wasn't much future in my future and so started to explore alternatives. I looked for legal work, but no one was prepared to employ me without a work permit. I worked casually as a laborer and carried millions of bricks as a 'Hoddie' but couldn't hold the job for more than a few days at a time without jeopardizing my employers status and so, often reluctantly, as I was a hard worker, I was told to take a few weeks off and return to do a few more sporadic days.

As I have mentioned, I used to often try to gain entrance to clubs by "lugging" equipment for the bands and now did it a lot more. I would try to get work in the mornings and if unsuccessful, would make my way, usually on foot, to the 100 club on Oxford road and wait for the vans to arrive and then "hustle" to get an opportunity to help out. Usually I was met with hostility and threatened but as time went by, I started to be better known and had earned a good reputation as I was one of the few, if not the only one who would be there at the end of the night to help load up the various band wagons. I helped many pretty famous bands and met "cult heroes" face to face without a stage between us and would sometimes sit with the band or be invited to the band room. This is where I got my "education" and learnt how to set up the sound and in particular the Guitar and effects. I would be there for all the band checks and for me it was where I wanted to be. It was all unpaid of course and the best I could hope for was that the band would stick me to a pint before the gig. I would do mainly the Punk nights but also metal or jazz nights. I helped Hugh Masekela a few times and watched him play. It was weird. I helped Motorhead and the guys invited me to roadie for them and I took a trip (literally) to Birmingham and the experience was mind boggling. Lemmy is the ugliest bastard I have ever seen up close and the whole atmosphere with all the Hells Angels was scary as Hades. I lasted two gigs before I decided to quit due to fear. I'm not joking. I would be spun out on "wiz" (sodium sulphate or "speed") and thought that it's a matter of time before I slip on the ice on one of the metal staircases with a huge amplifier or mixing desk and then I would be in for a good kicking and those dudes were MEAN. I was smart. I quit while ahead. I got paid though and the guys were pretty cool to me the whole time. They most certainly were the loudest band on Earth at the time. Due to them, I saw other kinds of Punk/Metal bands who influenced me for sure. I thought they were the cutting edge.

I worked it out later. I walked 19km that day. I had taken a bunch of speed and couldn't stop walking! I went down to the Kings road and "got" some Merrydown cider and a can of Tennent's and made myself a "snakebite" and walked and walked. The city was particularly quiet that day and I thought it was just my imagination but it turned out that there was a good reason for it. When I say quiet I mean that I didn't see any "street" people. I don't mean homeless, rather "alternative" people like Rasta's or Punks, Skins, whatever.

I somehow got to near Trafalgar square and as I was walking down the Strand I came across a most unusual sight. Half the street outside the Lyceum was blocked off by PUNKS! Loads and loads of them. More than I had ever seen in one place. It was about 8 or 9 pm and apparently the day had been "Stop the city" day. A day that was marked by protest marches through Fleet street and so on by all the "oddballs" and "freaks"

The Lyceum was host to 7 Punk bands that night and of course I was flat broke and so went about trying to find a way in. I met a Scottish guy outside and we got to talking and eventually decided to go to the amusement arcade and see if we could bump a machine or two and get a few coins together. This was disastrous and we were soon sprinting down the street with an irate Pakistani gentleman screaming abuse at us as we went. I eventually gave up on that and made my way to the back door as I was used to hoping to perhaps meet someone who recognized me.

No such luck. I was standing there with a group of Skinheads who had the same idea and were having the same kind of luck as me. By some twist of fate I nudged the exit door and found that it budged a little. I continued to encourage it and it slipped the catch. I looked over at the squad of hairless ones and said. You guys want to go to a gig? One of the beefier ones said. "Fuck off mate!" So I replied " Uhh Ok! See ya later" and disappeared into the darkness. It was only about a second later that he stuck his head through the door and whispered " How the fuck did you do that! We have been trying all night!" I just giggled and had him lead the way with his friends in hot pursuit. When the first one got to the auditorium he was of course blocked by the bouncer. Now the bouncer, finding he was faced with the prospect of single handedly having to throw out a Para military group of highly determined psychopaths, decided on the smartest thing and said. "Ok! 2 quid each!" The group fished into their pockets and I walked straight up to him with absolute Dutch courage and shouted in his face "I came 14 thousand miles to see this gig and you're not stopping me now!" He just moved aside while holding out his greasy palm for the silver.

The next scene is impossible to describe accurately but I'll give it a stab anyway.

The first 5 or so meters I didn't touch the ground. Not because of levitation but due to the fact that the floor was strewn with bodies passed out and inert. I simply had no choice but walk over them like the human carpet they were.

The entrance was at the side of the hall and below me there was another carpet of wildly writhing bodies.

The lights would show this sea of chest to chest crowd. Some on the shoulders of others as the Angelic Upstarts blasted out my favorite song of theirs. I couldn't hear the Bass. I felt it!

I made my way over more bodies and eventually to the floor near the front. Everyone was bouncing and the crowd was so densely packed that it was like a wave that would literally lift me off my feet for a few seconds and then back to Earth. There were the most outrageous spiky tops and one of the more hardcore guys next to me had put his hair up with Super glue! A fact I became aware of when I bumped into him and one of the spikes went cleanly through my cheek. At first I couldn't believe it but when I started spraying blood through the neat little hole I was convinced.

I went ballistic! I couldn't believe it. Here I was. A huge Punk rock gig and I was right in the thick of it.

Soon I got thirsty and so fought my way through the pack to the back where the toilets are and walked into a different zone. Before I even got to the door the stench hit me. I was about to step into about 3 cm sea of pure urine! I was too thirsty by this stage and so went for it but what I found inside was too much. The basins were all blocked of course and some people had taken a crap in more than one. This wasn't the bad *part. The bad part was standing there in shock as someone as thirsty as me pushed me aside and proceeded to drink from the tap while a turd was floating a millimeter from his nose. I stayed thirsty and went to the girls toilet but it wasn't much better.*

I went back in and saw each and every band and was the last person to leave that night.

I walked through the streets of a drizzly London with my ears buzzing until it became light and I watched the clouds become grey from the banks of the Thames.

Realizing that music was to be more than a passing phase and coupled with fact that I was looking for a way to stay in London permanently I looked towards the industry as a whole and thought about where I may be able to work and be happy at the same time. Record sales and merchandising didn't appeal to me at all and the "live " scene was a dead end since it required years to become a good sound engineer so I went to Tottenham court road, where it was my habit to stand with my nose pressed to the glass at night and dream about all the guitars I would buy when I one day could afford to. I love guitars and one day if I can ever afford to I will buy a lot of them. I can't play for toffee, but I would collect them if I were a rich man. All day long I'd da, da, da, dum, etc. Well I applied for a few jobs as a sales man but of course was politely shown the door due to my particularly unique form of dress and smell no doubt. I then discovered a small shop called Andy's Guitar shop which had a downstairs cellar where guitars were built and repaired. I would walk in every few days and asked as I had done to all the other shops down the street, for a job. It was my strategy to wear them down and impress them with my persistence and sense of humour as there wasn't a snowballs chance of getting a job. Well the guy in Andy's (maybe Andy!?) decided to inquire further one day out of pure curiosity I would imagine and I told him straight up that I just love guitars and all about my situation with nothing held back.

No visa, experience etc. He took me downstairs and showed me this small cellar workshop and said I was welcome to hang about if I could find a place to stand and not touch anything. The roof was so low that I couldn't stand upright but watched for hours while these craftsmen worked lovingly at their trade. One evening after work, one of the guys took me to Foyles to show me where I could find the best books to learn the basics of guitar maintenance and repair. It was the first time I had ever considered a career and was well keen. The highlight of this time was a weekend when a whole bunch of Robert Smiths guitars arrived from Germany and had to be fixed super quick and ready and back in Germany by Monday morning. I stayed all night and made tea and ran errands while they fixed up his quiver of black bodied beauties. I am a huge fan of Robert Smith and am proud to say that I have lovingly stroked his instrument! I was told that they may have a future vacancy for me as an apprentice in the future but it would hinge on my obtaining a work permit. It was to prove more difficult than I thought.

London...Its cold and wet and I'm dead tired. I have been walking all day and slept the previous evening near the entrance of Kensington High street tube station. The whole day was a schlep to stay moving and try to keep up my body temperature. I hadn't eaten a single thing.

I ended up at the 100 club and watched a band play and on my way back to the car park I was at yesterday as this is where I had hidden my sleeping bag.

I'm on the other side of Hyde park though and simply don't have the will left to walk around the park and so I do the obvious thing. I hop the fence and start to walk into the darkness.

It isn't long before I feel that I'm not quite alone and true to my hunch, I am immediately illuminated by a spot lamp and told by a mega phoned voice to put my hands over my head and lie face down. No funny tricks!!! I do as I'm told as it's no big deal as I'm quite used to being stopped.

I am approached by two imposing shadows and kept at arm's length while I am questioned. The usual, "who are you? Where are you from? What are you doing here? Have you got a valid visa? Where's your passport?" and so on. I'm a bit non plussed as I'm only taking a shortcut and haven't done any damage or been drinking or anything.

Eventually one of the policemen asks me "do you know where you are?" I laugh at this and explain that I am quite sober thank you and am quite aware of where I am. So he pushes me " So?... Where are you then?" I drop the smile and tell him "Hyde Park. London!" They look at each other and back at me. "You're not in Hyde Park mate." Now I'm really confused and it must have shown as the guy says " You really don't know where you are do you?!" I shake my head and they grin at me. " Hyde Park's over there son! This is Princess Palace!" I'm still a little confused and then it hits me. "Oh Shit! You're serious?" and begin to apologize but they stop me. And inform me that they had been watching me even before I had entered the property as it seemed likely that I was going to cut across. The fact that I was a foreigner and sober was what saved me.

It turned out that just a few days before, the Queen or one of them, woke up to find a strange man in her bedroom and duly the entire police force had been put on special alert!

They were well cool about it though and told me to continue walking and don't look back until I had hopped the fence on the other side!

My father is a British National. This fact alone, I thought would entitle me to British citizenship which is what I so desperately wanted. A complete break with the past and a new life entirely. Problem was that my father was born in India. Everyone said "that's nooooo problem!" I guess it wouldn't have been, except for the fact that apparently my grandfather had also been born there. This meant that officially my father was a second-class citizen. He had less rights to anything than a Pakistani who was born there and it used to piss my dad off no end. "Bloody Brits! I was ducking Japanese bullets in the jungle while they were drinking sherry and eating cucumber sandwiches!" and so on. I was told that it was a contestable issue and so I compiled the mountain of all the necessary paperwork and submitted it to the authorities in Croydon and waited for them to contact me which they did some 8 weeks or so later. I hopped the train and took my place in the line. Number 737! I was optimistic that the wait wouldn't be more than a week or so and kicked myself for not having brought a book. It took three days to get to the front of the queue. I had to train back and forth each day. I was not amused! When I eventually got within range of the booth, there was a woman in front of me with two kids and she had been waiting to complain about her dole check which was apparently not enough for her needs. The assistant was very polite and attended to her as a true professional would. The lady was from Nigeria. It was now my turn. The nice professional lady politely asked me how she could assist and I duly told her that I had applied for a British passport and wanted to become a citizen of the greatest nation on Earth. She was quite buoyant and said " country of origin?" I dutifully replied " South Africa" and the spell was broken. Her face lost its professionalness and became a scowl as she uttered the fateful words " Zola Budd!!?? Oh my goodness! NEXT PLEASE!" I was stunned. I didn't move. The person behind me moved up and I just stood there. The professional scowler said "sorry sir but there's nothing I can do. Please, people are waiting" I had been there for three days and knew where the supervisor's office was and stormed over there and burst through the door. Just ahead of the security guard and told him matter of factly that I wasn't about to be turned away and did not understand what my case had to do with Zola Budd! I told him that I had a genuine claim to citizenship and all the rest and he said to me " look, wait six months before you re apply and all this would have blown over and I'm sure that your chances then will meet with success" My visa had already expired and was unable to wait six months. I was stopped regularly as a punk by the police and there was no way I would manage another six months.

It's another day's end and I have just made a "run" to the pub and am on my way back to the hostel on the bus.

We haven't been on the bus long before a group of guys get on and come upstairs. I'm sitting in front and a friend is further back with a guy and his girlfriend behind him. One of the new guys sits opposite the couple and starts ogling the girl. This continues and the bus has become a little more subdued when the conductor makes his way up the stairs and breaks the tension. He asks the first one for the fare and is ignored. Very blatantly and at first the conductor tries to outwait him. At the next request the ignoring oggler turns to the conductor and issues forth a string of racialist abuse in the most threatening tone. The conductor turns and makes his way down the stairs as quick as he can. My friend turns to the guy, hoping to take the attention away from the girl and says "what all that then?' A second later the oggler is over the chair and is pounding my friend in the face. I stand up and one of the guys stands right in front of me and looks me straight in the face. We are about 5 cm from each other and he says " what? What?" I tell him "hey man that's totally fucking out of order!" I look him straight in the face and then I notice that his pupils are totally dilated. I mean TOTALLY! I cannot see any iris and it scares the shit out of me. He looks closer at me with his eyes pulled wider as a kind of provocation and I back down. Meanwhile, the guy with the girl has gotten up and he has summarily been thumped and kicked in the face by two of the group.

The conductor has meanwhile gone downstairs and tried to get the driver to stop the bus but the guy won't pay any attention and tells the conductor it's his problem. The conductor then noticed a policeman and leaned out of the bus and called for help.

A van full of police were passing by opposite and the policeman flags them down and the bus is stopped. One of the group who is lookout says a single word and like magic the group stop what they are doing immediately and sit down separate from each other. I am pretty shocked but nevertheless impressed by the move. I'm also more than a little worried as we now have a situation and I am a walking pharmacy waiting to be fried.

The policeman orders everyone out of the bus and asks for any witnesses to point out the guilty ones. The conductor is now completely confused as there is no more "group" and he can only identify one of them. The identified guy has undergone a complete personality transformation and if I hadn't seen him with my own eyes a few minutes before I wouldn't have placed him.

I go out and the policeman asks the conductor " Him?' The conductor answers " no! he paid" As the policeman looks at me I catch his eye and so move off to the side as he duly comes over. He asks me" are you willing to testify?' as he knows I can identify them. I reply" you mean in court?' he says " no just make a statement" I agree and nod in the direction of the guy who I was eyeball to eyeball with. The Bobby makes an imperceptible gesture to his friend, a hefty looking red headed policeman who would look more at home on a rugby field or wrestling ring. The redhead goes over to the guy and says" scuse me sir" and gets no further. The guy turns to the policeman with an animal like snarl and grabs him by the throat and lifts him clear off the ground and pins him up against the railing of the fence surrounding Hyde park. The policeman's feet are literally dangling in the air as his friends jump to the rescue and try to pull the ogglers friend free and bundle him into the van. It takes seven of them. I stand flabbergasted while one policeman is sitting on the guys back whilst being bucked around as if he was at a rodeo and the crack of fingers as another is bending back the hand and audibly breaking bones. The guy is screaming blue murder and looks at me and screams " you're fucking dead!" It's one of the few times that I have not had something cocky to say. I just shut up and sneered at him.

Eventually the lot of them are bundled away with the help of two more vans and as promised I tell the policeman that I can make the statement.

So we all go to the Earls court station and luckily we have to walk and so have a chance to hide the illegal stuff.

I make my statement with the sound of shouting in the background. The policeman was very decent about it and although my pupils were possibly as dilated as the ogglers group, he didn't mention it.

It turned out that the guy with the girl ended up suffering a detached retina and had to have surgery.

He was an ex French Legionnaire!!

I asked the policeman what would happen to them and he replied " they will all go down for six months and then to court' I said " Wait, six months first and then court??" He said " Of course! They knocked off a Bobby's hat!" I hadn't heard it before then and was really surprised.

After being tested it was discovered that the whole group had been on Angel Dust!!

I got on the train and went to Scotland to see my family and although they were a little taken aback at my appearance or should I say condition, they played it down and I spent a great time there and had an opportunity to spend a little time with my uncle who I had idolized and still do. He was a giant of a man. Six foot plus and smart as anything. He had a set of encyclopedias in his head and excelled at everything he ever did. He was in the commando's during the war and decorated for his bravery. He retired as a Colonel and worked in a textile company where of course he soon rose to the top. Upon retirement? He worked for the Red Cross and eventually became its president. Captain at St Andrews and a great golfer, he was simply an all-round extraordinary human being and I loved him dearly. He took me on a trip to Edinburgh Castle and took me to places not usually seen by tourists with soldiers in kilts snapping to attention smartly whenever he walked into a room though he wasn't on active duty. He told me things that the well-informed guide wouldn't have known as he had been a member of the Scots guards and knew it all first hand. He took me to a small pub for lunch and I had the best Guinness I have ever tasted. I remember that he took me to a bookshop to show me a book about the history of the commando's and there were pictures of him as a young man with Lord Somerset who he had rescued in Yemen and some chapters of which he was the author. He offered to buy me a gift and I chose a small pocket Oxford dictionary that I still have and use frequently.

We discussed the matter of citizenship and it was thought that I should return to SA and return later with a new passport and in the interregnum he would do some research and try to pull a few strings in my favor.

I thought it over and although I was totally against the idea due to my complete distaste for all things South African, I could see the logic of it and so went back down to London for a few days and then boarded the plane to JHB. I had felt more at home in London than I ever did at my real home and knew that it would be hard for me to cope, but was determined to stick it out and finally return. I was distraught and depressed. Sad and feeling like a complete failure.

My arrival at the airport was in keeping with my emotional state as my parents took one look at me as I walked into the arrivals area and turned smartly and walked ahead trying to pretended that they were not connected with this monster all in black and unconventional hairstyle and image. They had of course imagined that Europe would "cure me " of these silly notions and dress and so on and it had had the complete opposite effect. It was a most painful homecoming and I was determined to leave at the first opportunity.

Home Sweet Home?

The letter from the Air force was on the kitchen table when I arrived. I was to report for my "camp" two months ago. At least my air ticket would prove I was out of the country at the time and so would not have to go to serve time at the detention barracks for being AWOL. My dad informed me quite bluntly that I was to start looking for a job the next day and he expected me to have one and my own accommodation in two weeks time. Welcome home son!! Yeah right!

I moved in with my girlfriend sharing a flat with another couple in Berea and finally got a job working in a sport shop. I was expected to wear a work shirt with the company name and logo but at least could wear jeans and trainers to work. My responsibility was to meet a sales target of 700 or 750 rands per day I don't remember exactly. What I do remember is that it was the same as my monthly salary. I was expected to sell tennis racquets, shoes and running gear. It was a job I could cope with and my dad had gotten me a small Fiat to do the trips to and from work as public transport was a standing joke. Pun intended. The shop was situated in the northern suburbs and it was frequented by the stinking rich. I was definitely from the other side of the tracks and was curious to see how the other half lived so to speak. My boss was a beefy British immigrant and for the most part I thought that we would be able to connect but was sadly mistaken. His outlook was painfully stereotyped as I discovered on my first day when whilst being shown around asked what the drill was for shoplifters. He was very matter of fact about it and explained that if the guy was white we detained him/her and called the center security to deal with it. It was strict company policy to prosecute shoplifting and go for the maximum seek the maximum penalty. If the guy was black, and they were the majority then we simply took him out to the back alley and in his own words "kick the shit out of the fucker!" and added as an afterthought "last one had to be hospitalized" with a grin. It was a scene I knew so well and hadn't thought about for so long, it was like, " Oh boy! Here we go again" He was a new Karate student and trained with the guy who ran the camping dept and who was the senior salesman. They would come into work every so often and jerk each other off, showing the bruises from last night's training in front of the few other young salesmen who basically licked both of their asses as they were expected to do. I would sit on the sidelines and watch and keep my mouth closed. I had studied a little Shaolin oriented Kung Fu by this stage and had moved over to Tai Chi and thought it better to keep it to myself. All went well for a few weeks and I would watch as they would walk past a punch bag and throw a few feints or shots as a kind of ritual "keeping sharp" or whatever. One day on of the students from my previous school who was quite well known in the area came into the shop and was immediately welcomed by the boss and his top lackey and the conversation went straight to the relative superiority of Japanese over Chinese martial arts and vice versa. I watched from a distance and tried to remain unseen but was spotted by the student who let out a blast of a greeting as I cringed back into the shadows. Well there was no escaping it and now I was drawn into the stupid dumb bonding bullshit so religiously engaged in by the "jocks" Luckily there was a customer lurking close to my section and I jumped at the excuse to disengage and scooted over there as quickly as I could. The following weeks were painfully excruciating with continual comments, and requests to exchange techniques to see which was superior and I would stay as much as possible on the opposite side of the shop attending to anything I could think of to not have to get drawn in. It was my ongoing nightmare to be in a position to be in the shop when a shoplifter would be caught and be summoned outside to "do the honors" As a master of the illegal art of nicking things, I could tell straight away when a thief entered and would sidle over to him as soon as I was sure he had taken something and I would in a low voice tell him what he would be in for if he didn't leave the particular article in the change room on his way out. I would have made a great security guard but with a shocking arrest record.

I was saved in a weird kind of way. My military camp thingy had caught up with me. It had been a few months but the paperwork had obviously had time to be done and my arrival at the airport and receiving of a salary was enough for them to set it in motion. I had vowed previously, never to return to SA much less do a camp, but devised a scheme to get out of returning to Hoedspruit. I returned my final notification with an incorrect address in Cape town, knowing that as a "camper" they would usually try as much as possible to place you closer to home. I had not yet seen much of the Fairest Cape and thought that I may just do it at Governments expense. Which I did. Complete with days off to fictitiously go to JHB for a marathon that I was expected to participate in by my company. Sport is a powerful weapon and should never be allowed to get into the wrong hands. I reported to the base and was expected to stand guard in the middle of nowhere and protect a "bomb dump" as it was known. Contrary to my understanding that it was a place where old bombs went to retire or simply be dumped as in "rubbish dump" or "Take a dump" it turned out to be an Arsenal. An Arsenal that couldn't kick a ball to save its life. It was quite a dangerous job really as the place was surrounded by bush and on a few previous occasions people from the nearby location had taken a pot shot or two at the lone guard. There was a neat bullet hole from an AK 47 right next to my left ear, through a sewerage pipe which used to stink the little booth out in the heat of the day and provide a lovely fetorial ambiance in the evenings. I read a lot, drank a lot and walked around Cape Town a lot as we were pretty free to leave the base as long as we were there to do our guard shifts. To the other guys who had been posted there for national service this was normal! How different it was for us up north...

I completed my month and went back to JHB with a notebook full of new addresses and money in the bank as my work had to pay the difference between my Air force pay and my regular salary by law. A fact I was well aware of and that had prompted me to get a job in the first place, knowing full well that it was inevitable that I would have to do the reserve duty.

I couldn't deal with the job and the environment anymore and so much to the disgust and anger and disappointment of my girlfriend and family, I quit.

We're on set. I finish up for the day and want to get back to town as I'm not into hanging around for the whole day and then going back in the early evening on the extras bus. I go around and see that the actors driver is heading for his car. I scoot over there and ask him if he is going to town. He is really snotty about it and tells me "if I am or not it makes no difference!" I ask "why? can't you give me a lift if the car is empty and you're going anyway" He responds with a flat "No!" I try a different tack "OK, how about a lift to the main road and I will hitch hike from there?" He laughs at me and states " I only drive Mr Palance! Nobody else!" he gets into the car and drives off in a cloud of dust. I stand in his wake with my middle finger gently waving in the breeze. Bastard!

The next day is one of the final scenes and it's a critical one. The whole village will be incinerated and we all have to run around screaming and so on while the mock village goes up in smoke.

Its critical as its a scene that can only have one take and so we rehearse all morning before the final word and then its "action" and no turning back.

The call comes and the scene begins. The whole "village" has been constructed out of 4x4 planks and draped with burlap upon which a quick setting foam has been sprayed to create a kind of adobe building effect. But it's a set and not a village and as such it has some "real" entrance and exits and some "duds" Literally dead ends that bowl out behind at the end of an alleyway to contain the people that are supposedly walking through town on a market day or whatever.

All the extras know the place like the back of their hands but as it happens the "stars driver" is there on the day with his son to show him the spectacular final scene. As the flames quickly engulf the rapidly disintegrating structure, he and his son who are dressed as extras run like hell as is expected but duck down into one of the dead ends! I see this and although I shout it's impossible as everyone is screaming and pretending mass panic. I run off towards the crew and grab the director or assistant and scream it to him. At first he tries to brush me off but as we know each other he pays attention and its visible shock as the realization hits him. He rushes off with some fire fighters and goes round the back of the set to try and burrow a hole through and pull these poor guys out. They try and try but the place is an inferno and sadly don't succeed.

Both the driver and his son were burned to death.

I recall it with sadness and it makes me wonder at all the stupid little petty things that we do to each other that pale into dust when it is placed upon a backdrop that shows them up for the bullshit things they are.

Years and years later I was in Australia and after much searching I found the movie with Jack Palance and the others. I remember Russel Savadier was a co-star in this b-movie. I watched it with rapt attention and then again even rapter and finally found one scene in the "tunnels" where Jack Palance is speaking and I stagger around behind him with a huge piece of polystyrene that was supposed to be a rock and that's it! Hahahah!

It was like that a lot. You would spend days at a shoot and perhaps be lucky enough to be shown on screen for half a split second. I have a career spanning a total of 2.466663 seconds on the silver screen.

Hollywood!

I had moved into my own flat a few months previously and had only to make the nominal rent which I thought I would be able to manage. I was disillusioned with the relationship with my girlfriend and although I had remained faithful to her whilst overseas and loved her very much, was nevertheless aware of the rift that had occurred in my own thinking and also the fact that the next logical step would be marriage and kids and I was not going to go that way at the tender age of 20 something. Travel had worked its way into my blood and discomfort and hardship were nothing new to me and I knew that my girlfriend wasn't interested in the gypsy life. She wanted to settle down which was clear and I wasn't ready. Also my political views were pretty extreme and I viewed the "liberals" with the same disdain as I did the "right wing" and "ignorant sheep" which was my common blanket term for everyone who complied. The "establishment" Moral majority/minority" Whoever.

It took a VERY short time for me to revert to my previous state and with interest. I shaved my head into a Mohawk and played my guitar all the time. Writing songs that I thought were relevant to my situation in SA and not as some quasi "Pommy punk" wannabe. My lyrics were international as they rejected everything and were mainly against war. All my friends thought that I had "lost it" due to taking too many drugs in Europe and I slowly started to associate with the people in my immediate area and not so much with my previous circle as most of them were now doing there national service and had not had the experiences that I had had and so I saw them differently and in a big way "trapped" by the view they had developed locally. To me the world was still the one that I saw from an airplane window. Borderless and vast. It's only when you land on the ground that things like flags have any relevance. Borders between countries were to me just a way of keeping control and extorting cash. I still don't understand them. Flags should be for football teams. It's a good model to use to describe my attitude in general. I love football but could care less about supporting any particular team. It meaningless to me. I feel the same way about nationality. Its contradictory though which will be made more clear later on. It is the same when it comes to religion. I could not claim to support any one form of organized religion. I'm with Marx on this one but differ in the respect that I feel that it's good for others to follow whatever path they choose as long as they don't interfere and show respect for other people's choice to follow a different path. It's so rarely that case though and all the bloodshed etc... blah, blah, blah...

I'm in Malvern one afternoon. It's decided by my friend and I that its time to score some dope. So we collect the needed funds from our group of likeminded friends and since him and I are the "street smarts" We are naturally nominated to make the run. We get on his motorbike and go across the railway tracks to the George Gogh residents which is where the people who worked in the mines lived. I could actually see this barren expanse of blocks of quarters from my house yet had never dared to go there.

I walked into a world that could have been a different planet. No mans land for white people. Situated splat bang in an industrial area it was strongly recommended to avoid the area especially after dark.

We walked straight in and dropped a few names to the right looking people and were ushered directly to the right shebeen hastily as the ever-present police van on its regular rounds would home in on us like a bull to a red flag. There were many drunk dancing people swaying to African jazz being played far too loud and distorted to all hell. Everyone was very friendly. We make the score and as we are not on the street where smaller quantities are the norm, we have specifically come closer to the source to obtain a larger quantity for a substantially cheaper sum.

It is decided that I will carry the parcel on foot while he rides the bike and so make it more difficult for the police to apprehend us.

I set out and soon arrive at the flat where the others are anxiously waiting and we expect my friend to arrive shortly. Shortly soon becomes longly and then longerly and finally not at all. We guess that he has been stopped and so hide the parcel and sit nervously waiting for the anticipated visit from the boys in blue. They don't arrive either.

We later discover that our friend is in the JHB general hospital nursing a badly broken leg. It turns out that only a few meters from where we parted company he was struck by a truck that failed to successfully negotiate the bend. The point of impact was exactly where I would have been sitting had I returned with him on the bike.

Anyway... here I was just a few weeks after I had regained some semblance of respectability walking around town in knee length black boots and leather and finding out first hand what it means to shun a system and still have to exist in it. Back to sniffing glue for days on end, shoplifting books, food and alcohol. Living for the music that most didn't even acknowledge as such and my options for the future dwindling to basically nil in as short a time. I had to of course rely on my folks' support which was another nail in our relationships coffin and severe bouts of depression were constant due to the substance abuse and situation.

I was still funnily enough playing a lot of tennis. The only player in the first league with a shaven purple Mohawk. My teammates used to joke by telling the members of the other teams in all seriousness that my hairstyle was due to a recent brain operation which had left me highly unstable but nice enough as long as I had had a few drinks. I was always quite shocked at the response from the old ladies who lovingly used to ply me with drink. It was a long time before they let the cat out of the bag the buggers! I had to laugh though as I thought that the old ladies thought my unconventionality was somehow attractive and was always hoping that I could one day be cornered in a villa by one of the sugar mommies. Never happened though and now I know why. They were petrified!! Ha! Ha! Fact is that all the physical work I had to do, playing at a respectable level could have been what enabled me to keep my head above water, if only just so. It's amazing the physical punishment that I have meted out to this old carcass and still come back for more. The long hours of constant walking and days on end without sleep would have killed (and did!) other mortals. I don't have any other explanation for it.

Eventually I met up with two guys who said they already had a band and were looking for a guitarist and so I went over to "Highpoint" this was a 25 storey apt block on top of the hill of the aptly named suburb Hillbrow and it commanded a panoramic view of the city superior to the Carlton Centers panorama which was 50 story's but situated in town. It was dizzying. It was dizzyinger to think that this guy had lived in this little box in the sky for most of his life. He played bass and his friend was a "drummer" who bashed away on a kids set as it was all he could afford. He had 25% hearing which meant that he would mix up the snare and the bass. It didn't bug me in the least as it was all in the spirit of punk and DIY music and anyway I thought that it gave us a rather unique sound that even if I had thought of it, I would never have managed to find anyone who could invert the drums as effectively as he did. Our newly formed band was called 'Septic Lozenges" which I had no part in naming and we somehow managed to play a few live concerts around town. More about that later.

We were the "real" punks in JHB at the time. Centrally located, no income, delinquent, well informed and non-conformist. There was practically no "scene" to speak of but we weren't deterred in the slightest and gave it stick.

My routine was like a bus following the daily route. I would rise and start walking to Hillbrow. The morning mission was to try and "get" a box of instant soya based imitation minced meat and a packet of instant mash potatoes. Toppers and Smash. Yum! To be successful I may have to wander from shop to shop all morning as I couldn't hit the same place on a daily basis and even so it was dodgy for me to leave a shop without getting anything anyway. Once I had procured my sustenance I would go back to the flat and boil water and prepare the mixture and eat. I would then grab my skateboard and go back to Hillbrow where I would try to collect money by doing tricks outside the bookstore or record shop. This was hard as street performances were practically nonexistent and no one would believe that I would actually be asking money for doing such a thing. I had a lot of conflict doing this as I'm by nature very shy and would have to psyche myself up each and every day to do this. It doesn't matter how many times I may have had to beg on the streets, it was always humiliating and difficult for me to do. I would also have to endure a lot of heckling too and often had to grab my skate and run like hell from some irate bullyboy who wanted blood. I would approach it in a kind of fun way and say stuff like "20c per trick C'mon ladies and jerks How about it? I'll go away for 50c and if you don't help out I'm going to start singing and this you will regret forever!" whatever would come to mind I would blurt out and as I am quite good on the rebound so to speak I would be able to stay on a roll if someone responded with a wisecrack or insult. I would hustle and every day without fail no matter how long it would take I would make enough for a beer at least and sometimes for a box of dope as well. I would take the cash and go into the same bottle store as was my habit and buy the quart of beer and joke with the owner who would call me "dirty Pommie" "Go home Pommie!" he would say to me and I would reply" Yesss Sir!" With a click of my heels and a Nazi salute or say " I am already there and Jesus loves you!" whilst feeling the weight of the bottle of Southern Comfort that was stashed in a secret pocket in my leather jacket. It was the secret of my success. He would watch the obvious Alcoholics and chancers like a hawk all day and would catch them and lash out at them as they ran away with his trusty "shambok" a nasty type of whip that was weapon of choice for the SA Police in crowd situations. I would stop at his counter and chat and joke before walking off towards one of the many street people who I could trust not to rip me off when I got the neatly packed matchbox of "A" grade. It has to be said that dope in SA was freely available, top quality and dirt cheap, practically 24 hours per day. Straight home with the open beer stashed inside my jacket as drinking in public was illegal. Get stoned, start getting stuck into the Southerns and off to the bookstore to do some reading before band practice. More or less this was standard except for the times that I would lock myself away and sniff glue and listen to musik for days on end. It was a dismal merry go round on a downhill spiral.

Getting a job was not easy. Period. For someone like me, even if I wore a suit and "played the game" getting an anywhere decent job would be near impossible with my academic record. It would go like this...I would approach a particular company and after grooming myself into near respectability would go in "cold" like I did in London. The approach was unheard of in SA You went for a job interview after scanning the classified adverts and then phoning and then if you were lucky being asked to come in and then maybe a second or third time after as the "short list" became shorter. Walking into a place and asking for a job wasn't really done. I did it. Hoping to make an impression by displaying in initiative and drive. It never worked except for one isolated incident. I would say. "I'm keen, hardworking, a quick learner, I'll work for minimal cash, teach me! They would answer when it was positive..."we can't offer you employment without any prior experience!" I would counter " how do I get the experience if you won't offer me the opportunity?" They would respond..."yes we realize it's a bit of a problem but there's nothing we can do" I would counter the counter ..." if I had a university degree would it change the picture?" They would respond"

Of course! If you had a bachelors degree it would be no problem!" I would then ask..." How does four years at varsity qualify as work experience?" End of interview... The guys who had been new immigrants and so not having had to do any national service would be the guys with the jobs. They would be driving souped-up sports cars and have the sexy girlfriends and go to the expensive clubs. The university graduates who had opted and were privileged enough financially to study before doing national service would become the officers and have great prospects when they had completed their two years. For the rest I'm afraid it was the catch 22. I'm badly exaggerating here though. It wasn't that way for everyone, just the fools like me who had not followed the sound advice/admonitions of my schoolmasters when they warned that this would happen. That was what made the whole situation suck even more. The fact that with my opportunities and so called abilities I should have known better and "toed the line" as I was so frequently told to do by EVERYONE...and I know people personally who were less privileged and much less bright than I who secured a good life and supported their families through plain simple hard graft. I respect them and how often I have wished that I was able to follow their example and had frequently tried but simply couldn't keep it up for more than a token period at best. Unemployment benefits at stage operated according to the following system. You had to have worked for a minimum of 6months to qualify for a very meager unemployment benefit. This would be payable for no more than 6 months. The payout period was 6 months regardless of how long you had worked. The manpower people would send you to interviews and you of course had to go and the jobs they sent you for were of course the really bad ones. It wasn't London. The unemployment office was the best place in town to get mugged! No shit. I was scared of walking past there.

The next job I got was at a printing firm and I had answered the classified ad for a vacancy as a black and white stripper. No experience needed! Only the good Lord and a few of the chosen knew what the hell a black and white stripper was but I knew it was my true calling and so I went and duly got the position and as is the case with 99% of apprentices, was immediately assigned to making tea and fetching sandwiches when I wasn't sweeping up. After a few months I took the initiative and stayed after hours and sneaked time on the big computerized draughting machine and soon knew how to operate it although as to be expected, in a very rudimentary fashion. The average worker there was still very much in awe of computers and wouldn't have dared to try what I had. I have a knack for these things and go quite successfully albeit slowly by trial and error. I proceeded to move on and learnt to operate the special cutting machine that would transfer my draughted creations to a special double layered and very expensive type of plastic sheeting which could then be used to create prints. This was a very risky business as the average Journeyman was cut from the most typical worker stock imaginable and would have physically attacked me for having the nerve to use my initiative. It was not acceptable to ever do that. It was the same at school. I'm not joking here. I had been witness to more than one occasion where "my" journeyman, had physically smacked the old black guy around for missing a spot or something equally trivial with his mop and a few close ones where he nearly got in to a fistfight with the supervisor. I would have been severely slapped around for being "cheeky" and possibly or probably had my pay docked if not given the boot. None of this happened though and I was fortunate in that my immediate superior's superior was a fellow student at Kung Fu class and who would take a lot of flak from the workers. He knew full well what I was doing and respected it and through him I discovered exactly what my supposed apprenticeship was supposed to be for. It turned out to be a job that was on the cusp of obsolescence. In fact I was shocked to realize that there was a new computer program that had been purchased by the company that would enable one of the programming staff to do the very same task with ease, in half the time and without interfering with his current job as computer operator. I was shocked. I asked the supervisor what I was actually doing there then and he just shrugged. "not sure" he told me in his thick German accent.

It was clear to me that I was not going to have a brilliant career as tea boy sweeper upper and so I did the logical thing and confronted the boss and as I couldn't disclose the fact that I was aware of the whole software business due to having been told by my supervisor in confidence I took a different tack and said that I thought black and white stripping was a dying trade and that the future was in computers and I wasn't sure if I was cut out for the job as I was looking for a career with a stable future. He looked a bit sheepish and admitted that he had to agree with me and that the company had been re considering my terms of employment and were not sure of what course of action to take as they were afraid of being in breach of contract and there was the issue of settlement fees and so on. He went on and said that my enthusiasm and attitude had impressed them and he would recommend that I took a computer course and then they would be more than happy to re employ me in a different capacity. I sat there like the dummy that I was. I had been hopelessly outmaneuvered by my own stupidity and it wasn't the first time. Any normal scheming slinky thinking respectable member of society would automatically have been able to make the calculation and made a deal to either get severance or a very expensive computer course at the company's expense or ...anything! Not me. I simply felt I had let HIM down and stood up thanked him, shook his sweaty paw and walked out into the cold winters morning. I hadn't even eaten my home made and heavily chili sauced tomato sandwiches since it was not yet tea time.

I had given up hope by then of becoming a stripper. Black or white.

Needless to say, when my dad found out he hit the roof and we were back to square one. I was always amazed how both my parents would always immediately take the opposite side to the one I was on. They always seemed to bail me out of the shit towards the end but they never did things that I felt were supportive. I'm not moping about it and as a parent I now realize how hard it is to make the right decisions at the right time and so on but I was always of the mind that perhaps just a little of encouragement at the right time may give me the necessary material to be in a more commanding position the next time I may be faced with a difficult choice. Its wishful thinking of course as it's all done but I often think about the attitudes shown by some of my friends' parents towards them that showed support even when they were not in agreement with certain aspects of the situation. The result was positive and the particular person would seemed to have grown from the experience. I always seemed to be broken by it and have to compensate by strengthening my resolve in a stubborn, negative kind of way. It would be like "OK so that's the way it is ...FUCK THE LOT OF YOU!" Instead of "Ok so that's the way it is. I won't let that happen again" or something similar. I don't feel like I'm expressing it clearly enough. My mistakes always led to a huge confrontation. Being roasted on the spit. The times in between felt like breaks between barbeques. My response was usually rage and I would lose my temper and hurl abuse and things and go berserk in my anger and frustrated confusion which of course never served to solve anything and so the whole situation would be completely blown out of proportion. My mother used to actively enjoy egging me on to the point of no return and then sit there with her fucking smug smile as if she had scored a victory. I hated her. She was able to manipulate events to her advantage in ways that are hard to believe and we would all lose. My father, my sisters who were caught in the crossfire and were forced to take sides. My mother who would just deepen the rift and me who would leave these confrontations and embark in weeks of self-destructive behavior that would effectively serve as ammunition for the next round and the next and the next...

I went home in the middle of the day. As usual the house was locked and my parents were at work. I had come to see if I could scrounge some food and proceeded to walk around trying to find a way in without breaking anything. I eventually succeeded by bending the bracket that held the louver windows, releasing the springs and sliding out enough panes of glass to allow me to climb through the window. The next obstacle would be to gain entrance through the inside door. I had two sections of bamboo made of two pieces each that had been taped together. One piece had a coat hanger that was bent into a hook and was taped securely to the stick and the other had a mirror attached. I would slip the catch on the window, insert the two instruments and proceed to try to take the spare keys by hooking them with the hook pole directed by the reflection in the mirror of the mirror pole. The keys were on a hook behind a cupboard and one slip would mean that the game was over and I would be caught.

Success! I take the keys leave the two rods and go to the kitchen to make a cup of tea and eat a slice of bread or two. I finish and so do the whole preceding routine in reverse and hide the poles in the hedge for later use. The next time I go to the house I am not allowed in. It's nothing new and as usual I sit and listen to the string of abuse from my mother while I wait for my more rational dad to arrive home and try to reason with him. A police van drives up and the stupid sergeant storms in through the gate and makes his way straight towards where I'm standing. My mother stands behind the glass door and watches, smoking as usual. She is holding up the milk jug and displays the mark she had made a few days before when I had taken the milk and drunk about 3 cm's worth. She has laid a charge at the police station against me for housebreaking and theft. The sergeant greets her and they exchange a few words in Afrikaans and he turns to me without ceremony and grabs me by the front of the shirt and proceeds to slap me first forehand and then backhand, repeatedly as I do my best to back away but not daring to retaliate. She watches, smoking and a smug expression on her face as we do the two-step up and down the narrow strip of lawn. Forehand, backhand, forehand, backhand and all the while he is cursing me and telling me how I am wasting his time by making him come out for this trivial shit when he has work to do and so on. Forehand, backhand and so it goes for a few laps. Eventually he thinks it's enough and stands there panting and sweating and informs me that if anything like this ever happens again I will really be in for it down at the station. "now bugger off and don't come back!" I drag my sorry arse off the property as my mom invites him in for a cup of tea.

Later when I tell my dad he doesn't believe me and accuses me of making up a bunch of lies.

I went back to the seclusion and solitude of my little flat and send my semi-conscious time in a zone that was certifiably insane. There was a path through the garbage from the door to my mattress and another to the toilet with a middle ground between those and the fridge as it was sporadically occupied by anything and never merited a clearly defined permanent path. The dishes in the kitchen had been left and then so had the kitchen. My dishes had not been done for 6 months and at one stage some friends of mine decided to do them as they had become "Reborn" and saw it as a Christian duty that would lead to saving my soul from the foul clutches of the demon that possessed me. I stood by and looked on while they hauled out the stinkyest, weirdest looking black spore-like tendrils that I ever seen. It was better than National Geographic. I think the girl's rubber gloves melted and one of the faster-moving things made off with the dog from next door. It was scary. God works in strange ways.

I was behind with my rent as my dad was no longer prepared to subsidize me and day by day I was drifting further and further away and had no desire to stop the drift. I was perfectly aware that I was systematically losing my mind and could care less. In my more lucid moments I would fluctuate between being too angry with the world to be depressed and being too depressed to be angry. It may sound like I was oblivious to it all but it was more like the complete opposite. I was ultra-sensitive. The filters that we all impose upon ourselves to remain as close to acceptably sane as we can had been nuked long ago. I would sit on the roof of the flat in the middle of the night, freezing cold and watch as a police van would pull up and a cop would jump out and chase the bunch of little glue sniffing "twilight kids" as they were known. And beat the crap out of them with a shambok. It was an apt term for these abandoned little barefoot black boys who survived beatings and rapes and all kinds of terrible things by trying to stay as a group and beg at the traffic lights. It would frighten and disgust me and leave me in a state of mental confusion as I felt I had to do something and did not know what it could be. I was immensely afraid of the SAP I was scared shitless of being tortured as I had read others had been and in my drug induced hallucinating scenarios I would experience virtual hell as the reality would give way to the most realistic episodes of torture and captivity without any hope of being saved. The system and its injustices were burned into my mind and often I would have frightening "bad trips" that would have me in the Nazi concentration camps waiting in a queue to be experimented on by Joseph Mengele and the experimentation itself that would at some stage be blocked from my consciousness as I passed out and then "death" and resurrection in the next life and then recognizing the same guards as having somehow being re incarnated in to the current "system" as policemen or secret agents through a mysterious method that was connected somehow to the occult and different underlying dimensions. It was scary. It was real and it screwed with my mind as the distinction between "drug trip" and "reality" became indistinguishable and my day to day conscious reality was interwoven with paranoid delusions and the resultant fear that would accompany the ever frightening visions and "revelations" that I would experience without the aid of directly induced "altered states" It's one thing to have the mental anchor of taking a particular "pose" such as the Lotus position and going through a ritual that trains your mind to be aware and expect a form of reality shift. The brain makes compensation and so even the weirdest illusions can be taken with the proverbial "pinch of salt" but when things go way out of kilter without any precursor or drug taking activity whatsoever but rather as a result of prolonged chronic abuse, then the safety mechanisms get a kick up the arse and your sanity lies splashed all over the kitchen floor in a sniveling whimpering pile of pathetic confusion.

It's really late one night and I'm sitting on the bench up on the little hill next to my house. I occasionally hear a shot ring out from the southern suburbs where the "Porras" would be having a go at each other or perhaps their adversaries "the Lebs"

You were a heavy dude if you had a buddy who was "in the Porras or Lebs." Shots weren't unusual but it's not like there was machine gun fire each night or something. For the most part its dead still on top of the hill and the suburb I lived in was quiet as a mouse at night. I loved the peace, and looking at the glittering lights as I always had done since I was a child.

JHB is of course a city that was founded at its particular location due to the discovery of gold and it's quite possible that the early pioneers would have breezed right on by and continued north had it not been noticed that there were immense riches to be had. The city itself boasts some of the deepest mines in the world and is situated on top of a labyrinth of tunnels and shafts that go down and down and then even downer. Late at night you could feel the earth tremors more strongly which were caused by the blasting away of the solid rock 2km below the surface.

I started to feel a tremor and it was just run of the mill until I noticed that this one was a little different. I couldn't pick it up immediately but it wasn't long before I detected a rhythmic beat coming from within the earth. It became stronger and rose to a crescendo of pulsating beat before stopping almost at once and the returning silence was palpable. It was the sound of the thousands upon thousands of miners all clapping or beating or stamping out a particular rhythm in unison. It was fantastic. I had read about "the drums" that the Africans would beat and pass messages across the bush with and also heard about the riots in the townships where huge masses of people would be dancing or clapping as one. I had to shake my head and take a reality check as I wasn't doing any drugs and there wasn't any "Other" explanation for the occurrence that was immediately obvious and I wondered if it wasn't all my imagination. Perhaps it was but the fact is that I was sitting there in a state of absolute awe at the display of such a simple act of unity that had to be experienced to be believed.

The closing round of my stay in my little flat came after an episode where I did a really strange thing. I drank two beer mugs of coffee! That on its own doesn't sound like it could be out of this world but each 500ml mug was a combination of ...Water! lots of sugar and a whole tin of instant coffee!! Yeeeaaah! It was awesome. I remember swigging back this sludge whilst lying in the bath and thinking how famous thinkers had reached their "enlightenment" after drinking a cup of strong black coffee. I was heading for Buddddddaahhooooooddd for sure! It wasn't long after that I recalled that Nietzsche had spent his last days reclining in a state sponsored holiday home!! My mind worked! I could do mental gymnastics of the most complicated sort with ease and no purpose whatsoever and without any hope of comprehension from my fellow Earthlings. The whole thing is a little scatty but I remember somehow going to score some grass as I thought this was the only way I could knock myself out as I hadn't done any sleeping for days at this point. By some stroke of the miraculous I scored a bank packet of the most powerful dope I had ever had the privilege to stick to my finger. I was told that it was potent and so decided as was not my usual custom, to smoke a joint. Joints were for sissies and we real men smoked pipes but on this occasion I opted for sissy hood. The stuff was far too wet and had to be dried. It had the most unusually pungent smell and reeked the flat out before I had even lit the first spliff. Eventually I got my trembling hands to roll one and sat down and took the first drag. The world took a giant leap forward and MAN was I looking at it from the back of a long narrow tube. WOW! It was months before I realized that the smoke had gone out and so I lit it again, took a second toke and put the joint down while I contemplated my true underlying identity as one of the original Greek gods who resided on Olympus. I spent the rest of the night in the self-same contemplation and with the aid of some spectacular mental gym I had by early the next morning come to the true and very logically derived conclusion that my landlord knew my true identity and was waiting for me to make the quantum leap and pass my test of faith and conviction by appearing before him and claiming my rightful place among the Gods and in so doing be rewarded with lifelong occupancy of my current little flat. Rent free!!

I set off toward the property office and have to admit that I wavered a few times in my conviction but gritted my teeth and sat down respectfully in the line that was waiting to have a word with the estate agent. My turn came, I walked in, sat down and proceeded to feel more stupid than I ever had up to that point. My mind was still racing and going through some gym just to keep in shape

and I simply didn't know what to say. Needless to say, he was confused, but being a man of experience and living and owning property in a suburb where some pretty marginal characters lived, he no doubt had had some experience with Greek Gods of various descriptions in his time and so inquired if I was feeling ok. I replied" no" he asked if I had been drinking "no" Would I like him to call my dad" yes"

Dad arrives and drives me straight to the JG Strydom hospital where I am signed into the Psycho ward with the 2nd kookiest bunch I've seen since my last visit to such a place.

I am docile for the most part and have "sobered" rapidly. I am given valium late at night and as predicted wake up with a young doctor sitting on my bed and looking deep into my eyes. It's funny as its exactly what I tell the night nurse will happen if I agree to take the medication the night before. I'm an adult now and the different rules apply. I have not harmed anyone or resisted treatment and so have more rights. It is before the files are on computer and it will be a few days before my file will arrive. Long story short. I am exhausted and depressed but have a strong sense of resolve and realize fully how dumb and self-destructive my behavior has been the last few months and so take responsibility and sign out of the hospital to the protests of the staff and the doctor. He and they are all a very nice bunch of people but I know that even the nicest people with the best intentions can get a court order that will have me incarcerated for my own good and there would be precious little as I could do as my folks are notorious for being trusting and naive and ending up regretting a decision they had on my behalf based on the recommendations of nice and well-meaning but senseless people. Having your sanity questioned on a daily basis could easily drive anyone crazy.

I am accosted by the doctor in the parking lot on my way home on foot. He tries to convince me to stay and is genuinely concerned but I am adamant and explain to him that I appreciate it but essentially I am at the point already that they hope to get me to in a month's time whereby I can stand up and take responsibility and make my own decisions. He is far from convinced but is powerless to do anything. I walk across town. Along walk home. I'm tired and it takes every ounce of my much-fatigued mettle to make it home in one piece but I forge ahead. Upon arrival my folks are frantic but I manage to convince them I will comply with treatment this time. I mean it and so collapse into bed and sleep for close on three days straight.

Once partially recuperated I go back to re paint my flat and as my dad won't allow me to go alone we go together. As I walk into the battle zone I am knocked out by the smell of the dope drying on a magazine in the sun next to the window. I shrug and turf the lot of it down the toilet. It is a week before I manage to peel the paint off the bathroom walls and use paint remover everywhere. The landlady is disgusted and won't return the deposit even after all the hard work.

I move back home.

At first I had to move into my father's study where there was a bed and I and to sleep with the door open so they could keep an eye on me from their bedroom and make sure that I wouldn't sneak out at night and knock myself out with drugs. It bordered on the pathetic. My folks like most people of their generation had no conception about drugs and only had their terrible experiences based on my cookoo activities with glue to formulate their opinions and couldn't make the distinction between a "hard" and a "soft" drug. To them it was all the same. It had to be. Wasn't it like that with booze? Hard tack and beer or wine? Didn't they both knock you out and leave you disorientated when you drank too much? It was logical and comparatively to parents of "straight" children they were seasoned pros.

Eventually I could move down the passage to my sisters' old room and sleep there. It was basically a store room and I shared the place with all the boxes and odds and sods that were kept there. It was not long at all before my folks started resenting having taken me in and it was largely due to the fact that my appearance and views had undergone little change. It was all too easy for them to blame my ideas on "drugs" but less convincing to do so when they knew I hadn't been taking any. I hated that. "oh it's all because of the bloody drugs" It would infuriate me and I would blow up due to being treated like a non-entity and it would just convince them further "OH God!, He's been at it again!" whereupon my mother would go hysterically ballistic and my father would just stand there and nod in agreement. Becoming emotional was a sure sign of "being under the influence" being docile would mean the same. There was no way to win. My mother would be knocking back fucking Rohypnol at night and taking minute little "slivers" continually and this was cool. Even to my dad "but its medicine! Given by a Doctor!" I was disgusted. They were my folks who I had always loved and believed were individual thinking people and the realization that they were no more than normal misguided average people came as a great and very disappointing shock to me.

My dad and I could see eye to eye in many ways. We could get along great as long as my mom wasn't in the picture or present. If she was there he had to side with her and I hated it. She would do the cruelest things and get away with it and have everyone's approval and understanding. We clashed on the two most contentious points. Politics and Religion. She represented the system and I poured out my hatred in her direction in ways that I'm ashamed to mention. It had a twofold effect. I blamed her for the system and the system for her. I couldn't vent my anger on the system but I could dump it on her and then would hate myself and the system even more for creating the situation.

I had wanderlust and when a new friend arrived one day and said "hey let's go to Knysna!" I said "Uhhh...OK!" and within the hour we were hitchhiking down to the coast without a single cent between us. I took a bunch of books that weighed a ton and he took the Bible! I read the analects of Confucius and turfed the rest. Descartes and a couple of others that I simply got fed up with carrying. We made it after about three days and much hungriness. We went to the Knysna forest and walked through the most beautiful scenery you can imagine. After a week or so of this the whole thing wore off and so we decided to try and hitch back home. We were doing OK until one day while we were waiting for a lift and had been for hours, we noticed the yellow van approaching. "Here it comes!" I say to my friend and he just nods and smiles. The policeman gets out and swaggers over while his black constable stays in the van with a loaded weapon below the dash. "Good day Orificer1" I say as happily as I can. "Whats joose fink joo doing? Hey!" I look at him quizzically and ask what the problem is. He replies that hitch hiking is illegal. I realize that he is just harassing us and so I get difficult. Keep in mind dear reader that I am wearing a day glo lime green shirt that I got in London from Molly Ringwald! True!! The situation is bordering on unpleasant so I do the only thing I can think of. I attack. "Tell me Orificer, Why are you hassling us? We aren't doing anything except trying to leave here. Why is that a problem?" He scowls at me " You SHUTTUP! I am the law and I tell you no hitchhiking!" I laugh at this which gets him more ruffled and so out comes the gun toting constable and the Sargeant guy says 'OK open up! Let's see what's in your bags!" I comply and he is rather shocked that there are only a few things and a well-worn book. He tries a different tack and demands to know how we are managing to fund our trip. I interrupt and get to the point 'So your saying we can't hitch here. Where can we hitch then?" He informs me that he doesn't care what we do as long as it's after the toll gate which is only 16 Km away!!

I gape at him " You want us to WALK to the toll gate?!" he replies " I don't give a donner! But you don't hitch hike here. CLOSED!" I say "OK so were not allowed on the road? Yes?" He agrees. I slowly pick up my bag and walk off to the side of the road exactly 1 meter from the tar and make a big show of putting my bag down and using it as a

*pillow as I stretch out in the grass and put my hands behind my head "
AAAaaahhhhh! Maaan That's LEKKER!"*

*He stares at me as if I have just stolen the collection plate at church.
"WAT DE FOK!??" "WAT JOO DOOOING!?" I reply cheerfully as
ever " I'm on holiday and there no rush. We can walk tomorrow.
Maybe" He replies " Where do you get your money from to be on
holiday! HEY!" I smugly tell him " Sir. My uncle in England died two
weeks ago and left me 5 Million pounds! I never have to work EVER
AGAIN!" He stares at me incredulously as my friend is rolling his eyes
and trying to hide in the grass.*

*Off goes the policeman in a cloud of dust. We lie there for a while
and decide its useless. The best thing to do would be to start walking. So
we do. It's not long before the policeman comes flying down the road and
screeches to a halt. "Right you're both under arrest!" He screams " Go
on Rooinek! Run so I can shoot you!" he shouts. This is completely out of
hand and so I just look at him and eventually say" Why are you doing
this? What have we done? Your job is to protect people like us from the
bad guys and you just want to hurt us for no reason. It's not Christian!"
He is completely taken off guard and as he has seen my friends Bible he
isn't sure what to do so I push him in Afrikaans 'Hoekom?' (Why?) He
looks at me and says "I got to work for a FOKKEN living!" I don't know
what to say. He is nearly in tears!*

*I do the only thing I can think of and apologize to him in Afrikaans.
He looks at me quizzically and asks " How come you speak so good die
Taal?" So I tell him that I'm half Afrikaans and that my Great, Great
grandfather is a folk hero. He can check if he wants to.*

He gives us a lift all the way to the bloody toll gate!!

*When we are alone my friend teaches me how to say " I don't speak
English" In French so that in future I will shut up and he will do the
talking!!*

It just kept getting worse and my self-esteem was at an all-time
low. I used to eat breakfast after the dog had had her tea! It was a

morning ritual that would set the tone for the day. My mom and dad would leave for work without a word and I would be left to go through the classified ads looking at the circles that they had drawn around the jobs they thought I could get. That was in some ways worse. It was clear that they just wanted me to get the hell away and they told me so many times too. The evening ritual was having to give an account of myself for the day. Which interviews have you lined up? They wouldn't believe that I was unable to secure even the face to face 90% of the time. Contrary to popular belief that being unemployed is a cool thing to be it is actually a time of immense stress and pressure. It's not fun. I somehow got to hear of a computer course that was to be undertaken at Govt. expense for those people who were unemployed. The catch was that you had to have a minimum of high school graduation in order to qualify. I basically bullshitted my way in by claiming to have been at university and having decided to change my course of study and wanted to do the course to become computer literate to aid my studies. The ploy worked and I found myself as one of a multiracial group of young and old people who were looking to have some kind of career in computers. Some had studied programming course for the previous six months and were well familiar with some of the rudiments of computer programming. It was an intensive course and I spent most of the time next door in the library studying a brilliant book dealing with Chinese Philosophy. I would go in for a short while each day and pay attention to the lecture and then when it was time to practice the lesson like robots for the rest of the day I would check out and go next door and return in time for the final roll call. At the end of the course I wrote the exam and was convinced I had failed outright. Each part was based on the premise that the preceding part had been done correctly so If you screwed up at the start your chances were nil. I was sure that by this time they would have discovered my little fib and so didn't even go in on the last day to receive my grade. I decided to call them up the following Monday and do my best to explain my desperation to do the course and get a job and so on. When I called up I get the response "Ahh. Mr Myers!, one moment please, the director would like to have word" I thought 'Well here it comes" He came on the line and started off by saying" well you could attend the next one but the govt. subsidy doesn't really apply but perhaps we can arrange something . How does that sound?" I thought to myself: Hey It sounds great! What the hell is he talking about?" I explained that I was a little confused and that I wasn't sure what was going on and all I called up for was to inquire about my mark. He was a little confused and asked me if I had been in on Friday. I replied 'no" and so he burst out laughing. Now I was really confused. He went on to inform me that I had scored the best mark so far and I only made one mistake 99% "Congratulations!" I sat there stunned and then had to hold my breath as I was about to laugh so hard that I would wet my pants. He was actually offering me a job as a lecturer but in order to qualify I had to do a subsequent course that wasn't covered by the Govt. scheme! I would have to pay and it was expensive. I couldn't help but shake my head at the fact that it was the first time ever that I had lied about such a thing and the first time that I had met with such a degree of success! Honesty is the best policy!! Yeeeaaahhh Riiiiight!

This really set the cat among the pigeons as my dad was convinced that the future lay in computers. He was and still is dead scared of computers and holds the view that they are these unfathomable machines that are smarter than humans and one wrong move could result in one blowing up a minor country in South America by mistake. Funny thing is that if someone just took five minutes out to show him he would be bloody good as he is naturally gifted in the kind of methodical thinking required to operate this typewriter come TV.

Now I could go to interviews and lie with confidence that I had forgotten to bring my high school certificate but had my course results which kind of proves the fact as having a matric was a primary requirement for the course. I would then go to many interviews and get on the final short list for jobs with huge international concerns.

It was the first time I had seen the reality of what it would mean to work as a computer operator. Note I don't say Programmer. I had gotten to the last three people for the job that had had a cut off number of 1500 applicants initially. The company was Nixdorf. I went into this building that in which I had ridden my skateboard many times on a rainy day and been chased by the security. I went in to a waiting room and did the done thing. I waited. After a while of that, a guy arrived wearing a sweaty kind of cotton school shirt with no tie which made him look much less than professional and he quickly ushered me in through the security door. We quickly moved down a hall that resembled a set from the man from UNCLE and I was fully expecting the blond guy from the show to poke his head out of a swiftly opening door at any second. We went through one security door and then another and another with him opening each with a swipe from his special card. Al the time he says not a word or perhaps less. Eventually we enter a big room with all these lines of desks and semi partitioned off from each other to resemble something close to an ineffective open plan. He says to me " If you're successful this is where you'll work "as if he is disclosing a state secret and pauses with enough pregnancy to allow me the time to realize that I don't catch the subtle implication at all. We then go through another series of doors but before we leave the big room where all kinds of sharp cornered people are busily working away, a bell rings. The workers literally stop typing as a unit. In the very middle of a word, though or deed and stand up and proceed to storm out of the room. I think it's a fire drill and am ready to run but wait for my guide to give me the go ahead. I wouldn't get far anyhow as I don't have one of those nifty swipe cards that everyone seems to have dangling from a string around their necks. They look like rock stars with official backstage passes. The guide dude informs me " tea break" and I watch in wonder at the staff frantically drawing the death out of their hastily lit cigarettes while simultaneously pouring coffee. I follow him to his clammy little office and wonder how he can be so smelly of stale sweat and sticky looking. He asks me the question " Why do you want to work for Nixdorf" I think for a full nanosecond and reply " I don't!" He stares back at me with a mixture of incomprehension and card swipe fatigue and finds the word. "Eh!" I repeat and explain that if I don't go to the interviews that my folks expect me to go to I will get kicked out of home. He is fully pissed off at me and since it's the first time since we met that he has actually seen me in focus he explains what it means to have made it to the last three out of 1500 candidates and what a privilege it is to be considered worthy enough to be considered fit to be serving such an illustrious concern that specializes in cash registers and does a lot of secret work for Armscor. I reply " So what!, it doesn't look like you have seen the sun in ten years and although you earn more money in one hour than I will earn in a year, you spend about 10 hours a day in air conditioned office and then go home to sleep so you can start again the next day. What a crap life! I don't want that! You remind me of a bunch of Pavlov's pets the way you respond to the tea bell! Thank you very much. I'm sorry to have wasted your time" I think he would have punched me if he could have. He had the security guard escort me out who due to my formal dress didn't recognize me as the midnight rider!!

Getting back to the original course...It was the first time I had ever been in a classroom that was multiracial. There were whites, some Indians and some blacks. I found it very interesting how the different races would approach the learning end of it. During breaks the class would go across the road and sit on an open stretch of grass and then would automatically split into racially governed groups. The whites would sit together and then a short distance away the Indians and coloreds would make their circle and then some way off the blacks would sit in their circle. Now during class I had befriended a black guy by the name of Nelson and he proved to be well smart and I and I'm sure the rest of the class expected him to score the highest marks without a doubt. He actually would explain many of the concepts to me before I grasped them. He had done more than one course and although he was well clued up, was unsuccessful at obtaining a job. I took my sandwiches and without thinking went and sat down where Nelson was. His friends didn't mind and at the end of the first period he said " hey man its great! I can see you are one of us!" It took me a while to register and then it hit me. Of course! Stupid me I never realized and told him I didn't give it a thought and yes he is right. I have probably ruffled some feathers. We all laughed. The following break times of course I was more aware and would giggle at the way the white guys and girls would sneak a peek or simply gape. It was more than obvious that they would make derisive comments about me and later as time progressed openly sneer at me. I responded by being openly hostile after one incident where I overheard the word "Kaffirboetie" which translates roughly as "niggerlover" and a challenging look in my direction. I immediately got up and went over to this guy and asked him "Got something to say to me Whitey? Or are you too chickenshit like your buddies here to say it to my face!" It took them all by surprise and me possibly most of all as I was fully ready to go down fighting to the lot of them. The response was basically backing down and trying to save face by saying " why do you sit with them?' I answered " because I choose to" There were a few more tense moments while my heart was pounding madly but no one took it any further and so I walked back and sat down. I had given myself quite a fright. The black guys laughed and told me I was crazy. The cool thing about that whole set up was that I spoke completely openly with Nelson and his friends about political things and aspects of their lives that were news to me but realities to them. There was no sensationalism just matter of fact things and not really dwelling on the negative. They were all very curious to hear about overseas and the way of life there, not only in terms of racial issues but just all kinds of things. Prices, distances, food, entertainment, music especially and very general things that would be asked by any curious people who had not been there. They all lived in Alexandria township and I had never been there either.

It was a hot week. I was working as an extra on the movie "Gor" or "Return to Gor" I'm not sure. It was shot at a prefabricated set out on one of the open deserted mines on the reef. The first day I was a "trader" I had to wear all these robes and looked much like a Star Wars version of a Persian coffee vendor. Most of an extra's time is spent sitting around all day waiting for the moment when we would be called and have to do whatever routine for whatever time and then back to sitting around. It was a cool job if you liked that kind of thing. The second day I ducked the wardrobe person and was a Guard. Guards wore less and so it continued until on the fifth day I was wondering around in my jocks and running shoes with cheesecloth wrapped around my loins and feet. I was the proudest slave you ever did see!

I caught a great tan and pitied the theatrical types who loved dressing up as they boiled through an entire week in their "robes" Ha! Ha!

My routine of looking for jobs continued and it was some weeks later that a funny thing happened. I had a very good friend who was studying interior design and it was a real challenge for her as she was dyslexic. She would work until all hours just trying to perfect the many technical drawings that had to be done and so on occasion would skip a particular part of a project as she simply did not have the time. On one such occasion, she came to visit and said that she had a model of an office chair she had to make to scale and could I do it? She was going to fail the project anyway and didn't care how badly it turned out. I was given a brochure and a schematic, along with some polymer clay and four days to see what I could come up with. I was an avid scale model builder as a child and although I had never done something like this, I was keen to give it a shot. I got stuck in and made a pretty good one and put it in a box for my friend to collect which she did and without giving it a glance scooted off to class and I never thought any more about it. A week later I received a call from Julie telling me that she failed the model and the dean of the Technical college would like to see me! She made it sound like I was in deep trouble and so off I went to see the guy. We knew each other as I often used to hang around the college and was trying to figure out how to enroll because I desperately wanted to study but we couldn't afford it and I needed to wait a year or so to qualify by what was called "mature age exemption" I walked in expecting a lecture and soon realized that Julie had pulled the wool over my eyes when the dean informed me that he knew right away that Julie was incapable of producing work of that caliber and was pleasantly surprised to discover who the guilty party was. He was familiar with my situation and told me that there was an engineering firm that would be prepared to take me on as an apprentice with a recommendation from himself. I was over the moon. Model building was something I loved to do and was unaware that such a trade existed. I started at the beginning of the following month and would get up at 3.45 in the freezing cold, walk to the train station and stand in the dark. The only white face among hundreds of blacks. Get off the train and walk for an hour and arrive at 5.55 am at the front door of the workshop where I would immediately take the breakfast orders and start my day as the "Gopher" Go fer this and go fer that. I would take a lot of abuse but it was all in good spirits and without any animosity. The men were all highly skilled specialists and the work was exacting and demanding. They worked to a tolerance of .2 of a mm and after one mistake the materials had to be paid by the model maker. It went without saying that I never as much as touched the huge models of the Mosselbay Petrochemical plant. It was absolutely awesome. The whole refinery was created in miniature exactly to scale and it was where all the design problems were ironed out. Each valve was planned and a tiny mistake in the model making process would result in perhaps having a shut off valve situated meters from the place it should be in real life. Those guys were very well paid and for the first time since I had been in the guitar shop in London, did I think that I may have found the job I had for so long been looking for. The irony is clear. I worked diligently and took the jibes in good spirit and so gained the respect of the guys on the floor. They "rewarded" me by letting me make tool boxes for them or some salt and pepper cellars or something else that would enable me to become familiar with the special material and the machinery. I was pretty much at everyone's disposal and would often have to run errands for the man who was second in charge of the whole dept. He was an instrument technician by trade and had acquired it in the RAF. He was meticulous and the typical British expat living and working in SA. We got on well enough and I was flattered when he invited me to become a member of the model makers guild and attend their monthly meetings. It was strange as I had never even breathed on a model and it would be a long time before I did as no one had any time to spare to teach me anything with the pressure of work and I would have to wait until a new project would start or there would be a lull between two. One day he offered me a lift from work which would take me close to home and after getting out of the car and making my way to the bus station I passed by some black guys who said something funny to me and I laughed and we greeted each other in typical "street" style. A particularly complex series of handshakes that would immediately identify you as a person in the know or not. The supervisor had stopped at a traffic light and witnessed the scene and I didn't think much of it until a few days later when I went up to deliver something to his workstation and he was ultra cold and curt to me. I just took it as a bad mood but as time went by the attitude persisted and became nasty with insults and jibes at every turn. I put two and two together and tried not to take it too much to heart. I was disappointed but not surprised at all.

At this stage I was a member of a punk band as the guitarist and we would play the odd gig but nothing spectacular. I had recently founded a new band as a side project where I could play a more prominent role and play my own songs and only original material as opposed to the covers we were doing in the other band. The new band took off and we got a few mentions in the press and it was one of these that caught the attention of the guys in the model shop. They recognized me with my bleached white hair and thought it funny to post the clip on the notice board. It was all in good fun and the guys, having got to know me by then didn't see me as they would the average punk on the street and it was a kind of curiosity to them and resulted in ongoing discussions about all types of music and this intrigued them even more as I was quite familiar with their tastes and in many ways more clued up than they in their own genres. The clip of course was seen by the manager and he uttered a sting of filth that was heard right into the next office. I decide it was time for a showdown and walked into the room and asked him what exactly it was that offended him so and how he could direct his disdain at me personally when he knew me as more than simply a photograph in a newspaper. He went ballistic and threatened to beat me up right there I didn't "Fuck off out of his sight!" I shrugged and left. The guys in the workshop greeted me with silence and gestures to let it go, and play it cool for a while. It was a bad scene as this guy was a man who I respected and admired, although never shared his obvious bias towards blacks or whoever. The problem was that this guy was the chairman of the guild and a leading figure in the small and exclusive world of model builders and I most certainly wasn't going to go head to head with him and come out smiling. He could and would close any open doors at a whim and it irked me to say the least. Here I was singing songs about nine to five slavery and ridiculing the people who would allow themselves to be trapped by the expectations of the "bosses" and I was faced with the self-same situation. The whole situation came to a head when I received my papers informing me that I was once again due for my yearly "camp" and it was a problem as I had not yet been exactly six months with the company. I was only a few weeks shy and it meant that the company wasn't required by law to pay the difference in my wage. To make matters worse this manager made it very clear that I was free to piss off at any time and good riddance. The guys on the floor were very sympathetic and saw it for the bullshit that it was and tried to soften the blow for me by trying to justify his actions by highlighting his military background and so on. I went to the main manager and we had a long chat as to the options open to me and the verdict was dismal. I would have to resign and then after the month re apply for apprenticeship and it would involve a whole convoluted set of affairs due to the fact that no Technical college or university offered a course in model building and so the trade itself was in question due to all kinds of bureaucratic red tape that made no sense at all. One way to become a qualified model builder was to study architecture as they offered a course in model building but only as a side subject to the main course. It was all bullshit. The irony was that not one of the people there including the managers were actually qualified model builders! They all had trades of one sort or another that endowed them with suitable skill to become model builders. I really wanted to do that job and was well down in the dumps about the situation. The guys all wished me well for the future and it was little consolation that my dad seemed to understand it when I had to quit.

The last person I said cheerio to was of course the manager and true to form I wanted to leave with the hatchet being buried and so went up to him and thanked him for the things he had done as I did truly appreciate it and his response was" Piss off you fucking reprobate! You probably don't even know what that means!" looking at me with a smug mixture of contempt and disgust.

With a sneer I retorted " Someone with a poorer character than I wouldn't be standing here at this moment offering you the opportunity to show that you're not one of those ...reprowhatchimakalit thingeys yourself. SIR!" and I did a smart about turn and marched out.

I fully expected him to hurl something at me or pounce on me from behind but to his credit he took it quite calmly.

Toxiksox

It's all Johnny Rotten's fault! If I had been facing a different direction or chewing gum none of this would have happened. I might have gone on to better things and won the Nobel prize or found the cure to cancer. As it happened, I didn't do any of those things, and I place the blame squarely on the shoulders of the Sex Pistols.

It was the end of break at school. The bell had already gone and a friend of mine who was very high tech and owned a walkman cassette player said to me "listen to this" I knew it had to be good as the guy was a stingy bugger and would only have let me have a listen as the bell had gone and we all had to make it to class before the second bell went and so had no time to really give it a good sit down kind of indulgent listen. I put the headphones on my ears and adjusted my brain to dissimilate the incoming noise and was struck dumb by the line..."Hi ya boys I'm the chosen one CANT YA FUCKING SEE!" I was mesmerized. It was mind boggling. The most outrageous thing I had ever heard on vinyl was a burp on a Slade album and I had recorded it over and over to create a series of burps at the end of the tape that I had copied. This was in a class of it's own though. For someone to actually openly claim to be the "chosen one" and then the expletive was beyond my comprehension. My first thought was "how did this get past the censors?" Everything in South Africa that was even close to being "immoral" or not completely understood

was "banned" Jethro Tull's Aqualung was banned for the blasphemous statement that God was created in man's image, Pink Floyd's The Wall was banned because of the song "we don't need no education", pinball was close to being the only pastime for teenagers who used to hang about at the corner café and play for hours and it too was eventually banned as being considered a game of chance and thus "gambling" and not one that required any skill. Tell that to

George the Greek who could spend a whole day playing the game and only spend the first coin. When he left the shop there usually was a scuffle to grab the machine and play out the maximum ten games credit that he had "won" Chance!? Fat chance china! My guess is that whoever was on the censor committee that passed the law was a crap pinball player and it was his way of getting back for years of humiliation suffered by the many members of the "peanut gallery" The female body was never seen naked. The glossy magazine that was risqué enough to run scantily, costume clad centerfolds would regularly get into trouble for printing a picture that showed an outline of a nipple or God forbid, a pubic hair. Can you imagine the kind of people that were employed at taxpayers expense to sift through reams of pulp to isolate a sex scene that was too graphic. I can. They would be the type of people that would tack pictures of figures cloaked in sheets with pointy caps on their toilet walls and worship them in secret. The odd items that escaped the watchful eye of the censorship committee instantly became collectors items and of course "banned" in absentia so to speak.

That made this album a collectors item in the making and I immediately took it out of the machine to make a copy. To be fair, the music was not really that remarkably terrible as it was to be depicted by the press reviews that I would get to see in overseas papers like NME's that were always laying around the listening booths at the record shop that we used to go to like the devout music disciples we were. It was the dress and the aggression and above all the "ATTITUDE!" I loved it.

My first exposure to the word "Punk" was when I had given myself the DIY haircut a year or two before. People said "Oh! You look like a Punk!" I was ignorant and the only thing I knew about it was that the adherents would stick sharp things through their cheeks and tongues and I thought it was an offshoot of an Indian sect of some kind. After hearing "Never mind the Bollox" I naturally sought out anything and everything that was even vaguely considered "punk" It exposed me to a world of music and I particularly liked Ska as it was highly danceable. I also liked the whole Two tone movement that would borrow from the Jamaican roots and R&B it was cool and there were many lyrics dealing with racial issues that were highly relevant to me at the time. It was at this time that I became friends with the group of boys at school who were in the know about the whole scene and had been to one or two performances in SA that I would not even have dreamed of attending. I would much less have known about them as the word was spread by word of mouth and not advertised at all on the radio or in the local press. I was completely ignorant of the whole SA music scene in general as I listened to overseas bands exclusively and it was something generally considered to be a fringe interest in general. It was a commonly held "dream" by most people into the kind of music I was into to see a live gig. An inconceivable event as SA was blacklisted and no international group would come. Notable exceptions were a short visit by the Village people and a tour or two? by Tina Turner. The Village people event was one that deserves a mention. I, in my confused search for cult identity had decided to go and see these very popular and colorful group of sissy boys and "freak everybody out" as was the usual motivation to go and shock the public at large. Homosexuality was also "banned" by the way and I could have gotten into a fight for insinuating that these guys were less than the "macho men" that they so theatrically projected. The SA public was absolutely disconnected with the rest of the world and naturally about 50 years behind. It was a standing joke amongst ourselves at new year to toast ourselves into the new year and to follow it up with a " and of course the same goes to the Dutchmen who are being dragged screaming into the 70's!" and we would raise a glass with the well practiced expressions of the typical colonial that was magnamenous enough to include the "heathen" in the proceedings.

I was daring enough on that occasion to dye my hair green with food coloring and walked down to the shopping center where the Village People would make their miraculous appearance after being spewn out of a helicopter. It was hot! My jacket that may have looked totally cool in a London street in winter was not sensible summer wear in a sweltering JHB summer and I was sweating profusely by the time I reached the haven of the air conditioned mall. I was self conscious to start with and naturally terribly shy and it took all my resolve to get into the garb in the first place. It was easier at night at a party or at a club but in hard focus and sober in broad daylight? I was determined. The stares of total shock, snickers as I walked past, outbursts by the more brawny of "Jesus Krrrrriiiist!" comments such as "hey faggot!" from groups of boys all made me cringe but I was determined not to be gotten the better of and continued towards the huge crowd all waiting and singing lines from the string of hits that the group had had. "YMCA" and the accompanying dance gesticulations by the hardcore fan base comprised mainly of 12 year old girls and their "cool" moms. I could have puked which in hindsight may have been good for my street cred. The kicker came when I spotted my reflection in a shop window and was shocked to my shoes. The sweat had caused the food coloring to run down my face in green rivulets and I resembled something out of a 50's horror movie. Zombie from the black bog or some such like title would have been more fitting than Punk wannabe from Kensington SA!

I knew that wiping the sweat would just smear the drops into a green sheen and so I decided to leave untouched and continued to walk around with my arrogant sneer looking like a war casualty. I had achieved my objective though and soon was the resident freak of the neighborhood and had gained the respect of my new circle of friends which was a dubious distinction in any case.

In my early days as a Punk it was a usual Saturday morning routine to go to the Oriental plaza in Fordsburg, a predominantly Indian suburb on the west side of central JHB. We would club together and buy a six pack of Black Label and a dozen samoosas and sit around, drinking in public and look at the people who would be looking at us. These samoosas deserve a mention though as I have never before or since come across such absolute works of culinary excellence as those masterful little triangles of gastronomic wonder and too much juice. YUM!

After this we would make our way across town to a record library that would stock titles that were imported or simply unavailable and had no problem in selling you a handful of cassettes as you left to go home and put the whole lot quite illegally on tape.

In the evenings we would try to go to parties if we had heard of any and frequently this would mean a few hours of walking through endless suburbia to an unknown place based on pure rumor. If we were successful we would hopefully get in as it was almost closing up time anyway and then we would try to convince the dj to put on a tape of some more "tame" music and then maybe get to go nuts for a half a song afterward when the "Punk" would come on and we would be either kicked out immediately or more frequently be stared at by the "straights" and then kicked out. We hardly ever got into fights. We just walked a lot in the freezing cold.

Later on when I had managed to get to use the car, we would all pile into the Volvo which was nicknamed "the Tank" and had earned its name on numerous occasions when the guys had to get out and push since there was no fuel. We would drive around aimlessly with the tape player blasting out our chosen music and drink beer whilst singing at the top of our voices. The evening would end ceremoniously at the "P&C" The Pure and Cool Roadhouse. Each week was the same. Toasted chicken and mayonnaise and a chocolate milkshake! Often it would end up in a congealed mess on the sidewalk on the way home when all the alcohol abuse had properly kicked in.

We would sit at the roadhouse and tell jokes or listen to the tapes of Monty Python which we knew by heart anyway and would still kill ourselves laughing each time at a favorite part.

These were "the early days" of punk in SA. I would go to my bedroom on a weekday night as usual with the pretense of going to sleep and then listen carefully as my folks would retire and then when I thought all was quiet on the parental front I would hop out of the window very carefully and call out to our dog so that I wouldn't get eaten by him or cause him to bark and spoil the show. After the bribe of supper leftover meat, I would go to my mom's Volvo and proceed to as quietly as possible release the handbrake and open doors and so on and then push the huge monstrosity down the drive and try to get enough speed to get it up the incline at the end. It was a tricky business trying to push and steer through the open window and then at the critical moment dive through said window and engage the hand brake so that it wouldn't roll back down and I would have to spend the next hour or so inching it back to point of origin and making a second or sometimes a third attempt. It took many trial runs but I eventually got it down to a fine art and would start the car next to the neighboring house and so, even though it could be heard by my folks the hope was that they would be sleeping or that they would mistake it for the next door's car. Then the reverse backward down the narrow alley and off into the suburban night. I had no idea how to drive! I had not yet received my first driving lesson from my dad and so based my first few attempts on the sound principles instilled by years of riding a motorbike and rapt attention in recent months at the driving method of my parents. I got the hang of it quite quickly as I would drive through the back roads where there would be no police presence at 3am on a weekday. I soon became more and more confident and would then sneak into town and go to the underground and secluded clubs that would be open till dawn and play all kinds of music that was way off the mainstream. It was fantastic. I would nick some drink from my dad's liquor cabinet and slug it down on the way and then dance like a madman till just before first light and then shoot off home and freewheel the last few meters into the parking spot. Subdue the dogs bark as soon as I could and scoot over to my semi open window and dive stinking under the covers. I got away with it for a looong time before I arrived home one morning to find the window closed and had the embarrassing experience of having to be let in through the door by my very smug and bleary eyed mom who had been up all night as a victim of her overactive and fertile imagination waiting for me to return and vent her justifiable wrath. Apparently my dad just turned over and went to sleep with the comment " don't worry, He'll be back by breakfast"

The first live show I went to was at the Selbourne hall in central JHB. It was the only place that would give permission for the so called "new wave " bands to play and it was a strict 12 o clock pull the plug closure. I had nicked the motorbike on this occasion and had driven it through all the backstreets and parked it close to the hall in a shady alleyway. I never even wore a helmet and had I been caught by the cops I didn't want to think of the hot water I would have been in. To my amazement there were loads of punk rockers and a wide array of completely freaky people in attendance. We had come to support the only punk band on the bill called simply 'Dog" other bands were either reggae or alternative rock by categorization. Dog was awesome and I was an instant fan. I had the distinction of "gobbing" on the bassist and had been frantically bouncing around in the "pogo" which of course was the only way supposedly that a true punk would "anti dance" It was the first of many out and away concerts that we would make our way to, to support the band. I was an ardent fan and became quite friendly with the guys later on as I would do the "roadie" routine and carry a guitar into the place and claim to be part of the band. They later became more alternative in musical orientation and were considered by many early fans of having "sold out" but I never shared the view and for me it was a good lesson for me to fall back on later when I was involved in my band.

I was 11 or 12 years old when I first heard "Frampton comes alive" It was one of my sisters records and I would listen to the double album so frequently that I could and still can sing along and copy with utmost accuracy the fourth side which was mostly guitar instrumental. I used to and still do sing the guitar. Its weird as I was always unable to sing in public. I could do so as one of a group of people thrashing out the ever popular "country rose" at campfires but a solo was out of the question. It still is. On my own though I sing like a bird, albeit quite not as well. I decided that I was to play the guitar! My mom already owned a classical guitar that she had purchased many years before and threatened to learn to play as so many people do at some stage or other and never do. It was hers and as in all things hers, not to be touched. It was a thing that infuriated me. She would accumulate all kinds of tools and stash them away never to be used and they were considered untouchable and all hell would regularly break loose when I of course would consider the stupidity of it and go ahead and touch. On my birthday I was asked what I wanted as a gift and replied "a guitar!" my dad groaned and said "we have one" My mother immediately put on her flabbergasted shocked tone "What! My guitar..oh no, no, no ...forget about it. Not over my dead body!" I had foreseen this reaction and true to form had already found a "kids guitar" in the window of a toyshop that would be transformed into a singing, talking, living, walking demi god by my very own hands in a matter of minutes! My dad relented and avoided feinting when he heard the price by pouring himself a "stiff one" Forty hard earned rands later we walked out of the shop with the precious item and a book "how to learn" in the cardboard box that the thing was packed into. I immediately sprang to work and set about tuning the thing. It was apparently so easy, a chimpanzee could do it but I unfortunately didn't have a chimpanzee immediately available and so had to logic it out by myself. It seemed simple, you attached the strings and then pressed on ...uh, ..the fret! And uh..the next string had to be tightened so that it sounded the same! Hey! ...Simple! And so away I went. As far as the 3rd string that snapped with a most comical .Twang! and the whole spell was broken. They of course didn't include the tension of the first string which to them was obvious. " It's an E dummy!" Every human being has an inbred knowledge of these things. I went looking for a chimpanzee. The damn thing never managed to be tuned, even when I had bought a spare string and got a friend of the family to tune it up, he tried for an hour before giving up and accused it of being a "Toy" and untunable. I would use it as a prop in my air guitar sessions and lay the foundation to a unique style of theatrical guitar that would benefit me immensely when I would later go on stage. The sad end to the story is that I eventually demolished it at one of our concerts by smashing the bloody thing repeatedly over my head before ceremoniously tossing the remaining splinters into the frothing crowd.

I had never really had a job and the pocket money that I earned used to be spent quicker than I could earn. My knowledge and sensibility regarding cash in general is non existent. When I was 12 my dad sat me down and said 'well you're a young man now and so we have decided to give you a monthly salary that will be yours to do with what you like and payable on the proviso that all you're expected chores are sufficiently complete. How much would you expect?" I thought about it for a few days and settled on the princely sum of 15 rand. The proposal was rejected and the settlement came at the annunciation of the counteroffer and so I was now officially employed as a son for the substantial amount of 12 rand, payable at the end of each calendar month on condition that all odd jobs such as "picking up the poo" had been dutifully completed. On the memorable occasion of receiving my first salary I took the cash and secured an advance of another 50cents and within the space of 7 minutes flat had bought Thin Lizzys "live and dangerous" on cassette. My dad was flabbergasted and chewed me out for wasting my cash on such a stupid thing and enquired how I proposed to listen to said cassette as I didn't have a tape recorder! To me it was a minor detail.

My first guitar or rather, technically my second, was purchased in the same way. As a National serviceman I was the proud recipient of 200 rands each month. Payable reluctantly by the scowling paymaster at the end of each calendar month. I received my first paycheck and dutifully went to the music instrument shop and placed my one third down payment on a bright yellow electric guitar the would take me 8 months to complete paying for. The fact that I couldn't play a note or didn't own an amplifier was a minor detail.

It took six months of regular slog before I could play my only chord without placing my fingers one by one on the prescribed strings with my other hand before strumming like crazy whilst moving up and down the fret board at high speed. Its been pretty much the same story now for close on 25 years. The only difference being that I can play the bar chord in my sleep and in hundreds of ways. It was the guitar that I would take to London and eventually be stolen by a junkie who pawned it to get his heroin fix. I had written my first song by playing a chord with one finger up and down and in all the time I have played, only done about three covers which I interpreted in my own way and so destroyed as creatively as possible. Its been original or nothing all the way and currently my song tally stands at about 200 crap ditties.

I would play this guitar without amp every moment I could and when the time came that I was to join my first band, I could at least keep a fair rhythm.

Free peoples

The free peoples concert was a yearly event and one I looked forward to. I go down to the university campus and watch some of the bands and as is my habit, I go round the back to take a peek backstage. This of course is a VIP only area and the security is pretty tight. Not tight enough though and I soon make my way under the stage and through the plastic partitioning into the area and no sooner have I helped myself to a free drink than I'm spotted by the guard and he comes over to throw me out. I'm nonchalant and when he confronts me I tell him I have lost my VIP ID card whilst dancing to the previous band. He doesn't believe me and to be honest, neither do I but I stick to my story with as much innocence as I can while gulping down the beer. As luck was on my side that day, I spot Robbie Robb and call over to him "Hey Robbie! Can you help out here for a sec?" He comes over and without hesitation verifies my story and we both have a bit of a giggle as we go onto the stage and sit there drinking free beer and talking about Jimi Hendrix and the political situation with equal sincerity in between slugs. " Its great!" I think to myself. One minute I'm just a face in the crowd and the next I'm a potential troublemaker and the next a celebrities friend sitting in front of thousands of people drinking beer and chewing the fat. Amazing!

The last band has played and the whole show is over and I, make my way to the gates and then back to the world as I know it. As I get to within a few meters of the exit, a huge policeman gets out of his van and walks right into the midst of the peacefully exiting crowd and yells " This is an illegal gathering and you have 10 seconds to disperse!" Everyone runs like hell and I stand looking around to see what it is that must be going on to make the policeman behave like this. Where's the riot? Not being a student and so not being familiar with the frequent clashes with the authorities I was slow to understand that its not a situation that calls for debate. Run! That's the idea. In a few short seconds I am pretty much the only one standing, looking sheepishly around and so the policeman turns to me and shouts "Hey! You! Ponk! Why you don't run away? Hey?!" I look at him and say nothing but keep the puzzled expression on my face. He asks again and I begin to imitate sign language as spoken by the deaf people I have seen and mumble a few non descript words. Understanding registers on his face and he walks close to me and shouts into my face with exaggerated lip movements " FOK OFF!" and points to the gate. I nod understanding and say with a smile and a tongue wrapped in cotton wool "OK! OK! Sorry!" I walk to the gate and ignore his jeers while thinking to myself, "why does he think that he can make himself be heard by a deaf person if he shouts?!"

I wrote a song about the incident called "Social Phenomena"!

The first group I played with as I have mentioned was Septic Lozenges. We would practice on the 18th floor of an apartment block and after being threatened with eviction we played in the laundry room on the roof of my building. It was a room about 1 by 2,5 meters and we would start by sending the drummer known only as "Pasta" in and he would sit down. Then the bassist and I would carry in the drums, set them up in front of him and we would inch in sideways to stand practically face to face with both our guitars plugged into a home made amplifier and shut the door and thrash out our set.

We had our first gig in a newly established club that was owned by a club owner that both Ashley the bassist and I knew quite well. He agreed to give us a shot on a Friday night and so the stage was proverbially set for our first step towards rock stardom. We faced a slight problem though in that we didn't have a vocalist and both Ashley and I were so busy struggling gamely to keep up with Pasta's frantic inverted drumming that there wasn't a hope in hell of trying to play and sing. It was out. Totally. We solved? The problem by recruiting one of the more hardcore members of the hanger on club desperadoes who looked good and had the hugest ego on earth and issued him with the various dog eared papers that the sketchy lyrics had been scribbled onto and told him to let rip. He countered his obvious tone deafness and lack of talent by immediately trying to take over as leader of the band and within about 30 seconds we were nearly in the midst of battle. We somehow got through the only rehearsal which I had taped and sent him home with the strict order "PRACTICE!" I didn't care much and relished the chance to finally get up on a stage and fulfill the prophesy I had made a few short years earlier to make a band and perform live that was received with much mirth and merriment by my so called peers. I had something to prove and the mechanism had been set irretrievably in motion and I got progressively nervous with each tick of the clock.

The big day arrived and we went to the club early to set up and do a sound check. There was no sign of the vocalist! Early evening became late evening and there was still no sign of him. The club started filling up and a decent kind of crowd were standing around drinking and no one was particularly concerned whether a band played or not. My group of friends from the old days arrived and started whistling and cheering to get the show on the road. I was sufficiently lubricated at this stage and decided to grab my ax and get up there when one of the girls came in and said "Mark's here! He's outside! The bouncers kicked him out!" We all went outside to see this guy sitting on the pavement petrified out of his wits. It had turned out that the regular big mouth was a victim of acutely acute stage fright! To compensate he had done the smartest thing he could think of and taken a ridiculous amount of slimming tablets and was sitting in the resultant state with fully dilated pupils and incoherently blabbering about how he is too fucked to play. Ooooh boy! I looked across at Ashley and said matter of factly " I'm playing! With or without you sorry lot!" He smiled his usual mischievous smile and together we went straight in, grabbed Pasta and got on stage.

It was complete pandemonium from the start. We were loud and out of tune and out of time and I decided to compensate for our lack of ability with stage presence and struck glam rock poses and whirls and jumps which would have made Pete Townsend look like a block of wood. At one stage I took the initiative by utilizing the open area in front of the band (that was ultimately bare due to the crowd having retreated to a safe distance and were hugging the walls) by doing a record breaking slide on my knees that resulted in my much too short guitar cable popping out of it's socket and so I continued to play wildly whilst being unplugged. The show was abruptly brought to its close by the club owner storming on stage and literally pulling the electric plugs from their sockets before any equipment exploded and proceeded to rant and rave us off the stage and kick us out of the club. My so called friends had stared in disbelief all through the short set and along with the rest of the paying customers stood in stunned silence for a few minutes before going to get another beer and doing what it is that they usually did at a club. We were ecstatic! We sat outside in a communal pool of sweat and stared at each other periodically and bursting out in laughter that shook us to the core. We had done it! We had played!

Being kicked out never deterred us in the slightest as we were always "up against it" and were veterans of sneaking into clubs and gaining entrance to places we had been barred and so plans were immediately knocked out for the next evenings "Gig" We had been promised and this was good enough to serve as a green light and disregard the rantings of the club owner.

It's a Saturday night at the club. My girlfriend and I with a few friends decide to go and "make a blow" We go out of the club and make our way to one of the alleyways and as we turn the corner a police van drives up and screeches to a halt. It's a routine we are all used to and automatically small parcels are surreptitiously jettisoned and dead pan expressions adopted. This time it's a little different. As the van stops the driver gets out and rests his fire arm on the roof of the vehicle while the other one gets out of the passenger side and walks purposely up to me and without a word or a warning or reason, punches me full on in the mouth. Probably since I'm the biggest and it's the standard procedure to subdue a group when you are outnumbered. I go down to my knees and spit out slivers of my mildly splintered tooth. He then proceeds to search us whilst shouting abuse all the while. While I'm on my knees I shove the matchbox of cannabis under the van and stay down. He is now doubly pissed off as he is unable to "bust" anyone for possession or anything else like carrying a weapon or whatever. I stand up with blood trickling down my chin and I grin at him with all the arrogance I can muster. He punches me flat out for the second time. I look him straight in his blue eyes and Naas Botha blond hair but don't grin. He says " jou fokken panks fink jou soo taff hey!" He turns sneering and gets back into the van. They drive off. As he leaves I start giggling as the matchbox comes fully into view. Only one word is uttered by all of us just before we get stoned.

WANKERS!

The next afternoon I shimmied up the traffic light and then onto the balcony and slipped the catch to the door with my knife and stealthily sneaked through the club past the resting black watchman to let the others in. We entered the club with much noise and told the night watch that the door was wide open "what's going on!?" He was too startled and confused to do much and upon seeing the equipment realized we weren't thieves and allowed us to set up our stuff and then go back out to the balcony to drink the beers we had brought and stay out of sight. A few hours later when it was dark we went in one by one and kept a low profile in the ever largening crowd that was steadily streaming through the doors. The widest assortment of punk rockers I or any of us had ever seen in one place. We stood in a state of pure shock as the place filled out into a sheet of noise and anticipation. As I was buggered if I would hide in the darkness for the full period of our agreed period before miraculously appearing on stage to see if we could knock off the set before being kicked off, I went to the bar and ordered a beer. The club owner spotted me and rushed over. I thought the game was up before it started but I was in for a lesson in the smelly art of nightclub ownership. He was the happiest soul on earth and greeted me like a long lost wallet. I decided in one of my finer opportunistic moments to insist on an apology by way of free drinks for the band all night long. He promptly agreed and I went over to tell my low profile keeping fellow conspirators the good news. We all went straight to the bar and claimed our first down payment and after skulled it down and bounded towards the stage before our visaless Dutch courage failed.

The first song was blasted out and to our surprise it was all in tune and in time with each other. The crowd responded immediately and the floor broke out into a chaotic mess of writhing bodies and snot. I stayed close enough to the amp to remain plugged in and we soon got through the set and had run out of songs. I winked at Ashley and broke straight back into our first song which he immediately copped on to but Pasta didn't. It was a while before he did and then fell straight into the metronomic punctuation that we knew so well. We repeated the set with an added encore of one of the songs we liked most and no one noticed. They thought it was a sign of being very good and professional for us to be able to play the way we did, with me going off alone and the bass, seamlessly joining before the drums drew it all together into the cacophony. We kept shtum and simply nodded when we would hear this. "Oh yeah! It took us months to get that down!"

We had somehow managed to expose a hidden sub culture that slumbered in the many of JHB's suburbs and surrounds and met people from far and wide. Differing economic circumstances, grades of familiarity with the overseas scene but all united under one roof in the name of non conformity and confusion. We were surprised to say the least and the first thing I did was to sack the non performing vocalist.

We played in and around Joburg usually at about 2am when the other bands had finished and were packing up and the management and patrons were all too drunk to care. My main activity at this time was "liberating" equipment from the cruel captivity by the more affluent bands. The most audacious rescue was when I walked out of a club with a snare drum under my arm in full view of everyone. I employed the age old Ninja tactic of disguising myself in plain view. It worked! We now had a very expensive deep snare drum to bash and guitar effects that made us look good even though we had no idea of how to use them. Although we played a number of gigs, nothing quite compared to the first one and the band had to disband when it was Ashley's turn to do his duty and serve the country. He had to wear brown boots which he didn't seem to mind so much.

I then floated around for a while and eventually started playing guitar for a band called Sulphate and then Midget Submarine which had been around since the "Dog" days and had managed to continue playing various gigs every six months or so in way out of the way places. It was mostly cover versions and I would do my best to stay as close to the original as I could but was notorious for busting out spontaneously into a lead break or more frequently a rhythm break since I had no idea of lead and would just take the riff and go ballistic. This didn't go down too well with the other guys but they tolerated it as the crowd thought it was cool. The breakthrough came when we landed a gig at a combination colored and black club that would have live music and designated Thursdays as a "Rock" night. We played the first week and then the next and soon, for the first time in our lives we had a more or less regular spot. It was of course unpaid as these things always were but we didn't care and were grateful for the odd free beer that the owner would stand us after a good take at the door.

The club. It was such a total dive and I loved the place. Saturday afternoons and Sundays the place would be teeming with sweating , writhing bodies. You had to push your way through the people to get anywhere. I would go to the bar and Petrus the patriarchal figure would be in command and seeing me would grin and hand me an ice cold quart of Black label and I would go and sit behind the counter and watch the scene before me. Countless black smiling faces would come up to chat to me as they were completely amazed at a young white guy sitting there on a "black" or "colored" club time. I would talk to all kinds of people and laugh along as we would shout at each other to be heard above the noise.

It was a kind of "neutral zone"

I was slowly growing frustrated as I felt that playing covers was bullshit and as punks we should be playing our own original stuff and deal with issues that were more relevant to our situation than simply repeating songs from bands in England that, although forming a part of the historical context of punk if you could call it that, were singing about dole queue's and the rest that were tired and out of place themes. I wanted to play faster and heavier and do the stuff that was overflowing from my many notebooks and basically be a little more creative. I also noticed that the time was right for this kind of thing as the kids would be responding to the more aggressive music that was played by the DJ. It culminated on a night when I met a guy from my suburb who said he played drums and wanted to play in a band and it was pretty much the same kind of direction as my own. I never took these things seriously and had heard a million times before about people who were serious about playing on the Saturday night and would promise to pitch at a given place and time but never showed. We went through the ritual and I was more than amazed when I got to the practice room to find that he had transported his whole kit on his 50cc bike in a series of relay trips and was there as agreed and as drunk still as I was. We set up under the stage where I usually played with the other band and we proceeded to knock out a few of my own songs with just the drums and guitar. It was great! At the end of the session he told me he knew of a guy who was learning to play bass and would be keen to join us. It turned out that I knew the guy well and he hadn't approached me as I was already in a band. We met the day after and went through the few songs we had done before and it was a lot of fun for all of us. At the end of the practice it was clear to me that this was what I was into and so, told them that I was keen to get together but still had a commitment to the other band and it would of course have to take priority , but that it would be really great to have this band as a support band for the other one and the set up was already in place as we had a pretty regular spot and the club owner was open to these new things. I left it at that and went to the usual practice with the other guys and no one showed! I had been open with them and discussed the fact that I was interested in a side project but it would not effect my loyalty and they seemed fine with the idea as long as it didn't happen.

It's another Sunday at the club. I hear the warning "the kids are out today so watch out!" I haven't the faintest idea of what this means but as usual try to keep my eye out for any potential scuffles and try to stop them before they start.

Its not long before a fair sized group of young colored boys come walking down the sidewalk and before any of us have the chance to react, they quickly pick up speed and as a group stride past the line of people waiting outside. All of a sudden they scatter and run away in all directions. The main bouncer runs out of the club to the corner, drawing his gun at the same time and I wait for the shots because I know this guy is crazy and will shoot at kids without batting an eye. Tue to form a single shot rings out. I look across and see his gun skittering along the sidewalk and he is standing unsteadily. My first thought is "He's been shot!" It's an accurate thought but not what I imagined. He comes tottering over towards the club and I see the growing blotch of red on his shirt. One of the other bouncers walks over and sees that he has in fact been shot and tells him to wait by the car while he goes to look for the keys. There is no ensuing firefight as I have expected and its because as it happened this guy pulled his gun and it was of course ready to go as always and dropped the thing! Boom! He shot himself in the lung. Off he goes to the hospital while the guy who was standing in the line is sitting on the sidewalk bleeding. One of the kids in the group had stabbed him in the kidneys and run off when the group scattered.

It's a longtime after when the ambulance arrives and takes him away.

So here I was sitting on my own and strumming away when the drummer guy arrived with the bassist and someone else they knew who could actually play the guitar. They, had simply decided to come along and perhaps have the opportunity to play a bit when we had finished our practice. We all plugged in and went straight to it. The following evening too and one more when a mutual friend arrived with his leg in plaster and proceeded to shout along with the songs from a crumpled bunch of papers he had stuffed in his pocket. It was all good fun and we all agreed to meet again the following week.

I arrived at the club on Thursday evening at the usual appointed time and waited for the other guys to get there and they were late, very late. The club owner came out and recognizing me said "hey! Grab your guys and get on" I was about to explain that they were late but looked over at the drummer and smiled a challenging smile. He went pale, swallowed and ran away to find the bassist who would drive him home at breakneck speed to fetch his kit and the bass. It was no more than 30 mins later that we were all on stage complete with vocalist clutching papers and crutches for support. We dove straight in and knocked off the set to the usual crowd and they went nuts! After the set the club owner came over and said "why didn't you play that noisy shit before?" It was obvious that he didn't even know that I was standing there with a whole collection of totally new faces! We all broke down laughing at the fortunate mistake.

The die was cast...

The following week we got straight down to work as we had calculated that we had played our first live gig after an accumulation of only 7 hours practice in total! Two days later in the middle of practice the bassist of the previous band arrived with a muscle bound friend and walked straight in and wordlessly unplugged his amp and carried it out. I watched him as he left and thought how stupid he was and how he had without knowing it put the deciding nail into his bands coffin and in the same motion announced the birth of our new band. The fact that he took the amp didn't matter anyway as our bassist had long since turned the volume off as his taped up fingers couldn't handle the baptism by fire and he was simply pretending to play in any case.

It's a Saturday night at the club. My girlfriend and I with a few friends decide to go and "make a blow" We go out of the club and make our way to one of the alleyways and as we turn the corner a police van drives up and screeches to a halt. It's a routine we are all used to and automatically small parcels are surreptitiously jettisoned and dead pan expressions adopted. This time it's a little different. As the van stops the driver gets out and rests his fire arm on the roof of the vehicle while the other one gets out of the passenger side and walks purposely up to me and without a word or a warning or reason, punches me full on in the mouth. Probably since I'm the biggest and it's the standard procedure to subdue a group when you are outnumbered. I go down to my knees and spit out slivers of my mildly splintered tooth. He then proceeds to search us whilst shouting abuse all the while. While I'm on my knees I shove the matchbox of cannabis under the van and stay down. He is now doubly pissed off as he is unable to "bust" anyone for possession or anything else like carrying a weapon or whatever. I stand up with blood trickling down my chin and I grin at him with all the arrogance I can muster. He punches me flat out for the second time. I look him straight in his blue eyes and Naas Botha blond hair but don't grin. He says " jou fokken panks fink jou soo taff hey!" He turns sneering and gets back into the van. They drive off. As he leaves I start giggling as the matchbox comes fully into view. Only one word is uttered by all of us just before we get stoned.

WANKERS!

Toxiksox was born! I chose the name ages before, due to my many hours of walking to get jobs in my boots and returning home exhausted in the evenings and peeling the socks from my feet. Everyone agreed on the name and so we went back to playing with fervor and a sense of purpose.

We played the Thursday night spots along with other bands and once or twice also when the owner decided to do a Saturday night with lots of bands on the bill. It was all quite run of the mill and we would play the freezing winter evenings to the staff at the bar and friends of the band as it was a bad night and too cold out for most people to make the effort.

I'm walking to band practice after a long day at work. I'm really tired and trying to give myself a pep talk as to how something has to give due to my dedication and persistence. I was up at 4.15am and its now close to 9pm and I'll be lucky to be home before 1am.

I'm late and walking fast and as I get to the Jeppe train station I see a pick up truck drive past and stop abruptly. These guys are nicknamed "vultures" as they hang around listening to the police and ambulance frequencies and then when there is an accident they race over in their souped up trucks and tow away your car to charge you the earth when you want to get it back. They have a reputation for being a really rough bunch. I don't feel so good about this truck stopping and feel even worse when I see the driver pointing a gun at me and two of his friends running in my direction ducking behind a wall as they do so. I don't wait. I jump straight over the wall with barbed wire on the side of the railway line and look over my shoulder to see that there are two of them and one has a baseball bat and the other a bullwhip. The guy with the gun is shouting now and he cant see me as I bound down the broken stairs of a disused staircase and make my way towards the tracks. The bloody stairs disintegrate as I go down and my only consolation is that it will slow up my pursuers. I get to the tracks and its dark but I run like hell away from them. A shot rings out and then another and I hear the whine of the rounds as they scream past. No more shots as the shooter gets into the car and bombs down the road to try and cut me off further along. He nearly succeeds but I find my way out of this recessed and sunken track with sheer concrete walls and run zig zag through the back streets towards the Belgravia hotel. I know this is where these guys usually hang out and figure it would be the last place they would look. Out on the streets they could easily spot me and so that's where I head. I duck into the back and hide amongst the garbage for almost an hour. Eventually I pluck up the courage to move and my stiff joints ache as I climb my way over the small koppie not far from my old primary school.

The only real effect of the incident is that the guys in the band are pissed off at how unreliable I am.

Apparently the reason behind the unprovoked attack was due to a fight that one of them had had with some skinhead types that were known to us but were a separate group. They had badly beaten one of the "vultures" and as a result it was thought that all "punks" were to be targeted to try to even the score.

Its not the first time I have been shot at and I have to say that on both occasions I couldn't really relate to the fact that I could be struck by a ball of hot metal that could kill me. I guess if I had been shot before that the gravity of the fact would register somewhere.

One evening we arrived as usual and were speechless to see a line of people lined up right around the corner waiting to get into the already packed club. We were let in and went down into this subterranean hellhole and stood around sheepishly drinking our beers in shocked silence. We got up on the stage at the signal and plunged into our first song. We were loud, fast and particularly tight that night and it was a chaotic mix between pandemonium and open warfare! Bodies flying around and people diving off the stage with the security guards trying as much as possible to prevent the pressing crowd from damaging the equipment. At the end of the frenzied set we got off stage to chants of "Toxiksox! Toxiksox!" We went to our section that was reserved for the bands and sat down, barely able to register the congratulations of the other members of the bands and sat in a dazed and confused state of post play nervous excitement adrenalin buzz. The drummer, Martin summed it up in one phrase as he was apt and gifted enough to do " FuuuuuuuuuuuuuuuuK!" we all laughed and laughed on our way down from the magical world of live performance to this one.

Sunday afternoon at the club. I have managed somehow to convince the manager that I can handle the task of being one of the many bouncers and duly arrive at the appointed time with a three sectioned staff folded up in the secret pocket in my leather jacket.

I'm standing around trying my best to look tough when all hell breaks loose. There is a rival club a few blocks up and many people are there and so business is relatively slow. To counter this the manager has sent a couple of guys over there with baseball bats to beat the crap out of the place and a couple of bystanders for good measure with the objective of closing the place down for the afternoon and gleaming the spare customers. There is a pretty chaotic scene up there and people running all over and being chased around and so on. I stay put and then watch as one by one the other guys arrive back sweaty and exited. The largest of the guys, Jimi comes strolling up with his ever present grin and says "Aish!! we broke them!" and punctuates it with his usual laugh. Jimi is HUGE. He is my best friend and I would feed him if he were hungry and let him drive my car, live in my house, borrow my sister or all of the above while I run him a warm bath and feed him plates of his favorite snacks. Like my dog or small Japanese motorcycles. But friends we will be.

I notice that he has blood on his shirt and on closer inspection realize that he is bleeding. I say "Hey Jimi! You get poked or what?!" and point to his shirt. He looks down and his expression changes and says" that little bastard shot me!!! I'm going to kill him!" and walks out back in the direction of the other club.

Some time later he comes back and informs us that the little bugger got away but his days are numbered. Jimi pulls off his shirt to reveal that he has been hit 4 times in the upper body.

He wasn't even aware of it.

Beers all round and an announcement that the club would now shuffle its usual schedule and open on Saturdays as a 'Punk" night. Not an "alternative" night or some other watered down phrase but "PUNK!" in loud capital letters.

The club owner was a crook and we both loved and feared him. He has my eternal respect for having an ex con who was a sign writer, paint "Punk's Not Dead!" in enamel paint complete with a picture of Wattie Buchan on the side of his white Mercedes Benz! I thought as we all did that that was a pretty hardcore thing to do.

The club was called "double image" probably due to the fact that the main idea was to get off your face plastered. It would cater to the coloreds who had their club at a specific time and then was hastily practically hosed down and would be packed chest to chest a few hours later with sweaty drunken dancing blacks much as the place had been before. It was very dangerous and had its fair share of stabbings and shootings. I had witnessed a few as I practically and literally lived there at a stage and would double up as a bouncer.

A group of young colored kids would walk up together and then one of them would stab the intended victim a few times , drop the knife and then the group would disperse in all directions and it would be impossible to catch the perpetrator. There would be no whites at these shows and on rock nights the crowd would be mostly white with a smattering of blacks who would come to see the reggae. It was technically speaking a multiracial club and I was free to go down and get the barman to give me a beer when the club was in full swing on any of the days. I used to be looked at kind of strangely and I had to keep my eyes open but for the most part it was no problem to be the only white in the club. I would be considered as a kind of staff member anyhow so I'm not sure I could be considered a patron in the true sense of the word. Parasite more like. At our gigs there were a few black punks and they were well cool. They would support the band and mix with the others without any problems but were in many respects a minority within a minority within a minority that formed the miniscule fringe of the societal minority as a whole. It was a cool scene and the only one as punk type people were not welcome anywhere and it was "open season" for the cops and miscreants that roamed the streets in search of someone to beat the crap out of. I loved it and we formed a kind of family where everyone knew everyone and there were rituals such as "perve hour" where the usual group would gather near the door at 3am and along with the manager have a joke telling session that was better than any stand up comedy show. The manager was a kind of Godfather in both the criminal and traditional sense. He ruled the roost with an iron fist and didn't tolerate any shit. True to his frequent warnings, if you overstepped the line you were expected to pay in blood. He would champion us though and was powerful enough and experienced enough to tell the raiding policemen to "fuck off and come back with a warrant or I'll have you shot full of holes for trespassing!" and they would. He didn't bluff and wasn't intimidated. It would give us the time to "stash" our illicit goods and if on a wanted list as so many were, to split out the back entrance or over the roof. The manager eventually offered the band "Residency" and a contract that was as one sided as the chances of us ever being successfully managed by someone in the music industry proper. We didn't mind and I must add that he would slip me a ten rand note or two during the week when he knew I was desperate and needed to eat. To buy drugs was strictly out and he knew I would respect his rules.

The band was my lifeblood and I was its only full time member in the sense that the others were either at college, school or had jobs. I would go to the office and scheme with Roland the manager how to shake up the roost and get some free press in very inventive ways. One day I clearly remember going into the Star newspaper building. It was funny. Here I was, six foot and a smidgeon extra. With a 30cm bright orange Mohican. Dressed like something out of a science fiction movie, with a quart of beer in one hand and a large brown envelope in the other casually strolling in through the heavily securitied doors of SA's largest newspaper and instantly being shuffled to the door while giggling and explaining that I have an appointment with Gus Silber/Sibler?? the papers main music critic. A guy who by virtue of his position could make or break a band with a casually penned full stop, period. He was notoriously difficult to get hold of and in high demand by live music venues and bands who constantly harassed him to attend and hopefully get a positive review. For him to lower himself and be seen at a dive such as our place to see a band that couldn't play would be way below this mans dignity. I got kicked out as expected and swiftly walked around the block to give the guard the impression that I had got the message and get him off to that side. I then returned and walked in through the "out" door and bounded up the stairs with the security in hot pursuit. I knew my way around and entered the press room and haughtily waved at the gaping bunch as I had seen the queen do on TV and said " I'm looking for Mr Silver! You know, the critic dude!" The security entered and I playfully dodged them by running behind desks and pretending it was a game, much to the amusement of some but by no means all of the journalists who were sitting back enjoying the show. Soon enough a gruff old man said "what hell do you think you're doing?" I immediately stopped and took on a serious tone and said to him quite levelly " I am the guitarist of the legendary punk band Toxiksox and I have here in my hand an envelope with our press package that I was hoping to deliver to Mr. Gus Silver in person as I know that if I don't it will stay out in the lobby and not even gather dust before it is turfed out! I phoned before and was told that it was fine. However.." and I turned to motion to the two security guys. "these gentlemen have tried to prevent me from entering the building due to their obvious bias towards me based on my attire and so in effect are preventing me from legally following the many and varied activities that comprise my chosen career as a musician! So if you would direct me to Mr. Silver or at least his desk I will make my delivery and be on my way. Thank you!" There was a pause that could have accommodated the entire maternity ward of the Jo Burg Gen before the gruff man in question said" My name is Silber not Silver!" Where upon I shouted "Gus! Is it really you!" and the whole room erupted in applause and laughter. I handed him the envelope, turned on my heel and walked out with all the dignity I could muster. "carry on!" I said over my shoulder with a grand wave as I had seen done by royalty in the movies.

We never got the review but it was rumored that he had attended a gig once but it couldn't be verified as he was heavily disguised. He did see us when we played a few months later at larger venues and had begun to carve our initials into the bark of the rapidly emerging SA alternative music scene.

Sunday afternoon. Bored shitless. My girlfriend and a friend decide that we can go and jump the train as there are no conductors working and it beats wandering around aimlessly. We go down to the bottom end of town and ride the train up and down the reef eventually getting out at the Ellis park station. Somebody had the bright idea to get off there as there would be loads of black spectators watching the soccer that would be played on Sundays at the Rugby grounds and we would somehow manage to "score" It was a dumb idea but something to do and in any case I had never seen a football match with the two main opposing teams playing each other. Orlando Pirates and Kaiser Chiefs. They were great teams and we were sure we could at least sneak in.

The first surprise was that there was no charge at the gate! So we waltzed straight in to a jam packed stadium and the cloud of smoke from the crowd. Now at a white sports event such as Cricket, you would be greeted with the smell of barbecuing meat, but here all we could smell was ...DOPE!

Wow! I was amazed. I stood staring at the crowd and would be totally shocked to see a guy stand up off the telephone book he was sitting on and tear out a page. Then take a wad of green leaves and roll a joint with the whole page! He would take few puffs and pass it down the line and another one would come his way and take a few puffs and so on. I was like "WOW! Where are the cops?"

There were people standing on each others shoulders to see and it was wild. I was awestruck. The atmosphere was unbelievable and the place was all of 2.5km from my house. I had only been there once or twice as a kid when I got my first "job" selling milk and orange juice to the fans at the rugby matches. This was something else completely.

The match ends and we move off to the station with of course the idea that we will accost one of the guys and ask for some weed.

Now I am standing on the platform and taking swigs from a bottle of Amaretto while looking around to see if there are any people who would be conducive to giving us a little of the green stuff. I have also got my eye on a skinny little black uniformed policeman. It's not long before he wanders over to me and takes the bottle from my hand and looks at me questioningly. I smile at him and look over at almost every black guy standing there with a bottle of beer in their hands and shrug. Now drinking in public is basically illegal in SA but as always there can be, and usually are exceptions to this rule/law. His answer is to take the bottle and empty it over my head. I keep a straight face and ask him if he is going to do the same to the hundreds of people standing on the platform or only me. He replies "I don't see anyone with alcohol, only you!" I reply "Ahh!.....You don't? I see many people, one Whitey and one Asshole!" He starts to get angry but backs down as we are starting to attract a crowd.

We are standing on the platform and I hear the snippets of talk from the younger ones and I don't like much of what I hear. They are thinking of "taking" my girlfriend and dropping the two of us (my friend and I) off the train a little further down the line. I realize the danger as I am the only one who understands a few words and my girlfriend and friend are being ultra friendly and being slowly maneuvered towards the front of the platform so that they can be easily bundled into the approaching train. I go over to my buddy and tell him with a straight face and smile that were in deep shit. He knows I'm not the kind of person to joke around and it's been more than one occasion that my "smarts" has saved both of our hides. My girlfriend is a different story. She is determined to score and I know she is not the quickest on the uptake when it comes to these things. As I am making my way over to her, one of the black guys pinches her butt and she turns to me with absolute fury and demands that I do something. I tell her straight out "Time to go!"...."NOW!" She doesn't want to listen and things are turning nasty. I turn to my friend and tell him to grab her and walk away. I turn to the crowd of guys and try to take the attention away from them by addressing them and beginning to deliver a lecture about the fact that we are not racist and so why are you treating us like we are? and so on. All this, while the precious Amaretto is dripping off my face. My girlfriend, who is completely oblivious to the danger pipes in and wants to get some answers too and I am doing my best to try to stay calm and get out of the steadily worsening situation. It's at this point that a chubby black guy comes up and tells her "Don't try to reason with the mob! Just go! Quickly!" She begins to backchat him and he takes out his ID and shoves it in her face. She takes one look and turns around and walks off down the stairs, my friend in tow. The man is a policeman and tells me to go too. I turn to everyone and let rip with a string of abuse. Basically that I am not going to be forced through fear to do such and such and blah, blah, blah. I see that they have made it safely away and so I continue to hold the mobs attention by talking about peace and the future and all kinds of shit to buy some extra time and sow confusion. I then turn and walk off slowly and purposefully. As I get to the staircase the train arrives and the protagonists in the group throw cardboard boxes at me and proceed to pee a rain of urine down from the platform as I refuse to run and continue walking with the under cover policeman close behind me. I get to the subway and turn to him and thank him as he risked his life to help us and he tells me to run as fast as I can for as long as I can before turning in the opposite direction and doing the same. I take his advice and its not far before I realize that no one is giving chase and I slow to a trot.

A few blocks further on I get to where my friend and girlfriend are waiting and see that he is pale and sitting down. She however turns to me with all the venom in the world and accuses me of being a coward for not punching the guy who pinched her ass.

???

The whole alternative affair was spearheaded by Barney Simon. A character that I was familiar with from the early days of my club trawling and had seen him carve up a mannequin with a chainsaw one night during a performance of his band "Naked Lunch" Burroughs would have been proud. He rose to the rank of DJ with own show in the SABC. And became a favorite on Radio 5 with his show that played pretty mundane but far out stuff compared to any other station. He started out as a sound engineer and eventually got the show. He would host a series of big gigs that would give the SA bands a chance to get up and play before large audiences. The first one we made it to was a concert held at the Portuguese hall and attended by a 5000 strong crowd. Roland had specifically employed a young lady who's job it was to chaperone me everywhere I went and with the sole task of, in his own words "make sure he doesn't get too cooked!" So she followed me everywhere and would do her best but was hopelessly outclassed and out maneuvered as my girlfriend would take a huge slug of gin from her babies bottle and then kiss me full on the mouth and deliver a gin injection. It was a cool way to get drunk and I can highly recommend it if you are ever faced with the same predicament. Before we got up to play we could hear the crowd from the back of the stage chanting "Toxiksox! Toxiksox!" I was cornered by Simon the bassist and forced to tune and re tune my guitar which always went out of tune and he didn't want me to go through the regular ritual of tuning up while 5000 people had to wait. The tuner wouldn't work as it was picking up interference from the booming racket being kicked up by the band before ours and so I went on stage with a dubiously in tune guitar. Just before the moment we were supposed to walk on, Barney Was doing the "Who do you wanna see?" routine "I cant hear ya!" and I thought it's now or never. He had a whole crate of beers to himself and all the bands were given a crate to share between themselves and so I quick as a flash lightened his load by half and hid the evidence under my leather jacket in the band room. He came off stage just as I returned cursing and disgusted as one of the fans in the front row had told him to shut up and piss off and punctuated his request by spitting on Mr. Simon's brand new, ultra expensive and still squeaky leather jacket. This was thought a good idea by a substantial number who followed suit and rained a storm of phlegm in his direction. I remember his comment as he trundled in our direction " My God! I wonder how many diseases there are here!"

We went on and I immediately antagonized the crowd by going to the mike and hurling abuse at them. We started playing and I remember very little. Not because I was drunk or anything, simply due to the fact that I couldn't hear a thing for one and was progressively becoming more and more embarrassed as the set progressed. I looked over at Simon who was a bright shade of crimson himself and was sure we had bombed on the biggest occasion so far and would never get another chance to play a big concert like this one. It was over as soon as it started and I ran off the stage and passed the now furiously screaming Mr. Simon who had discovered that his weighty crate of beer had gone on a crash diet. I ducked the scene by diving into my girlfriend and practically had sex on the spot. After the gig had finished and we had all gone our separate ways we discovered that our new vocalist had topped the show off by doing a stage dive and landed on in the photographers pit unceremoniously and concussed himself. It was the item of interest that got us a dirty great headline in the papers. I encouraged him to do it more often as we sat giggling at the practice the following week with him sitting there with his head bandaged. We all felt the same way. We thought we had played the worst set ever and we were the only ones who did. Everyone else thought we were bloody brilliant. We were all left scratching our unbandaged heads as we were informed that the response was so positive that we had been included on the bill of the next show which was to be held at the top venue in town. The Thunderdome!

The Thunderdome was the undeniable highlight of all the gigs we played as a band. We played twice and both times were good although the first was out of this world. I'll never forget it. I was a regular non enterer at the Thunderdome. I would walk up and down the line outside on a weekday night and beg a few coins here and there to make enough to pay the cover charge. The head bouncer was a mean piece of work who would on occasion chase us away and we would go chop- chop as he was as unstable as his stupid haircut. The night we played I walked proudly up to the VIP entrance where he was standing and his words were " what can I do for you handsome?" I replied with undisguised glee " You can tick off my name on the VIP list my good man!" He knew I was in a band but was skeptical none the less and I was saved from a scene when the manager walked up and greeted me with a smile and ushered me through the door. I had waited for that moment for years and recall it now with relish.

The outstanding point of the first gig was that I had convinced my parents to attend! They tried to weasel out of it a few hours before and I prevented them and they arrived nervous as anything and feeling totally out of place as without a doubt the oldest people there. I escorted them straight up to the VIP lounge and had to giggle as I handed my dad his drink and he reached into his pocket to pay. They had never believed me about free booze and always suspected that I had stolen the money to get drunk for years. I just laughed and remember the expressions on their faces as they recognized the various celebrities that they were used to seeing on TV and one or two that knew me and wished me well for the upcoming set. The lounge had oversize monitors all over and of course a commanding view of the stage as it used to be the upstairs balcony of the theater before it had been converted into a club. The screens were displaying the most popular band of the time "the Psycho Reptiles" who were a pretty decent Psychobilly band. My mom was curious to know why the crowd were shouting 'Toxiksox" in between songs. I had to laugh as I was asking myself the same question. It was time to go and so I left them there with my mom staring wildly and totally enraptured at the myriad of spiky topped characters that filled the auditorium. Although she had been a social worker and had worked with youths all her life, this was beyond her comprehension.

I went into the band room to find the others in a state of shock and being teased by their girlfriends who thought it hilarious to see their big tough, hulking boyfriends reduced to blubber. The drummer who didn't smoke was lighting everyone's cigarettes for them and Simon was catatonic. I just busied myself with checking my equipment and soon we heard the Reptiles returning through the tube that led backstage and their front man was cursing wildly. Apparently one of our fans had hurled a bottle at him which had very nearly made it to home base and he was pissed as a snake. I passed him and said " Nice gig!" and he replied "FUCK OFF CUNT!" I blew him a kiss as he went berserk and I headed for the stage as usual the first one out. I was physically struck by the sound as I walked out there. It was awesome. In true alter ego fashion I strutted up to the mike and screamed "Good evening you fucking wankers!" and prominently took out my bottle of Old English cider that I had walked miles to steal from a shop that imported the stuff and opened it and proceeded to slugg away at the bottle throwing the top into the crowd and letting rip with a burp that could have demolished a block of flats with ease. I turned to grab my guitar while the center stage was taken by two friends that to my knowledge performed the first original RAP routine ever on a SA stage and at the end my friend Max took his baseball cap, turned it back to front, looked at me with a crazy look on his face and dived straight off into the crowd way waaaay down there... I looked to Brendan our drummer and he went straight into the explosion that started our first song. It was fantastic. The crowd had people of all descriptions going nuts. Metal fans , Skinheads, some of the Psycho Reptiles fans, straights, trendies, the lot. I was in heaven and very nearly landed in hell. If it were not for Simons warning I would have plummeted off the stage in a howling mess of broken body and guitar that would have struck an augmented chord with the fans and press alike. I was standing right in front of a smoke machine that would periodically blast me and leave a puff of white haze where I was standing for the longest time before it would dissipate and I would appear majestically like some Arthurian character or so it was supposed to go. Truth was that I couldn't see shit and had to guess where to play and subsequently inched forward and eventually took a peek over at Simon as I would do when trying to figure out if we were actually playing the same song. He was frantically shaking his head and looking down. I didn't understand and at the same moment stepped out into space. My foot stopped in mid air and hovered as I regained my balance and stepped back into the bloody fog. When I re emerged and snuck a look at Simon he was shaking his head and rolled his eyes. It was very close but went down very well with the crew that would only watch me and not the band for most all of our performances. I looked down at them with a grin and winked. They thought it was put on but I so nearly created a head line of my own that night.

I'm living in my new flat just across the road from the one I was in when I first got my own place. It smells of sandalwood as it was occupied previously by some Hari Krishnas who had painted a really wicked picture on the lounge room wall of Dishnu and Vishnu and Gashnu and Lobsang Rama Rinpoche and a few of their buddies like peacocks and cows and stuff. It was cool. The one dude was completely blue! I never had the heart or wish to paint over the mural.

I had been living there for some time and it was round about the period that the band was becoming quite popular. One of the upshots of the old block of flats was that at the other end of the corridor was an old black lady who sold the most wowzer dope you ever saw. Dead cheap and completely unbeknown to me for ages. I used to wander the streets and eventually through a long and roundabout way I managed to track the seller of this potent dope down. It ended up being the kind and friendly lady a few doors down! I would never have guessed.

So I was not surprised to look through my window one day to see a very out of place gentleman leaning against the tree opposite my flat, reading his newspaper. Upside down! I swear! It was straight out of Laurel and Hardy except that Stan Laurel had been sent off to get a couple of doughnuts. I was curious and not nervous at all as I didn't have any of the green stuff in my possession and thought that our sleuthful/slothful protagonist was watching the "hot house" so to speak. I became nervous very quickly however as I noticed that this guy was watching MY house!! That wasn't so cool. A little later he was replaced by a guy sitting in his car.

As is my habit when I'm not doing anything illegal or not...I decided to confront the guy. I opened my front door and walked straight over to him and leant into his window whereupon he pretended not to notice me! Now that's pathetic! Anyone walks up to your car in Hillbrow and you close the window first. I asked him straight out " Listen you guys are bugging me. What do you want?" I got the usual bullshit about not knowing what I was on about and so on but I cut him short and said "well if you're not a cop then you're a thief and so I'm going to call the police to see what they have to say" Now he had to do something as we both knew he wasn't a thief and me calling the cops was bullshit but he came clean and stated simply " why do you tell the kids to bunk school?" I had to laugh as I wasn't sure about this guy and which dept of the police or even not he was from. Telling me about something that I had said onstage the previous Saturday night identified him as some kind of policeman other than one from the narcotics bureau. It was relieving because those guys are exceptionally mean. I countered" I think you may have heard me incorrectly. I said something else entirely and would never encourage kids to cut school. Not live on stage anyway" He immediately reverted to the self righteous power position that I knew so well from people with some kind of authority invested in them. He said" what?! You calling me a liar?" I responded by asking him to wait a second and to relax as I wasn't going to fetch a gun or something. I went and fetched the cassette tape that I had been listening to all morning as was my habit when I had managed to get a tape of the gig. I brought it back and got him to put it in his car radio and we both listened very clearly to my words to the audience "Hey! How many of you fucking misfits bunked school to get here tonight!?" I looked at him and he looked back at me angrily. "You fucking punks think you're so clever but we will get every one of you scum!" I said with theatrical earnestness " Well as a public servant in the police force you should catch anyone who breaks the law, whether they are punks or not. That's your job" He said something which disturbed me "Catching crooks is for the stupid police not us!" He started the motor and went off with tires squealing. I blew him a kiss as he sped by.

I never did find out who these guys were but it was not long after that an illegal organization was busted by the police who went by the name of "The civil cooperation bureau" The big wigs of this group were upper management employees of the JHB City council amongst others. The shocking thing was the discovery of a "hit list" What exactly was meant by "hit" I couldn't say, but according to a friend in the police force, the band and some of the close fans were among those targeted.

The gig was a roaring success and the highlight that made all the suffering and hunger and bullshit worth it for me.

My mom was the last to leave and had to be dragged to the car as she would have stayed for the after party if she could have.

The irony of the whole thing that I was so broke at that time that I couldn't have afforded to get in to the club to see us had I not been in the band. I got paid 30 rand after performing to a crowd of 2000 who paid 20 each to get in and hadn't even drunk a beer yet. I was in the wrong business for sure.

We continued to play at the club but wanted to expose ourselves to a wider audience and so, mainly through the efforts of Simon and Anti (Anthony) our vocalist, we played a few gigs elsewhere. We also had a few on air, radio interviews and cut a demo with two songs that was played on Barney's show but as Anti had decided to leave for the UK and my continual abuse and bullshit, we only played a few more gigs before the whole thing ended up disintegrating and Simon teaming up with our original drummer to join a more Metal oriented band called Urban Assault. They had a far more successful "career" than we ever had and were influential pioneers in the early SA metal scene.

To me though, those days were the definite highlight of my life in my twenties and although there were many unpleasant things that happened, the positive outweighs them by far. The colorful characters that I would never have met otherwise and the side of life in my own city that I possibly would never even have seen. Too many things to mention. We had a scene that was tough to beat. Very little violence in a diverse group of youngsters that by and large were out to enjoy themselves and did. To the MAXIMUM!

Toxiksox! Toxiksox!........

Not Normal

I was still living at home and it was a particularly turbulent period. I had however kept my sense of purpose and was making calls and going to interviews when it was possible and on the whole just sticking it out and hoping that something would come up. I had a few times where I would "open up" to my parents in the hope that it would serve to bring us together somehow and heal the festering wounds. On one occasion we touched on my abuse of glue and I remember being asked something to the effect of what it was that so attracted me to it as they knew I wasn't physically addicted and the prognosis from the "Experts" was "psychological dependence" It was a subject that I didn't discuss with anyone as it was something highly personal but on this occasion I relented somewhat and tried at least to touch on one or two things that I was continually intrigued by. I started off by explaining that glue sniffing for the sake of escapism and experiencing hallucinations was exactly the opposite of what I was doing. I went on to attempt to describe some of the strange experiences that I had had and that couldn't be swept under the carpet as a strictly drug induced state of mind. Now you have to take certain factors into account here as I am ultra aware of what shaky ground I am on and the shakier nature of the ground I'm going to try and cover.

First. My abuse which it most certainly was, was undertaken in a very methodical and ritualistic fashion. I would cure the mixture as I have previously noted and sit in a prescribed position and inhale the fumes through my nose in a very controlled way for hours on end. The result would hardly ever be the same but there were isolated instances where I would feel "removed" from the drugs effect and experience something far different from the usual array of effects. I put this down to the fact that these incidents would occur when the elements were often extreme and the actual quality of the glue very poor. Meaning that it had lost its potency and was "flat" if that's the right word to describe it. I would continue and there would be subtle changes that I was aware of and that would act as pointers for me to either alter my posture slightly or concentrate harder or regulate my breathing more strictly or whatever. I would then approach a rather different state and in the following years would recognize these in my readings and experiences with methods of meditation! I would be amazed at the similarities and came to the conclusion that although I had been initially disorientated by the obvious effect of the active ingredient in the volatile stage I would slowly transition into a meditative state that allowed me to engage in an enormous amount of introspection that would leave me with profound insights into certain aspects of my existence. Don't lose me respected reader.. I sense your cynicism and I don't blame you. It is only now, years later that I can close the circle and draw a semi rational conclusion. It's a shaky premise and in those days it was far shakier and rickety bordering on ethereal. They dutifully nodded and so on and I hoped they would appreciate the very difficult and personal nature of the kind of things I was confiding in them. I was wrong of course.

It was a few days later, early one morning after our usual squash game that I was sitting with the paper and ready to start the list of circled ads when my dad came up behind me, put his hand on my shoulder and said " I'm sorry I have to do this fellah but you're just not right" I was puzzled for a second until I saw the policeman walking down the steps towards the front door. It was immediately obvious what had happened.

The young constable was let in and explained to me that I need to pack a toothbrush and so on and would have to accompany him. I went to my room and then to the bathroom while he waited like the stupid ignorant farm boy that he was and stood staring at the second sculpture I had ever made. A Crucifix out of clay. I could have run straight out the back door or casually walked up behind him and clonked him on his empty head with ease. I had packed and walked in to the room and said" I see you like my work" He turned and snarled at me" Jou fokken stjoepit! You *must* be crazy to think you could make a thing as beautiful as that!" "KOM!" I followed him up to the van in which the sergeant was waiting and climbed in the back. He drove off and to my amusement it was in the wrong direction! The police force was quite often manned by staff that were posted to an area far from home and had not the faintest idea of anything. The constable was a prime example of an out of towner and would not be able to catch a bus on his own if he ever wandered unaccompanied from the police residence for some strange reason. The sergeant wasn't much better. We drove around the area for a while and I tried again to "help" by informing him that I knew the way as I had lived there all my life. I was promptly told to shut up if I didn't want to get a few slaps and they continued. Nearly an hour later we were miles from the station and the sergeant turned and ordered me to tell him how to get to the police station. I just looked at him and shut up. He eventually radioed in and got directions. The police station was exactly 2 km from my house and he couldn't find it. I was jostled into a stinking cell and as the roofs are open walked around to keep warm and did some Kung Fu forms to while away the time. Eventually I was ordered into the cell and locked up for the night. There were army blankets folded up in the corner but I was disgusted to discover that they were smeared with semen stains and had been used as toilet paper by many many previous occupants. I was faced with the choice between hyperthermia and disgust and chose the latter when I selected the cleanest one I could find and curled up fully clothed with the blanket over my eyes to shade me from the wire mesh enclosed light that would remain on permanently. I eventually fell into an exhausted sleep. I was later awoken by the cell door opening with a clang and before I could register, a rough hand plucked off the blanket and I was slapped full force across the cheek whilst still lying down to the accompanying tobacco breathed scream " Any complaints! Ha!" I was too stunned to respond. I was lucky as one of the others said to him " its OK he is just here under custody. He's kookoo!" "That so!?" said the brave one and went into what he may have considered a funny imitation of a crazy person to amuse his crones. Rolling his eyes and making spastic gestures whilst waving his arms about. Not to be one that didn't appreciate his own good humor he then burst out in what I would describe as "cruel" laughter. The kind of laughter you would hear at a boxing match when directed at the loser. I sat there stunned with tears in my eyes while my face was on fire and felt unadulterated and absolutely pure, ...hatred.

The following morning I was shoved back into the van and taken to the dept of health where I would have to meet with whoever. I knew no details, didn't, ask and simply kept breathing deeply and squeezing my squash ball. It was a long wait and so I stood up and noticed the young cop tense up with his hand on his holster. I looked across at him and said that I really wasn't going to run anywhere as I had nowhere to run to and I was tired of scrounging for an existence and it was far better to have regular meals and safe accommodation at states expense and I was going to walk around the floor and if he wanted he could shoot me right there. I proceeded to slowly wander around and eventually noticed an open office with a famous picture that was a copper pressing of the "Black Knight!" I looked at it closely and a voice came from inside the office " Do you like art?" I turned to see a smallish woman with fiery red hair and a gentle smiling expression on her face. " I live for it" was my answer and continued gazing. " what do you see in the picture she asked in true psychoanalytical form " A misused childhood and an Oedipal complex, with suppressed homosexual tendencies" was my answer. " I see!" she said with an amused chuckle " how do you arrive at that?' she asked. "Well, this is William Mac Watchamakalit 1333 and he was a brutal barbarian who earned his immortality by being famous for slaughtering people with that distinctly phallic object in his hand. It always astounds me how the barbarians are treated as heroes and the meek who should be inheriting the earth are ether slaves, cannon fodder or wormfood" " Why are you such an angry young man?" she asked in all sincerity. I thought for a while at that as it was a great question. I was seething with subdued rage. " possibly because I am a sane person in an insane world" I answered with a sigh. I looked at her and smiled with a sense of resignation. "Could be "she said.

Our short exchange was interrupted by the constable ordering me to "KOM!" and so I walked down to the door that he was holding open and entered. I was faced by two women sitting next to each other with a file on the desk in front of them. They told the policeman to holster his gun and to wait outside. He started to protest with "But I got orders" and one of the ladies cut him short with a dismissive smile and said " you're obviously new here. Please close the door when you leave" and turned her attention to me. We went through the formalities and soon we were all engaged in a pretty informal conversation. They asked me straight up what the problem was and I told them matter of factly that I thought it was a combination of many different facets. I felt that a lot of my problems were created by my mom and that she was able to manipulate my life in ways that were unfair and unjust and I simply would not back down and insisted on being my own person and taking whatever came because of it. I touched on the day to day conflicts I experienced in a system I could not become reconciled to and the various things like drug taking and unemployment and positive dreams but negative realities. It was a good conversation and I didn't care if they sent me to the loony bin for shock treatment or not. I was still reeling from the fact that my dad had had a court order forcing me to be "observed" by law and could not get over the feeling of having been betrayed at a time when I desperately needed them to just be there while I worked things out. I had seen the charge sheet and in the section marked " reason for complaint" in my dad parker penned instantly recognizable print were two words " NOT NORMAL" it burned through my head like a branding iron. Two words would give total strangers the right to arrest me and keep me in custody and subject me to tests that were far from conclusive and would alter the very course of my life in an instant and have the added distinction of being able to affect my life for years to come at any moment as it would all be on record.

I did not deny the fact that I was in many ways my own worst enemy and that it would take more than a day to learn not to be and it could only be done by me and not some outside party. We concluded the conversation and before the end I asked them outright. "Off the record, do you think I'm crazy? Honestly?" They both put down their files and the more senior of the ladies spoke to me while looking me straight in the eye. It went something like this...they thought that I was absolutely not nuts by any stretch of the imagination but it wasn't as simple as that. They had to compile their report which was a "joint" report which meant that they tore their files into separate pages and then re stapled them together with alternating pages of both reports to produce two new ones that were in effect combined! I thought that was pretty zooty and the first time I had heard of such a thing. They would then give it to their superior who would read it and much like the supreme court judge, make a decision that was as good as any made by a judge in a court anyhow. It was totally in the hands of their superior and there was nothing more they would be able to do once the papers had been bound and sent off.

"How long do I have to wait?" I asked as I knew these things usually took weeks if not months and I would be incarcerated for the waiting period for sure.

"Not long" I was told, expecting weeks. "about an hour!" I was so relieved it was painfully obvious and it eased the tension a little as they realized I wasn't keen on being locked away and so pulled my leg about it a bit. I was told to wait outside until called which I did whilst trying my best to annoy the cop by bouncing my ball against the wall repeatedly. A very short while later I was called back in as the policeman was told to "heel!" and walked into the room. The two ladies were standing more or less at attention while the very important and powerful woman who had my life in her hands sat down and smiled that sweet gentle smile at me. It was the fiery redhead from down the corridor! She said "go home my boy" I just looked at her as the tears welled up in my eyes and nodded. Before I walked through the door I turned and in a broken voice could say the only two words I could "Thank you"

I was officially free to go, much to the obvious confusion and indignation of the stupid policeman who was convinced I was crazy. It was obvious and just by looking at me you could tell and of course he had heard with his own ears that I had claimed to make a statue of the Lord that I quite clearly couldn't have since I was ...crazy! He could do nothing and I walked the full distance home without regret. I secretly smiled as I imagined him calling in to get directions back to the station!

The only action taken after this event was that for the first time ever, My mom was required to attend the so called therapy sessions with me and squirmed through the first session trying to be her usual evasive self. There was no second session as she had found that she could beat the court order by voluntarily going to a therapist of her own choosing which she did. He turned out to be an old acquaintance who automatically filled out the forms to enable her to sidestep the therapy and gave her more prescription medicine to "help" and collected his bulky check without a backward glance. Life's like that.

Not normal.

Rehab

I was a tramp. Homeless , destitute, hungry and frozen most of the time. My folks had gotten a court order to keep me off the property and so I was sleeping on the koppies in my army sleeping bag. I had realized that if I did not get my system cleaned up, my folks would be able to have me put away by law and there was precious little I could do to contest it in my current position. So I quit. Totally. I tried to get to speak with my dad a few times as he was the reasonable one and eventually did, and explained that if I was to get out of this situation I would need his help. He said OK on condition that I would once again "sign in " at SANCA and go for treatment. I agreed and so would still be sleeping out in the open and would walk to town each day to take the tablets that they said I needed under the watchful eye of the sister. The fact that I had been "clean" for ages now meant diddly squat and I knew it was useless to argue and so I had to go on drugs to get off the drugs that I wasn't on. Obviously! I did this routine and attended all the meetings I was supposed to and after some weeks my dad agreed to help me pay my share of the rent in a flat in Hillbrow that I shared with a great group of my punk friends. It was a real relief as being out in the open in a Jo burg winter was no joke and hyperthermia claimed the lives of twilight kids and vagrants on a daily basis. I had a roof over my head at least. I had been on the street for months.

My mother meanwhile was continually pushing for me to be locked away somewhere far away from her. I guess it was due to the fact that there were some things she could hide from others but not from me and was dead scared of being put on the spot or being exposed. She had high blood pressure and hypertension and was an active hypochondriac. The result was that as an adult with loads of charm, she would manage to get the most horrendous arsenal of prescription drugs from her doctor and it was all accepted. Each morning she would swallow a small mountain of pills and a couple to prevent drug interactions and so on and as far as I could tell (and a few of my friends too!) she was buzzing like a bee for most of her waking hours. Of course any attempts I made to try to make my dad aware were met with indignation and seen as an attempt on my part to use dirty tricks to get the focus off my problems. Now that I was clean, clear headed and more confident I presented more of a problem to her than before and so for some strange reason the focus of the whole issue of me being out of kilter was directed towards the fact that at age 20+ I was still riding a skateboard! I swear! I would just laugh at the complete stupidity and obvious desperation of the ploy but was soon left scratching my head at the fact that the therapists started to pick up on it too. It culminated in having to go to court and appear before a judge. On the morning of the trial/ hearing, whatever one of the therapists said to me "why don't you take your skateboard in to the court with you" in the most pathetic condescending tone I have ever heard. Coming from a therapist who worked at a drug counseling centre I was amazed that she would take the common tone that was used by the many completely ignorant people who thought that one aspirin without the express approval of the doctor would turn you instantly into a vegetable. I had had this experience all too often. They would talk to you as if you were a naughty 3 year old and quite often discuss your case with other people while you were standing in the room but of course wouldn't be able to understand due to your mental condition. Much like the old person who shouts into the telephone when receiving a long distance telephone call.

I went into the court jand stood there with my mouth open while a therapist who I had only just laid eyes on proceeded to address the judge as if she was well familiar with my case and we had been bosom buddies for yonks and although she had done her best it would require the work of true professionals to apply themselves full time to my case

"SO sorry you honor, I tried my best but..." she would have received the Oscar for best supporting actress in a non fiction comic tragedy if it was up to me.

It was a simple formality on the judges part and I was sent to rehabilitation for a period of six months. I got outside and asked my real therapist what in hell was going down. Hadn't I complied to treatment? Wasn't I clean? What? She couldn't look me in the eye and then took me out of earshot of the others and told me that they could not hold me by law if my urine was clean and that my only chance was to insist on a urine test and even a blood test as soon as I arrived at the institution. She understood full well what I was in for and of course how ineffective the treatment was. I got the distinct impression that she had been just as shocked as I at the decision and it may have come from higher up as I truly thought that she was on my side right through the whole saga. She was the only person I would speak to regarding personal things and I could not believe that she had simply "sold me out" On the other hand it was a saga and perhaps she was just tired of it all and it provided an easy way out. Who knows? I was on my way to the funny farm.

I was completely disgusted. The fact that I had confided in them meant shit and that their jobs were nothing more than people processing just left me with a bad taste in my mouth.

I felt betrayed by the people who were supposed to help me and the people closest to me and the irony was that I hadn't taken anything for ages and had done it on my own steam. It seemed like my life was running out of control in reverse.

The whole skateboard issue was nuts. It wasn't like I was sleeping with my board and talking to it or anything. I had been taking part in the circuit that ran throughout the year and would hitch hike across the country to participate in the competitions and do demos to get food money and then hitch back to go back onto the koppie and survive till the next one. I was ranked on average 5th all round in the open division for around 5 years consecutively and it wasn't as though I had just started. Their attitude in their self righteous ignorance and power wielding megalomania was that skateboarding was for kids and you gave it up at around age 15. I didn't have a leg to stand on. I was outgunned.

An interesting minor incident happened at the courts. I was told by the judge that I was to be taken by "state transport" which meant I would be cuffed and bombed in to the back of a van and possibly spend a day or two in the cells before going anyway. My parents piped up and said. "No its ok , WE will volunteer to take him!" the judge , not being one to want to waste well earned tax funds agreed. I was pissed off to the maximum. I was now ordered by the courts to go with my parents who had me previously ordered by the courts to stay the hell away! I stood up and asked the judge if I may say something. He, getting a little tired of the stupid scene and becoming visibly irritated said "Yes! What?' I replied that I refuse to go with them and request to go in police custody! He fumed at me " You will do as I say! Perhaps 6 months in jail before you go will help to remind you who is in charge of this courtroom! CASE CLOSED!" Bang! With the gavel and that was that.

At least I tried.

I went to "the farm" with the sole intention of getting the hell out of there as soon as possible. I spent six fucking months there! I never learnt a single thing except perhaps that the system was run by people who turned out to be far, far stupider than I had ever imagined. How they managed to remain in power for so long was beyond me. Fear, was the closest I could get to an answer.

We drove in silence. It was quite a way as this place was situated near a small one horse town called Cullinan. It was made famous by a man by the name of Cullinan who had found a humungous diamond there and lived happily ever after. I saw no sign of the illusive horse as we passed the place and drove up to a huge gate that was guarded by a uniform clad guard toting a machine gun. After inquiring as to our business he waved us through and we drove past fields in which prisoners were working the fields and closely guarded by more guys from the machine gun club. We arrived at another gate where the guard had forgotten to bring his gun and were allowed to pass through into the compound which was surrounded by 3m barbed wire fences and had unmanned guard towers on the corners of the periphery fence. The place used to be a prisoner of war camp that offered its hospitality to the Italian inmates during the 2nd world disagreement. We got to the front of the admin block and I was told to wait and not move a muscle while my folks were taken to see whoever it was they were supposed to. I watched the inmates tending to the garden beds and was relieved to see that they were wearing civilian clothes. Not like the guys we had just driven past. My folks appeared and started to go through the motions of greeting and I walked straight past without the slightest acknowledgement of their existence and told the orderly "Lets go"

I never as much as looked back.

I was taken straight to the hospital as they were determined to offer me their hospitality and I was told to change and get into a hospitality gown. I asked the guy why I had to be in a hospital and he answered curtly ""detox" I laughed and said that wouldn't be necessary as I was clean. He smirked and said' Ja! You and everyone else hey!" and walked off.

I wanted to have my "piss test" but was told that it wouldn't possible before my 10 or 14 day detox period was over. I thought "that's dumb" as it would take about that time for the body to expel most of the accumulated toxins anyhow so what was the point? I was stuck in this stinking ward and was unable to see anyone of the staff until the two week period was over. People would come and go. Most of the people who arrived were guys who had managed to escape and had been caught again and so had to go through the whole procedure again from the start. One of these guys had been in the place for 7 years! Each time he ran away he would get totally drunk and return after being arrested by the police and then start from the bottom again. There were 211 alcohol patients and 11 drug patients in the population at large.

After being admitted. I was to have a meeting with the therapists or whatever they were and straight away told them I wanted out and was told that I have to be released by law based on the results of my urine test and I wanted it now! They just laughed and told me stuff to the effect that it would all happen in good time and if I wanted to "refuse treatment "I had to make a written statement and submit it to the director and she would take it from there. Meanwhile I should be a good boy and go with this nice man who will show me were I must sleep. I was shown to my bed in the dormitory and would be taken around the next day for a haircut and so on.

The following day, true to their word I was escorted about the place and eventually brought to the barber who was to give my beautiful 40cm bleached Mohican the chop. I sat down and the barber who had tattoos right up his arm started giving me the most hideous "Dutchman cut" I had ever seen complete with combing my hair down straight towards a neatly cut fringe. I was holding my breath the whole time but this was too much! He made me look just like the fucking people I hated most and so I asked him politely " can I see the clipper for a sec?" He told me it was against the rules as I could try to commit suicide. I said for him not to worry as I could possibly do so with a pair of scissors but with a clipper? How? He relented and I took it in my hands and said 'Well..If I'm to be a mental patient I may as well look like one!" I then took the thing and ran it straight down the centre of my head as he stood by and gaped and I continued to shave my head leaving only a few mm of bristles. I stood up, made a theatrical show of checking myself out in the mirror and said " Yeeeaaah That's much better! Thanks Mr. Mineerr!" and handed him back the clippers. He looked at me and said "Jou's fokken MAL!" I laughed and countered " well I'm in the right place then aren't I?"

We had to address the "wardens" as 'Mineer" it's Afrikaans for Mister but translates directly as something closer to "My Lord" it's an old expression and a formal form of address. I refused to call these dumb bastards anything resembling a respectful form of address and as the slang term for Afrikaaner amongst the English is "Rock" I got a kick out of pronouncing the word "Menhir" as in the objects that Obelix would tote around and would visualize the vertical boulder each time I spoke to these fools. As they would treat me as a 'Pommie" and speak to each other in Afrikaans right to my face thinking I couldn't understand. I would mostly be able to stay a step or two of these canine sapiens. I hated them and they hated me. Neither of us ever tried to hide the fact. There would be occasions where I was made to stand in their office for no real reason except that they could make me stand there and they would say things like "If you ever walked on to my farm I would slaughter you like a dog, Pommie! You know that? You're lucky we are here and the law protects you" I would answer them " If you ever walked on to my property I would offer you a cup of tea and then pray for your souls as you know not what you do!" They would only last a round and a half before threatening to get physical

I spent most of the first two weeks in bed with the most horrendous Pneumonia! Now I don't want brag but as the guitarist of a brilliant band I have been in bed with far more sexy things.

I thought I would die. I would stagger over to the sickbay and wait in the line and be refused even a headache tablet. I was coughing and so asked for a lemon and was laughed at as lemon juice is used by the junkies and was totally out. I just suffered through it.

I'm in rehab. It's the first few days and I'm in the hospital supposedly detoxifying.

A guy arrives who was late returning from a weekend home or he had run away, I don't recall and he gets the bed next to mine. He knows the scene and everyone seems to know him and he starts wangling his way around as soon as he arrives and is constantly out of his bed trying to get in touch with his buddies in the general population that are not really allowed to visit the people in the hospital freely. Every thing is fine until the evening when he starts to complain about a sore stomach. This continues way into the early hours and I'm pissed off as he is groaning away and it's impossible to sleep. The orderly in charge of the ward who is just a patient at the farm like we are, kind of like a trustee, is not authorized to issue more than a generic over the counter type of painkiller and repeatedly ignores the guys request to see the doctor as its late and he doesn't want to wake him up and drag him out in the freezing cold. It's a common ploy for patients to feign sickness and then try to be taken to hospital where they can escape more easily. It is obviously surmised that this is the current situation.

The guy eventually pleads with me to call the orderly as he is too much in pain to move. I tell him to piss off and go himself but eventually his moaning and groaning drives me out of bed and I storm off to the idiot in charge and tell him to either come or move this guy somewhere else or he will really need a hospital. The orderly refuses and I go back and tell the groaning dude. A while later he manages to crawl out of bed and crawl on all fours down the corridor to stop at the main entrance to the office and wail and continue un till the orderly relents and calls the doctor. A short while later the doc arrives and is well pissed off and gives the orderly and the groaning moaner hell. The doctor reluctantly agrees to call out the ambulance and have the guy taken to the hospital with stern admonitions that if its just a ruse to get out he will throw the book at him when he gets back. The guy goes. The ward is quiet and cold and we all go to sleep.

The next day we get the news. The moaning groaner was DOA.

A common practice for the more serious drug users to resort to when they know they will be given a urine test is to drink a few drops of disinfectant in a spoon of water. Another way is to get someone who you know is clean to pee into the container and then when you go for your test and are observed to see if you are actually filling up the container with your own pee, you distract and switch just before handing the thing over. The guy in the next door bed opted for the former, only problem is that he was nervous and so drank a whole spoon or perhaps more of pure disinfectant. He waited much too late to confess to the people who may have been able to help him through fear of admitting his guilt.

I felt like crap but there wasn't much I could do about it. The thing that really got to me was that he would go down statistically in the records of the "rehabilitation" center as a patient who was considered as successfully treated and make up the 2% of patients that are.

It was more than a month before I was ordered out one morning to do a "piss test" I would have to stand at the bog while the main warden would stand by and witness that the urine flowed right from my willy into the cup. I looked at him the whole time with a grin and blew him kisses and tried my hardest to fart but never managed. He took the lukewarm container of pilsner and dutifully delivered it to the nurse who was sitting there wishing she had his job. Predictably the results were negative. I had long since realized that there was no way on earth to get what was essentially the legal process to work. I had written out countless "declarations" stating my position and requesting release and discovered from one of the guys who cleaned the directresses office that they were automatically binned with out even a cursorary glance. I wasn't surprised.

The therapist that was assigned to the drug group was a woman by the name of Mrs Balt. She would manage to smoke the same number of cigarettes as the entire group at one sitting. In one hour I counted her smoke 11 head to tail while the guys who of course were prone to addiction would manage one and perhaps another at the end of the session tops. The favorite pastime for the guys was to try and rifle her bag and steal her ever present bottle of valium if she was called outside or went to the toilet and forgot to take it with her.

I was supposed to have one private session with her per week and at the first such meeting interrupted her halfway through some rambling nonsense and told her flat out " I have had more therapy in my life than I care to think about and all of it was bullshit. We both know that having me here is a farce and so I will simply abide by the rules until my date of release but I am not coming here once a week to sit through this. You are by far the worst excuse of a therapist I have yet met and so I will go somewhere quiet and read my book for my hour!" I got up and walked out. Before I did she said that it was her duty to send me to "D" group as I had used an expletive which was immediately punishable by ...going to the bottom of the ladder and then having to work your way back up again. Sounds trivial but it could mean another few months in the place and was no joke. I replied " Do what you have to do, Just remember that it means having my ugly face around for a lot longer"

I never went to another session or to "D" group. You would be sent to "D" group for any kind of so called serious offence. Swearing or running away meant that you came back and went to "D" group. Being there meant that you were last in line for any and everything. No phone calls or visits. No tuck shop and a host of other things designed to get you to toe the line and become a good tax paying citizen. Many of the "patients" there had volunteered for treatment.

Some had been sent there by their places of work. Many of the guys there were basically prisoners from the next door prison and other penal facilities around the country who had managed somehow to claim addiction and through hook or crook landed at the farm from where it was dead easy to escape or simply much less harsh than prison. That was true to the extreme. Life at the rehab was not hard at all. No real instances of rape or beatings. They happened but it was rare. The main thing for me was the utmost stupidity and hours of waiting and watching your life slip away.

The funny thing was that the majority who were for the most part absolute hopeless drunks looked down on the drug patients as people who had "blown their minds" and were brain damaged. The treatment was thus geared towards alcoholism and the tried and trusted method of "saving the lost souls" was to try to convert the inmates into God fearing alcoholics as opposed to heathen ones. We would receive "lectures" basically the person delivering the talk would be reading from a step by step illustration of alcohol dependence and simply substitute the word "drink" for "drugs" It was pathetic as some of the drug patients were heavy drug abusers who had pinned their hopes on being helped at "the farm" and were receiving zero help from people who were operating at maximum capacity as they knew zero in the first place. I walked out of a talk by some uniformed head sister one day when she was berating us as being disgusting sinners who were destroying our bodies. I asked her if the comment was made from a medical or religious standpoint. Not to be cornered so easily she replied" both!" and I was about to attack when she continued " what do you think all that Mandrax is doing to your stomach!"

All the heads in the bored shitless group popped up in unison and then looked around at one another with bemused expressions. I took the bait immediately "Aaaaw its not that bad!" she then started shouting as she was apt to when moved by the power of the spirit and continued to rain insults down in my direction. She then went into detail to show how superior her medical training was and proceeded to explain in minute detail the actual process of swallowing the tablet and then it going into your stomach and afterwards into your kidneys and then lungs and bladder, before being forced through the liver to emerge in the left ventricle and then off to run amuck in the brain, killing brain cells with wild abandon that will never be replaced and so leave you mentally deficient and in a perfect position for the Devil himself, cowardly sod, to take advantage and poses your soul for all eternity and you! you impertinent little brat! daring to question the logic of it all just proves that you have been destroyed by the destroyer and stand no chance of redemption unless you confess your sins before Jesus Christ our LooooOOOORRRD! AMENN

Now we all knew that was a load of horse since you *smoked* Mandrax!

So it went. It was like speaking in tongues.

Mornings were particularly painful. We would have to assemble in this auditorium type place and the Directress would bound in and stand at the podium and say " maak julle ogies toe!" Which is difficult to translate, as literally it means close your eyes, but it is said in a way that is reserved for children. Young children. Very young children. It was said in the same kind of sing song style that you would use in a kindergarten and it still makes me angry to just relate it here. It was just so totally demeaning to have to stand there and be subjected to it. Now, *IF* this was a technique such as the humiliating scenes created by such dubious, albeit relatively successful methods such as "tough love" then I would have been able to brush it under the carpet but it was just sheer blatant in your face contemptuous behavior that burned me like a red hot poker. I used to keep my eyes wide open and stare at the grown men who would simply stand there and do as they had been told.

There was no therapy to speak of. The guys who had serious problems effectively started taking other kinds of drugs while they were there. Blood tests were very rare as they were expensive and urine tests only really checked for cannabis. We had one guy who arrived and joined the drug group and although I forget his name I recollect his face clearly. He was very young, about 16 or perhaps 17. The minimum age for being put in an adult facility. He had been sent down for sniffing petrol and as I had been elected group leader I was put in charge of showing him the ropes and so on. He wasn't anything special and was relatively smart but misguided as all of us are at that age and more so the ones of us that experiment with drugs. I was really stern with him and told him as a kind of "independent" that sniffing petrol was just plain dumb. He countered that I had sniffed glue so how could I say that and I then proceeded to inform him about lead and its effects on the human body and mind. All went well for a while and he was a real spoilt brat and a handful to say the least. He had tried to run away a few times and so was put under the constant supervision of the main warden who would make him stand outside the office for hours as he had to me until he thought he had sufficiently worn the boy down. I bumped into him at supper a few days later as he had now been given a job and so on and with one look I noticed that he was "less clean" than he was when I had been with him. I confronted him straight out and told him I knew for a fact that he had sniffed petrol very recently. He of course played it down and denied it but I could see I was right by the way he behaved. And a tell tale blue tinge to the whites of his eyes. I decided to keep and eye on him and the very same evening I saw him sneak off and knew something was up. I saw him go to a fire hose box and take out the container that obviously contained the gasoline. He was about to sneak off to his private spot and I cornered him straight away and said "Everyone's and asshole except you! You're so fucking smart that

I can catch you only a few minutes after you treat me like one, so what does that make you? Einstein!"

He was shocked and thought I was going to crack him one but I just said " look, I'm not a policeman and I have explained the lead deal to you. If you want to kill yourself why not blow your head off? Its cool with me as I respect the choice but don't do it in my face as its an insult and I wont tolerate it OK?" and turned around and walked of leaving him with the petrol and his choice. He surprised me by coming up to me the next day and saying sorry and thank you for not turning him in and he had thrown the stuff away and was going to try to clean up his act. I said fine and went back to the mindless things we were doing and he went off to the head warden as usual. I paid no more attention to it and never really saw him much until one night I walked into the showers to find him sitting stark naked in the basin with feathers in his hair and staring

at himself in the mirror. All the guys were laughing at him and he was blissfully unaware. I walked up calmly to the basin next to his and proceeded to smear toothpaste and brush my teeth completely ignoring him. He saw me and spoke to me quite lucidly for a sentence or two and then went off into his fantasy world and in and out of the whole separate universe he was existing in. I asked him why he was sitting naked in the basin and he laughed hysterically and continued acting kookoo. I wasn't sure if he was putting it all on or if he was under the influence of something, I just don't know. It wasn't long before the head warden and his henchmen arrived and completely unnecessarily jumped on him and put him in a straight jacket and took him away. The next morning I was called in by the whole senior staff and some other big wigs that had come in from the outside and the head warden was there as well.

I was asked to give my account of what happened and there was much talk and speculation. One of the "outsiders" asked me what I thought may have happened. In a very serious and direct but professional way that respected me and my opinion. This was of course someone who wasn't familiar with the day to day of the institution and I noticed the head warden stiffen up as it had been me and not him who was asked the question. I thought a bit and then said it straight out " I think the guy has been secretly sniffing petrol for awhile now and possibly suffered from toxic psychosis" There was a stunned silence before the head warden exclaimed "What! Nonsense!" I was amazed as I didn't think the guy even knew what a toxic psychosis was. "How could he have got petrol? Huh?" shaking his head challengingly at me. I battled to keep a straight face but the other less discreet therapist didn't manage quite as well. Now I had personally seen him with the stuff but didn't know how either so I asked him " well he worked for you. What did he do?" the warden responded " he just cut the grass all day long!" I nearly fell off the chair and the "outsider" just slumped down with his head in his hands. I looked at them. I wasn't going to ask the obvious question and my silence and expression was enough anyhow. The outsider then straightened up and said " Minheer, did he use a lawnmower?" The warden answered " of course! Do you think we would make him cut it by hand?" I turned and looked at him in utter disbelief. He had not yet made the connection that was painfully obvious to all in the room. I could have punched him right there.

We later heard that the poor little bugger had totally lost it and ended up being permanently institutionalized. I often wonder what may have happened if I had turned him in instead of doing what I did.

Things were bad and the guys in the group were complaining terribly, but only to each other which wouldn't change anything. There were a few more incidents that got me to thinking about trying to get someone from the outside to do something about the dismal situation. It was pointless going to the press as it was illegal to report anything as the farm was a government institution. I thought about trying to go to SANCA and telling the therapist there what the real situation was and see if she could do something about it. My idea was to do a runner and go directly to the offices and then come straight back with her knowledge and then they wouldn't be able to throw the book at me. I was in two minds and the deciding blow came when I was told very smugly by Mrs Balt that I would not be going to the "A" group for some or other reason. I remember saying to her" You cant do that!" and she replied "here I can do anything I like!" I thought that's it! I'm not going to let you get away with it any longer.

Now here's the thing...as I'm walking up towards my living quarters I see the group standing together and they're deep in conversation. They call me over and tell me " Listen Bro.. We are going to hop that fence today and were going to go to SANCA and tell those people what's happening here. Now you know how to talk and so we thought to ask you if you will come with us. What do you say?" I started laughing and told them I was on my way to grab my leather jacket as I was on my way over the fence myself with exactly the same idea in mind!!" we all laughed and went nuts and it was no more than 10 mins later that we had hopped the fence in
broad daylight and were walking through the bush.

We hadn't gone very far before we noticed a van on the hill opposite and two people looking at us with what seemed like binoculars. We continued walking and sure enough they came over and stopped on the road next to us. The guys got out and sure enough they were guards from the prison. They asked us what we were doing. I immediately explained that we were a six a side soccer team who were on our way back to Jo Burg after playing our match and were taking a short cut through the veld to get on the right highway. They said that we were close to the prison and maybe it would be a good idea if they gave us a lift to the highway to avoid any trouble. What could we do? Running was out as we would get shot and declining the lift would arouse more suspicion and so cheerfully we thanked them and hopped straight into the lions jaws. I joked that at least we would be back for supper. We weren't of course.

We drove into the prison and when we got out we were surrounded by guards with shotguns who screamed blue murder at us and we were strip searched and chucked into a cell. A little later we were shoved into a van and taken to the Culinan police station and put in a cell. 12 people in a tiny cell. Freezing cold and of course everybody nervous and smoking like chimneys which I just couldn't handle and so grabbed a mattress and bedded down at the door.

The occupants of the cell welcomed our company and told their stories which left me more than a little discouraged at our chances of getting out of there any time soon. The one guy was dressed in the filthiest suit I had ever seen and his story was a bleak one. His wife had conspired with her lover to get him arrested and since the lover was a policeman in the small town it wasn't hard to prefabricate a charge and have him held. According to the law in SA you are guilty until proved innocent and so a charge of wife battery for example was one where you could be locked up and then face the daunting task of trying to contact legal representatives to handle your case and so on. Its not like you see in American movies where you get the telephone call and the lawyer rushes to your aid and you go out on bail. His wife had apparently only wanted to get him out of the way for a short time and it turned out that he had been in the cells for 5 months! He had been to Pretoria to appear in court once and his case had been postponed and here he was. In the same suit he had gone to work in that fateful morning. No one had stepped in to help.

I thought it was a pretty rough thing to have the lot of us stuffed into a cell like that until I looked through the drain pipe at a grinning black face that was in the cell next door where there were 19 people. And some of them had been there for nearly two years!! I was subdued and pensive for most of the time.

We were transferred a few days later to Pretoria Central Prison where I spent two weeks in the "stockade" before having to make my court appearance. It was a short time due to pressure created by my brother in laws lawyer friend and the other guys stayed between 2 and 7 months before they went to court. I was very grateful to him. I would look forward to the time that they would lock us up in our single cells with the stinking metal bucket in the corner and our one square of toilet paper. It was better than being out in the population.

I was thrown into the van with on of the others and driven back to Cullinan.

After eventually making it to the courtroom we await our turn while the day to day cases are being done by a stern looking ultra strict judge. The bailiff was a chirpy black constable who was continually wheeling and dealing with the prisoners. One case in particular shook me. An old black guy gets brought into the court and the charge is read. "Drinking in public" The judge looks at him with utter boredom and says " how do you plead?" the black guy says "not guilty Baas!" The judge clenches his jaw and bores a look into the public prosecutor who is a dyke bitch notorious for handing out the maximum penalty to anything that pees standing up. A word of clarification is called for here. A lesbian is a homosexual female and deserves the same respect as anyone, irrespective of sexual orientation. This woman was not in the same category and I don't apologize for the derogatory description. Man hating Dragon lady could also suffice but then I would be showing disrespect to Dragons that I love. But I digressionate.

She turns to the bailiff and tells him in Afrikaans " take the dog outside and teach him some manners!" the bailiff complies in his particularly bouncy way, escorts the old man out of the room with ever present ear to ear grin and proceeds to beat the crap out of the old guy right outside the door to the accompanying stream of abuse that he no doubt learnt from his white colleagues.

The door opens and the old man takes his place with bloodied nose and bumps starting to form of his forehead. The judge repeats " how do you plead" the black man responds " guilty Baas!" The judge looks down at him and says "why are you wasting the courts time Hey? Do you think I've got nothing better to than sit here with you kaffirs?" ..." Two months for drinking and one month for contempt!"

We all sit in apprehensive silence. Eventually the first name is called and I'm surprised to find out that we will be dealt with separately. Mrs Balt walks into the court at this point and takes her place next to the prosecutor! I think.."wait a minute, that's a funny place for her to be..??" and she starts chatting quietly and looking around and gesturing with her head in our direction every so often. They're obviously good buddies.

I look at the charge sheet and see the charge "escaping from government rehabilitation facility" I sigh with relief as I know that cant stand up since we had not yet been noted as missing when we were caught and so couldn't be charged. I lean back and watch. The first of us gets called to the stand. As the prosecutor starts speaking she takes out a permanent marker, draws a line through the charge and pens in " trespassing on prison ground!" I'm flabbergasted!

I blurt out "Hey! You cant do that!" she turns round to me and says "Oh yes I can!" with an expression of pure spite. I say "Really? According to what law?" and she replies " MY law. The one I studied at university for seven years to get!" The judge slams down the gavel and declares "Silence! One more peep from you and I'll throw you inside for six months!" I duly shut up.

The first one of us is an English guy who had volunteered for treatment. He has no prior offences and the judge takes this into account and postpones his case to a later date to allow for the relative paperwork to be done as there isn't a question of a plea. We were on prison ground. We couldn't have been otherwise unless we somehow managed to levitate as the farm is situated within the grounds.

Another interesting point is that if you asked about the status of the "farm" you would be told flat out to your face that it was an "open" facility and there were no constraints on movements to and from the place. "You can leave anytime! No one is stopping you!" Is something we had to bear all too often.

My turn. I stand. The charge is read and the procedure goes on and I ask the judge if I may represent myself. He looks at me with amused interest and grants my request. I figure that I'm going down anyway so I may as well get a chance to have my say on record. If I were to be represented by a state appointed lawyer I wouldn't say a word. I start off by calling my first witness. The guy who has just been center stage. I ask him the questions. Why did you admit yourself? Do you feel like you are being helped? Will you continue with your treatment? Why did you hop the fence? Were you coerced into doing so by anyone or was it your own decision? Etc. Next witness. Mrs Balt! You should have seen the expression on that womans face! It was without a price. You could even say "priceless" and you wouldn't be far wrong.

Questions. Name? occupation? Qualifications? What is the success rate for the rehabilitation center? Who makes up the 2%? Why do you think the patients that hopped the fence feel the way they do? "Thank you"

I look at the judge. He has just heard the woman admit that only two percent are considered successfully rehabilitated cases and they are comprised of the patients who die during treatment!! No shit. The judge looks at me and says " do you realize that in effect you have just entered a plea of guilty?"

I reply to him that " if I am guilty for jeopardizing my release date by agreeing to act as spokesmen for a group of human beings who by their own admission are desperately seeking help to re assimilate into society, as a patient who has never once been punished for not complying with treatment, then yes I am guilty. I have the utmost respect for the law and accept whatever consequences my actions create. This is the basic idea of rehabilitation I would imagine. To get to the point where one can make choices and understand the repercussions and do "The right thing" regardless of the discomfort it may create. The public prosecutor here is manipulating the law in a way that borders on contempt but more importantly she shows by her actions that she is blind to the bigger picture. By throwing us all in jail for whatever amount of time doesn't solve anything. It makes things worse because it exposes these people to the real criminal elements in society and then releases them back into a rehabilitation that isn't effective and all of this at states expense. Wouldn't it just be better all round to try and help these people so that everyone benefits? The sooner they get better and manage to maintain stable lives, the sooner they will be able to get work and so contribute to society and not be a burden to it"

Its not word for word, but that's pretty much the gist of what I said.

He looked at me. Well, he stared at me, unblinking for what could have been maybe 3 minutes and I struggled to hold his gaze levelly without arrogance. Eventually he said " 6

months jail" Whack of the gavel " Suspended for 6 months"

The tension left my body like the air from a balloon and I thought I would collapse. The prosecutor glared at me and I looked her straight in the eye without any emotion until she looked away.

So I was the first to return to the farm and the first time I saw Mrs Balt again she took the attitude that all was well and nothing bad had happened and although I was a naughty little boy she had it in her heart to forgive me. I remember it well. She was sitting in the hospital and I arrived for the "detox!" I was changing out of my clothes and she was sitting with a new arrival as she was supposed to and never had before and she looked up at me and said" Oh my teddy bear! You're back! Well I hope you learnt your lesson my boy!"

I was openly hostile to her "I'm not your little boy for one and don't patronize me with condescending terms like teddy bear either. You may be able to fool the new people by pretending to be a therapist but you don't fool me. Why don't you take another Valium and shut up!" We never exchanged another word the whole time I was there.

You could get visitors on a Sunday and I only had one visit from my mom once. I was called out as I had a visitor and so went to see who it was. I thought perhaps the guys from the band would perhaps have found a few hours on a weekend to drive out and at least say hello or phone but sadly, nothing. My punk buddies visited on two occasions and also came to pick me up the day I was released. They were great and I loved them. The visitor was of course my mother who had come alone possibly due to guilt or whatever. We loved each other but somehow couldn't communicate and caused each other so much unnecessary pain. I said hello and "what do you want" She took the usual tone " well I wanted to see if you had come to your senses and were ready to start behaving like a human being"

She hadn't come all that way to see me. She had come as usual to see herself. I took the packages of food she had brought turned around and walked away without a word.

On the date of my release I took my small bag and headed for the gate. As I went through the head warden said to me "See you soon Pommie!" I stopped and turned to him and in fluent Afrikaans said " I was here for 6 months but you are here for life!" and blew him another kiss. I didn't pause to see the effect it must have had on him.

I got to the car where my friends were waiting and as I got in was handed a bottle of Southern Comfort to the loudest cheer you can imagine. We drove out past the fields and the guards with the music flat out and our heads bobbing in unison. There was no need to say a word.

It was over.

Skate or Die!

It was three days after I arrived back in the civilian world that I smoked my first 'Button" This was a Mandrax tablet that would be crushed fine and then the powder would be mixed in or/and sprinkled over the top of a "bottle neck" pipe which was packed to the brim with dope. Usually pretty poor quality dope. I hadn't smoked buttons before as it was something I didn't want to get into but for some reason when I was called up by a guy who had just been released from the farm and going to meet him to find he was already smoking and offered me a "cream" I went for it. Buttons were a world of their own. The people who used them were pretty much more hard core than the average pot smoker and the places where you went to obtain the stuff were rough as hell. You had to watch for the ever present undercover police and the dodgy characters hanging about who would rob you if you were a little too dozy, or not. We used to usually go in two's with some kind of concealed weapon. Buttons were expensive and highly addictive and knocked your head off. But only for a short while which made it an excellent drug to sell if you were that way inclined. I kept it to a minimum but even so it caused me to visibly lose weight and become short tempered if there were none around. I had seen long time abusers in the dingiest tin shacks who would smoke all day and all night constantly and when they coughed it sounded like two strands of cotton blowing in a football stadium. The average pusher was usually a chronic abuser and a common ploy would be to get you to sit down and smoke there and then they would basically wolf the lot down and there wasn't much you could do or say as you were on his turf and one whistle and you could get badly carved up by the many who didn't want whiteys to come around their neighborhood attracting attention. It was a crap scene and I was aware of it before I started and didn't stay into it for long. Instead I would spend more time skating and working really hard to get better and try to compete with the younger guys who were financially in much better shape than I was. The natural thing was to hang around the shops that sold skate gear and so, after placing quite well in the SA Championships, I managed to first get sponsored and then offered a job at one of the stores. I had moved into the servants room at a friends house and would go to work each day and sell skate gear. The manager of the shop took me aside one day and told me about his scheme of opening up a shop of his own and since he had been a surfer and tried skating once, claimed to be a "Skater" the deal was that he wanted me to go in with him and run the shop. It would mean we would be taking a huge risk and that I would be paid the princely sum of 20rand a day but I thought it was great. The whole industry was getting bigger and the scene was run by outlets that were run by sharks in for the quick buck.

Our idea of opening a "skater" run shop was a good one. We soon got premises and I made the logo and we got T shirts and stickers printed and due to our obvious street credibility we managed to assemble the hottest team of the day. It was truly great. I was fulfilling my dream of being in effect a "pro" and although I pretty much sucked compared to the other guys in the open division, I would give it stick and try my best to keep up. I particularly liked to do demo's as I liked the relaxed performance in front of all kinds of crowds all over the country and the signing of autographs and throwing stickers and all the things that went with being a skateboarder. It all went well and although the business seemed to be staying afloat my salary wasn't improving and it came to a head when I was idly buggering about at a skate facility one weekend when I was approached by a "skate dad" and shown with great pride the board that he had made in his garage. Now this wasn't the first time I had seen such efforts from parents with a quick cash fixation who would knock something up out of plywood or some wildly out of place material, thinking that they were going to retire when the "craze" had bitten the dust.

I reached over and virtually at the moment I touched it I handed it back to him with a laugh "Oh no..forget it" The guy looked at me and pretty non plussed said "What! What do you mean? You haven't even looked at it!" I replied " I don't need to. I've felt it and its way too heavy. Nobody can skate that!" He was indignant and countered with "But its ultra strong! I rode my four by four over it and it didn't break!" I laughed at that and pretty much jollying him along challenged " how do you expect to sell the second one then?" And looked him straight in the face for a while before shrugging and getting on my board to go and do some "work!" I thought no more of it until the next week when he walked straight into the shop, stopped in front of me, pulled a brand new board out of the bag he was carrying and issued the challenge "what about this then?!" I took it and gave it the once over and saw that although still on the heavy side it was a very well made board and the best "garage job" I had ever seen. I gave him the verdict and noted the shortcomings such as the shape itself being a little questionable.

. "OK! Why don't you make me a shape then and I'll make you a board!?" I went straight to my bag and hauled out one of my many templates that I used when I cut factory produced boards into my own personal shapes. He turned and walked straight out and I was more than a little curious about this "skate dad" He seemed to be quite serious. Needless to say he appeared before the weekend with the first of what were to be many prototypes for me to test and give him feed back on. The first one took me 4 hrs to break !

I was well curious by this stage and so took him up on it when he invited me to his "factory" I was shocked to discover that this guy was really serious and that he had sectioned off an area of his existing business to make a space where he proposed to make internationally competitive skateboards in SA. The companies name was aptly Skates International and he wanted me to head the design dept and be the first signed pro! What could I say? I was blown away. Problem was that I had made a commitment to the skate shop and wasn't just about to dump my partner. I breached the subject quite openly explaining my dilemma and announced my decision that I wanted to give it a shot. My partner was naturally none too happy about it but understood that it was something that held more positive prospects than the current one at the shop with him. I agreed and promised that although I was moving to essentially a new team, I would still represent the shops team at the upcoming nationals. Which I did, much to the annoyance of my soon to be new employer. I managed to gain a respectable third place in the freestyle that year and was beaten out by the two best guys in the country for sure. I reckon that any of us could come out tops on a given day and I didn't feel disappointed at all. I remember just before my run looking over at Simon and Manuella (the Toxiksox bassist and his girlfriend) and them laughing at me as they recognized the expression on my face they knew so well from the band days. I remember grinning at Wa as we used to call her and looking down at the front of my T shirt to see my heart visibly pounding. It's an amazing experience to compete in events such as this. I can equate it to gymnastic routines or figure skating more like. You go and work on your routine until you can do it blindfolded and then after months you finally find yourself out in front of a huge crowd and you know your name is going to be called next and there's no way out. How many times I had to suppress the urge to run I couldn't care to remember. I would treat it like a test of courage in a way. It was the same when getting up to play in the band. I was always ultra shy and dreaded the stage. I had to appear a few times as a child and on one particular occasion I remember having to recite a poem in front of the whole school at age 11. "I must go down to the sea again. The lonely sea and the sky...." I remember a few seconds before my queue and then ......nothing. My only recollection is of being aware of my face and particularly ears burning with heat.

Its still the same today on the odd occasion when I perform. It doesn't show apparently, but inside it is total chaos. I struggle with a whirlpool of swirling emotions all flowing around and reaching different climatic intensities that make me want to scream. Somehow I don't.

I think I also got third in the slalom event which I was disappointed with as I new I was faster than everybody and could cream em!

The following year I did and it was with immense satisfaction that it happened to be the bassist of the first band that came in that auspicious night and dragged his amplifier out of the band room who was to be the runner up in the final. The irony was that I was now independent and unsponsored and he was working for Skates International and had a special board made out of carbon fiber and space ship materials that he was certain would give him the edge. I skated a standard street set up and hastily put my shoes on without socks! Ha! Ha! I have to be fair though, it was close. But the gold medal went to me that year and history will remember me as the SA Slalom champ for 1991. I still slalom on my own every now and again and the irony is that I'm faster today than I was then. I'll take on any challengers age 40+!!!!

Sunday afternoon. Bored shitless. My girlfriend and a friend decide that we can go and jump the train as there are no conductors working and it beats wandering around aimlessly. We go down to the bottom end of town and ride the train up and down the reef eventually getting out at the Ellis park station. Somebody had the bright idea to get off there as there would be loads of black spectators watching the soccer that would be played on Sundays at the Rugby grounds and we would somehow manage to "score" It was a dumb idea but something to do and in any case I had never seen a football match with the two main opposing teams playing each other. Orlando Pirates and Kaiser Chiefs. They were great teams and we were sure we could at least sneak in.

The first surprise was that there was no charge at the gate! So we waltzed straight in to a jam packed stadium and the cloud of smoke from the crowd. Now at a white sports event such as Cricket, you would be greeted with the smell of barbecuing meat, but here all we could smell was ...DOPE!

Wow! I was amazed. I stood staring at the crowd and would be totally shocked to see a guy stand up off the telephone book he was sitting on and tear out a page. Then take a wad of green leaves and roll a joint with the whole page! He would take few puffs and pass it down the line and another one would come his way and take a few puffs and so on. I was like "WOW! Where are the cops?"

There were people standing on each others shoulders to see and it was wild. I was awestruck. The atmosphere was unbelievable and the place was all of 2.5km from my house. I had only been there once or twice as a kid when I got my first "job" selling milk and orange juice to the fans at the rugby matches. This was something else completely.

The match ends and we move off to the station with of course the idea that we will accost one of the guys and ask for some weed.

Now I am standing on the platform and taking swigs from a bottle of Amaretto while looking around to see if there are any people who would be conducive to giving us a little of the green stuff. I have also got my eye on a skinny little black uniformed policeman. It's not long before he wanders over to me and takes the bottle from my hand and looks at me questioningly. I smile at him and look over at almost every black guy standing there with a bottle of beer in their hands and shrug. Now drinking in public is basically illegal in SA but as always there can be, and usually are exceptions to this rule/law. His answer is to take the bottle and empty it over my head. I keep a straight face and ask him if he is going to do the same to the hundreds of people standing on the platform or only me. He replies "I don't see anyone with alcohol, only you!" I reply "Ahh!.....You don't? I see many people, one Whitey and one

Asshole!" He starts to get angry but backs down as we are starting to attract a crowd.

We are standing on the platform and I hear the snippets of talk from the younger ones and I don't like much of what I hear. They are thinking of "taking" my girlfriend and dropping the two of us (my friend and I) off the train a little further down the line. I realize the danger as I am the only one who understands a few words and my girlfriend and friend are being ultra friendly and being slowly maneuvered towards the front of the platform so that they can be easily bundled into the approaching train. I go over to my buddy and tell him with a straight face and smile that were in deep shit. He knows I'm not the kind of person to joke around and it's been more than one occasion that my "smarts" has saved both of our hides. My girlfriend is a different story. She is determined to score and I know she is not the quickest on the uptake when it comes to these things. As I am making my way over to her, one of the black guys pinches her butt and she turns to me with absolute fury and demands that I do something. I tell her straight out "Time to go!"...."NOW!" She doesn't want to listen and things are turning nasty. I turn to my friend and tell him to grab her and walk away. I turn to the crowd of guys and try to take the attention away from them by addressing them and beginning to deliver a lecture about the fact that we are not racist and so why are you treating us like we are? and so on. All this, while the precious Amaretto is dripping off my face. My girlfriend, who is completely oblivious to the danger pipes in and wants to get some answers too and I am doing my best to try to stay calm and get out of the steadily worsening situation. It's at this point that a chubby black guy comes up and tells her "Don't try to reason with the mob! Just go! Quickly!" She begins to backchat him and he takes out his ID and shoves it in her face. She takes one look and turns around and walks off down the stairs, my friend in tow. The man is a policeman and tells me to go too. I turn to everyone and let rip with a string of abuse. Basically that I am not going to be forced through fear to do such and such and blah,

blah, blah. I see that they have made it safely away and so I continue to hold the mobs attention by talking about peace and the future and all kinds of shit to buy some extra time and sow confusion. I then turn and walk off slowly and purposefully. As I get to the staircase the train arrives and the protagonists in the group throw cardboard boxes at me and proceed to pee a rain of urine down from the platform as I refuse to run and continue walking with the under cover policeman close behind me. I get to the subway and turn to him and thank him as he risked his life to help us and he tells me to run as fast as I can for as long as I can before turning in the opposite direction and doing the same. I take his advice and its not far before I realize that no one is giving chase and I slow to a trot.

A few blocks further on I get to where my friend and girlfriend are waiting and see that he is pale and sitting down. She however turns to me with all the venom in the world and accuses me of being a coward for not punching the guy who pinched her ass.

???

The reason for my not being a part of the company was due to the fact that upon my arrival back at work in early 91 I started making more frequent trips to the drug merchant in my company car with the predictable result that it would eventually lead to problems with work. I was not surprised or even upset about the deal which may sound strange but the situation at work was not what it was when I had started a few months earlier. The first incident was when a new sales rep was hired. A true blue asshole. He had been an employee for a very well established international skateboard company and in his obvious opportunistic way, could see the very real future with the people I was with. He had become kind of a "friend" by dropping by at the house that I was sharing with Simon whenever the weather was fair and on occasion giving me equipment to test and so on. It of course culminated in me recommending him to the boss and after a short while he was the official rep. I had a ulterior motive for this as I was currently having to fulfill the role of 'Everything" and the selling thing was what I hated most. It was on the fateful occasion of the 90 nationals that he came with in the car and after being exposed to the hard core non stop party on the way down he used as much leverage as he could to manipulate his way closer to the boss. I had been warned of this kind of behavior by him on previous occasions by almost everyone who knew him, but he had been ok to me so I didn't take much notice. I eventually split with him and his response was to inform the boss as to all my misdemeanors (of which there was a list of what he knew of and a longer one he couldn't have dreamed about!!)

The boss's reaction was to cool somewhat and then to freeze over completely at a later stage. I was slowly becoming more and more disillusioned with the whole scene and after one particularly bad weekend the boss arrived at my doorstep and demanded the keys to the car and informed me that he wanted to have a meeting with my father present!! I was more than a little curious. What on earth would he want?

Turns out that the guy was very interested in employing me for a very long period of time. He told my father and I that he would be prepared to fund a full university education and offer me "real" employment in his company proper and not just the kind of "sideline" affair the skate company was compared to his real business. All of this was dependent on me undergoing "treatment" full time at whatever place he had in mind. I was to consider his offer.

It was a very lucrative firm and had operations way up into Africa. He had taken me one day to the brand new office block that he was constructing on prime real estate land overlooking one of the valleys in the very affluent northern suburbs of Johannesburg. He had taken me to the very spot where "My office" would be complete with where my drawing board would be situated and the secretaries office and so on. As much as I was impressed by all this I was at the same time a little un nerved as I felt that pretty soon I would be owned, so to speak. Being a fierce individualistic kind of person, this was worrying. More so when he sent me for a haircut one day!! Or tried to anyway...

Long story short, after carefully considering what he had offered I reached my decision when one day while working in the factory knocking out hundreds of boards I was being ordered around by a guy who I had personally brought up to JHB from Cape Town and secured a job, working at the factory. Not only that, I had agreed to let him stay at the house and moved into the lounge to sleep on a mattress whilst giving him my bed!! He didn't do a stitch to try and get a place and would lick the boss's butt all day long which eventually led to him being given the title of "foreman" He took to the task like a sergeant major and proceeded to start ordering me about and walking about with puffed up self importance and come around and "inspect" my work. I was well pissed at his turn around and lack of gratitude and the ironic thing was that he was taught how to do the job by me!! So lording it over me wasn't such a cool thing. We nearly got into fisticuffs one day and I was ready to vent all my pent up frustration at that point. I stopped in mid swing and walked straight up to the boss's office and quit on the spot. I walked home.

From there things went flat out downhill and one day after being picked up by the cops for loitering suspiciously I went to my sister and told her that I needed help. I had reached the end of my tether and knew that I was going to end up brain damaged or dead if I didn't drastically change my attitude. The result was that I volunteered for treatment at a clinic in Pretoria where I was expected to go for an interview and be "accepted" as a genuine case before being checked in. The treatment cost money and my sister and my folks paid. I was accepted and for the first time ever received something close to what could be considered fair treatment. The whole turning point was that I was genuine. I had stopped many times before and was determined to make it permanent this time. I succeeded of course and had many very good sessions and some very challenging personal experiences that made me see myself in a light I had thought had been extinguished long before.

After being released I stayed with my sister for a while and would go and judge skateboard competitions. I eventually got elected as head judge for the national circuit and would be paid for my efforts. At one of these events the boss from the skate company came up to me and in front of everyone,

Climbed up the stairs of the ramp and on the platform that doubled as a stage shook my hand! It sounds like no big deal but the skate community is a small and intimate group of people and it was his way of showing publicly that there was no bad blood between us as had been rumored. I thought it was typical of him and although I had some very clear differences of opinion regarding racial attitudes I immensely respected the man and admired his strength, drive and professionalism. It meant a lot to me.

I eventually went down to Cape Town to where my parents had moved to retire and although our relationship was still rocky at the best of times and there were still isolated incidents of drug abuse and family upheaval, there were also glimmers of light and moments where I felt very positive about myself. Sadly though, not about my future. I had been a relatively successful skateboarder and managed to skate with legends like Tony Hawk and appeared in the same magazine when he came to SA to do a demo tour. I got the front cover and the interview and he got the article and center spread poster.

What was next? I got an opportunity to work as a ramp builder and did that for a while and loved the job. There wasn't much full time call for a ramp builder though and so something had to be done.

The break came when on one of the "explosions" at home I took to staying with a friend for a few days and somehow started working where he was on a herb farm weeding the organically grown plants. I could move onto the plot and stay in a tent and although there was no hot water I would make do by sneaking a shower when I got too smelly at the caravan park close by. I was earning 25rands a day and was dead happy. This continued for months and the added bonus was that the boss of the place would also take a Tai Chi class once a week which I attended religiously.

I really loved working out in the open and although I was forced to work in our huge garden as a boy I never really knew much about plants and even less about herbs. I was hooked! I was amazed at the variety and the absolute wealth of the world of herbs and their various medicinal and culinary uses. It was a lot to absorb and the boss of the place who was known to all by his nickname "Spook" was a walking encyclopedia of botanical names, classifications, uses, things to watch out for and if your goldfish had hay fever he knew at least twenty readily available things in your neighbors garden that you could use to fix the poor sneezing bugger in the blink of an eye. He even knew how to fix your eye if it blinked too much. He was fantastic. He was also married to a Jew and perhaps this is why one day when the conversation drifted there, that he suggested that I go for a visit to Israel. I was anti the idea as I never saw the appeal of the place. All those camels and sand just didn't do it for me. He explained that it was a good place to learn about growing things as the climate was quite variable from place to place. Also, I didn't have to go to a Kibbutz where I was expected to volunteer, I could go to a Moshav which was much the same as a collective farm and where I could be paid for my work. It was VERY hard work though but the whole deal, according to him was well worth the adventure. I was more than a bit interested and as my mom was always keen on me going to Israel and my dad had on more than one occasion suggested that I go to a Kibbutz to sort myself out, I thought they would be open to the idea. Or rather paying for the ticket that would play a major role in making the idea a reality.

They were..and after much telephoning and information gathering I was informed one day that my dad had taken out a loan and through some "agent" had secured a ticket and the whole thing was sorted for me to go to work on a Moshav in the Holy Land. It turned out that this so called agent was a bloody shark who stole my folks money and didn't do a thing to help me except tell me at the airport where I could catch the bus to the Moshav office!!

So it was not long afterward that I found myself standing in the departure lounge at the airport with a bag, a skateboard and an electric guitar (without an amp!) saying goodbye to my folks and soon to be boarding a plane that would take me out of South Africa to the so called Promised Land, years and years after I had landed at the airport in JHB to the chilly reception and vowed I would leave at the very next available opportunity!!

HALELUYIA!

CODA

Its hard for me to write this last chapter. Firstly because I don't have the cassette I originally captured my thoughts on and because I am unsure of how to finish. I have actually not followed the cassettes at all. I would start to listen and then begin to write and the thoughts would flow and I would just keep going. When I would listen a little later I would find that I had almost used the exact words to describe the events. I may have kissed the girl before sipping my beer instead of sipping first and kissing after, but it was clear that there had been drinking and kissing! If you know what I mean...

The thoughts and memories would flow and I would battle in my "hunt and peck" style to keep up.

Ridiculously so. The other day it was raining and I sat for 12 hours straight! When I tried to stand it felt like my body had been cast in painful cement. That's a first for me.

I have cried a lot while writing this. I have had to stop on occasion and just sit here and sob. It's a skill that I have spent more than 20 years trying to regain as I stopped crying at a very young age and I don't think I'm good enough at it yet to be able to do it in public. I'm still unsure of what exactly I'm trying to say. If anything. I think about these tears immediately feel stupid as I don't consider the reasons worthy enough and really couldn't tell you why I feel such a welling up of emotion. I have touched on some of my experiences with black people and made comparisons to our relative distance. "They" have more reason to shed tears comparatively than I ever could have but that's not the issue. Pain is personal. No one can say "his is worse than hers" no one. Pain is pain and South African history in the Apartheid era was written in it.

I have spoken at length about the two dominant black people in my life but must stress that they were not the only ones, black or white. I was blessed to be exposed to the most extraordinary human beings in my lifetime. Both then and now. I couldn't begin to mention them all even if I wanted so its enough to say that there were many. Both good and bad. People seem to try to negate the "bad" things but to me, although they are not always welcome, they are important. It depends on your attitude. You can live life as a victim to circumstance and rejoice when its good and be filled with self pity when its bad and bemoan your fate. The black people showed me what it is to be positive. Struggle when its hard and persevere until things get better and then celebrate. Celebrate life! Jabulani! A word that rolls off the tongue and even Americans can say it. It embodies an attitude and way of life that is hard to describe to an outsider. But that provides the glue that keeps the colorful fabric of African life stuck together.

I never went back to South Africa for any substantial length of time after I left for Israel so many years ago. I learnt about the release of Mandela and then the dismantling of Apartheid and never went out to celebrate or anything like I saw others doing. It never really struck a nerve until I went back on a visit and saw the changes that are usually noted by people who leave a place and then return years later. I wasn't caught up in the day to day politics and familiar with the usual groans and gripes about new injustices and stories of corruption. None of that. I could see with a fairly objective eye. I liked some of what I saw and didn't like others. In some ways nothing had really changed. In others it was a world away from the country I had left behind to rot in its own fetid juices.

Being away from your country of origin and living in a foreign one serves to expose you not so much to the new culture. It's a misconception. You go to China thinking you are going to learn all about the people and all you are bounced against continually is not their culture but your own! I learnt what it is to be a South African by being away from the place.

It was said by (I think) Sir Lourens van der Post that deep in the heart of every African there beats a drum. Something to that effect. A drum that beats there under the surface and that is connected to the land and place that is Africa. It doesn't matter if you are black or white at all. Growing up in Africa makes you connected to the soil and the people in a way that is not possible for others.

I was quizzed and am still by my students from around the globe about South Africa and about my attitude to the "change" and I don't know what to say really. I never thought it would happen in my life time!!! But I thank a God I'm dubious about anyway that it did. Those guys could have taken all the perpetrators of torture and terrible acts of suppression and put them all against a wall and machine gunned the lot of them!! The world would have made a huge fuss about it for a day and then gone back to the sports pages. The constant fear whilst I was growing up had it's opportunity to play out and it turned out to be a huge anti climax!! How lame was the truth and reconciliation committee!! Sorry dudes, but forgiveness and rising above your animal instincts. Justifiable animal instincts I may add. Just does not sell enough news papers!! Thank God for Bosnia!! Now that's something that will keep the circulation within the expected parameters.

How cool was that? Face your tormentors and openly admit where you were wrong. It's a whole new concept in human relations and I whole heartedly applaud the people involved in choosing this plan of action over and above the historical one that arrests our dubious evolutionary ascension as a species. I would love to meet Nelson Mandela. He is one cool Madiba and I would like to give him huge hug and a sculpture! He's my man and my major inspiration as the embodiment of everything I have always recognized as inherent in a race that, different from my own and looked down upon by most of my fellows, possessed a wisdom that is enviable. The dead cow story comes to mind. An ability to go straight to the heart of a matter and maintain a simple outlook in a world of devious, convoluted, complex, confusion.

I must remind the reader that this is wholly my current opinion and can not be considered as an opinion that is contemporary in the sense that I'm looking backward from the outside and have not lived in SA for years and so cannot speak on behalf of anyone else who may be living there today. The last time I went to visit I was asked on more than one occasion "Where you from! Hey?" I found it amusing and hard to answer with the ease I am accustomed to doing elsewhere.

Imagine if the American Empire took our old pal Saddam Whatsisface and gave him a cool job like using his Arabic skills to translate ancient texts or letting him help out by washing sheets in a Kuwaiti hospital or weeding the gardens at the white house or making him earn his living so that he could afford to pay the expenses incurred by his incarceration and so take some pressure off the taxman????

Kooky ideas I admit. And a little on the lenient side for a psychopathic mass murderer and committer of crimes against humanity. A humanity that is aptly proven by his death sentence and execution. Seen as a backdrop to the truth and reconciliation committee that was dreamed up by a bunch of legislators and primitives from the jungles it makes me wonder at the miracle.

I grew up completely ignorant. A fact that boggles my mind even today. How could I have been so bloody dumb? I grew up in the shadow of a constant fear and it resulted in me being a coward on too many occasions to mention. I'm not so much ashamed as awed due to the fact that I'm a little older and have the advantage of hindsight and I realize I cant change the past. If you ask me what I would have done differently in hindsight, I would think of many, many, many things that would have changed but in reality I realize that not only is it a pointless speculation to try and make since what's done is done it is all wishful thinking. Life is a learning experience and all the dumb things I did I did completely committed to the moment and that's what I still do today. Life is a wonderful, magical gift and each experience forms part of a wider and deeper tapestry like matrix that cannot be seen in terms of isolated events, much in the way a court case is managed. Life is interwoven and not simply a chronological series of events. The person who I am today and the country that South Africa is today are products of such a multifaceted interactive process. You cant make an equation so simply and I wont be tempted to do so. Instead I would much rather try to move forward and see how to avoid the mistakes of the past. How to instill infrastructures into a societal framework that would prevent such things from recurring. South Africa is faced with a whole busload of different problems today and it is far more pertinent to address them than to dwell on the past. We should never forget but not be caught in the quagmire of dwelling in the past which is simply a breeding ground for the re emergence of bitterness and hate that doesn't serve anyone. Least of all ourselves. I'm preaching I know but it's the way I feel and have always felt. Punk rock was the cultural movement that embodied those ideals. Lets forget about the past and move into a brand new positive future. Idealistic as all hell but I still feel that way.

I'm older now and try to live the healthy life. I'm successful for the most part but there are still the sporadic instances of "losing my mind" I marvel at the fact that I have managed to survive at all and am thankful for each day I am alive. I am a professional sculptor and proudly represent South Africa all around the world at sculpture symposia that I am lucky enough to be accepted by and create clouds of dust and make a horrendous noise while standing under the multicolored flag that I love so much. It is my most fervent hope that I will one day participate on home soil and be the host to sculptors from other countries that will come to South Africa and be enriched by the plethora of artistic wealth that abounds. Maybe soon.

It is a quote I read that was made by a Zen monk and sadly I am hopeless at remembering names but I remember the words clearly "sometimes you have to completely annihilate to reveal what is indestructible" It's a little akin to the other one that says "what doesn't kill you makes you stronger!" I'm pretty much sure that wasn't a Zen monk! Probably one of the Rolling Stones!!

Its with this in mind that I look forward and ironically, when I do look back I realize.

I wouldn't change a thing!

Maybe....

Also by Jon-Pat Myers

Incranium
Got Change?

Watch for more at https://web.facebook.com/jonpat.myers.7/.

About the Author

From playing with punk legends Toxiksox in 1980s Johannesburg, to working as a roadie for Motorhead, to singing with The Psykotix and trying to kickstart disc golf in 21st century South Africa, Jon-Pat Myers has done it all.

Now he tells it his way, ranting and raving about a world he claims he cannot change.

Jon-Pat is not a writer. He'd be the first to tell you that. His books were created using a Dictaphone, a cellphone, and an antiquated laptop. At his own request, they have not been professionally edited. They are raw. Like JP's life. Brought to you from the back alleys of Hillbrow, and from the war-torn streets of Israel. Come journey with a Madman. Sculptor. Musician. Composer. Painter. Traveller. Speaker. Disc golfer. Poet. Clown. Juggler. Teacher. Student. Doorman. Gardener. Current occupation - unknown.

Read more at https://web.facebook.com/jonpat.myers.7/.

About the Publisher

We've all had those nights where drunken sex with a witch in a blood pentagram under a full moon on the roof of your favourite Johannesburg nightclub summons a hard-drinking demon who changes the fate of the human race forever. Right? No? Just me, then? ?♠? Enter Burning Books' decadent twisted world of mystery, music, magick & mayhem at www.FaceBook.com/BurningRosesNovel